XIII - purpose / XVII (XXII q) ___
                    XXIII q
XX - films (10)
8 - ♀ & psi. ★   [XXV] ★ -102q
                          50q
12 - cr (15-yes)   cha[___]
                          & "we[___] [___] "strong"
25 - lobotomier   1940s-60s   156±
                                                cr
26 - ECT
                      ψα (6) // *Couching*
54-55 - films ⓐ   **RESISTANCE** e.g.
                                          (89)
65 - cr   CR: more jargon in
                      film analyses + info
71 - Eve ahistorical ⑬   than in text info in
     ↑   chapters (12) (convoluted
TEXT = FAILURE of STRUCTURE   syntax)
TO CONTAIN OPPRESSED
   ★ theme is familiar to historian (& ψα) more
      than to film/lit cr. how artefacts
e.g. (e.g. "Hollywooden" movies) reflect
94   times — w/in & w/o "artists'" control
cr   but what else about these "films"?
96   (what other things went into them
      which might infl. elements analyzed
      here? ② what, if any f/x did they
      have on soc. y viewers, proj, etc?
   ★ ③ how much read into films by interp. model?
89 - films ⑥   ★ most evident in microanalyses
1[3]3 - films ⓒ - 138   while macroanalysis = familiar,
                          even obvious themes   e.g. 98 ★
                                        Foucault
                                          160q - ambiv
   ★ 1st chs best (: (these) films not best f. eluc.
      points? give them too much credit? 104
                      (not the authors)
   9102 [___] on [___] theme y auth./resist. as
   ↳ Lacan "text" escaping control y "author"
                      also not give authors any credit
                      for manipulation y material for
                      purposes y entertainment (134)
            (123) + accident - all 3 y course

Couching
RESISTANCE

Women, Film, and Psychoanalytic Psychiatry

Janet Walker

University of Minnesota Press
Minneapolis
London

Portions of chapters 1, 2, and 3 have appeared in somewhat different form in Christine Gledhill, ed., *Home Is Where the Heart Is: Studies in Melodrama and the Woman's Film* (London: British Film Institute, 1987), and E. Ann Kaplan, ed., *Psychoanalysis and Cinema*, a volume in the AFI Film Readers series (New York and London: Routledge, 1990).

Published by the University of Minnesota Press
2037 University Avenue Southeast, Minneapolis, MN 55455-3092
Printed in the United States of America on acid-free paper

Library of Congress Cataloging-in-Publication Data

Walker, Janet, 1955–
    Couching resistance : women, film, and psychoanalytic psychiatry / Janet Walker.
      p. cm.
    Includes filmographies.
    Includes bibliographical references and index.
    ISBN 0-8166-2232-9 (hc : acid-free).—ISBN 0-8166-2233-7 (pb : acid-free)
    1. Women and psychoanalysis. 2. Women in motion pictures. 3. Psychiatry in motion pictures. 4. Motion pictures—United States—History. I. Title.
    RC451.4.W6W34   1993   92-23509
    791.43′656—dc20   CIP

By-the-by, that very word, Reading, in its critical use,
always charms me. An actress's Reading of a chambermaid, a dancer's
Reading of a hornpipe, a singer's Reading of a song,
a marine painter's Reading of the sea, the kettle-drum's Reading of an
instrumental passage, are phrases ever youthful and delightful.
    —Charles Dickens, *Our Mutual Friend*

Dedicated to my sister Mim
for integration

Contents

Acknowledgments

Since this book was written over a number of years the people to whom I am grateful are numerous and their contributions much greater than can be reflected in the pages and ideas of a single book. To all of those who have taught and believed in me, teachers and students alike, I owe a debt of thanks. Let me single out especially the early inspiration of Robin Wood and Janey Place, who led me to recognize the inherently political nature of cinema; Raymond Bellour, who showed me *Whirlpool* for the first time in the context of his interest in hypnosis; Christine Gledhill, who commissioned my first commitment to paper of this research; and the students of my University of California, Santa Barbara, seminar on psychoanalysis and cinema, particularly Geoff Burdick and Dave Cash, who took up this material and ran with it. In the early stages of this project I benefited greatly from Janet Bergstrom's lucid questions, careful readings, and general encouragement; from Steve Mamber's clear organizational sense; and from Ann Bergren's example of how intellectual commitment may enhance life's other pleasures. Ellen Evans, Claudia Gorbman, Ann Kaplan, Christine Gledhill, and Connie Penley offered editorial suggestions on earlier versions of various chapters and in so doing affected substantively my thinking about the project as a whole. In the later stages of writing, the intellectual and personal generosity of several friends and colleagues kept me afloat: Julie Carlson and Brad Newfield offered friendship as well as insights from the disciplines of history and feminist critical theory, respectively; Frank Tomasulo, Dana Polan, and Diane Waldman read closely and commented lucidly and at length. Diane Waldman deserves additional and very special thanks for sharing her own published and unpublished ideas about film, women, and psychoanalysis and for what she has given me through our collaborations, and finally for her unfailing support of my endeavors in every area.

I am grateful to the American Council of Learned Societies for the fellowship that made possible the transformation of this manuscript from doctoral dissertation to book and to Edward Branigan for crucial editorial advice on the matter. Thanks are also due to the many helpful people at the University of Minnesota Press, in particular my editor Janaki Bakhle, for her belief in the book and her energetic efforts to bring it to publication.

I am convinced that all scholarly books, and especially one's first, grow out of the author's social experience and also, very profoundly, out of his or her psychological and family background. Since this book is no exception, I would like to thank my parents and sister for the positive experiences that gave me the strength and volition to write this book at the same time that I acknowledge the troubles that led to the book's subject matter and to the repressions that still may limit its depth. Final thanks and love go to Steve Nelson, who has seen me through from the very beginning of my film education, for his help as an incisive lay reader and for his sustaining efforts on behalf of my work and my well-being; and to our young daughter, Ariel, who has respected my closed office door, helped me with library returns, and enriched my life in ways I never could have imagined.

Introduction
Women and Psychiatry
Reading the Cultural Texts

Evolved from a basic feminist goal to understand the patriarchal edifice in all its facets and incarnations—to understand it, moreover, in order to help change it—this study is concerned to show how two institutions, American psychoanalytic psychiatry and Hollywood cinema, at a certain point in history were absolutely central to the formation of feminine psychosexuality and women's life experience. Between World War II and the mid-1960s, American psychiatry enjoyed both its greatest institutional strength and its most controversial concentration on women. It was then, too, that the largest number of Hollywood films on the subject of psychiatry and women were produced. This book offers readings of a group of films about psychiatrists and patients informed by the history of psychiatry and women, which history itself is read through a collection of sometimes coherent and sometimes contradictory texts.

The intellectual climate described is one that was inhabited by real women: women involved as present, past, or prospective psychiatric patients, as material for case histories and theoretical elaboration; as the relatives, friends, and co-workers of psychiatric patients or even as psychiatrists themselves; as the subjects and objects of magazine articles offering philosophy and guidance on women's perceived problems; and/or as imagined and eventual cinema spectators at films depicting psychiatric intervention in women's lives. The following pages represent an attempt to read the physical and mental experience of these numerous individual women, to read it through the multiple and varied central texts that reported, mediated, influenced, interpellated, expanded, and restricted that experience. The operating assumption is that it is impossible to comprehend a social subject/spectator without direct and substantive reference to the very specific filmic and nonfilmic discourses at hand. As Patrice Petro has pointed out in the conclusion of her important study of women in Weimar film history, "Questions relating to spectatorship and gender can only be answered within history and understood as defined by the historical representation of sexual difference."[1]

For the purposes of this study a distinction is made between texts (films, books, magazines, journals, written correspondence, etc.) and contexts (organized psychiatry, education, mental institutions, film studio production, etc.), but it is made for the purpose of detailing their mutual influence without recourse to overly simple models of reflection or direct causality. By reading as texts both films *and other sources through which we come to know contexts*, I aim to explore how similar ideologies operate in different media and registers. Also, I have tried to give weight to the *content* of films, stressing that the use of psychiatry as thematic material in films is *not interchangeable* with the use of any other patriarchally determined set of ideas, but rather that it specifically informs the meaning of these films.

In his preface to an edited volume of literary-historical essays, Sacvan Bercovitch proposes a desirable "*problematics* of literary history." His premises are as follows:

> that race, class, and gender are formal principles of art and therefore integral to textual analysis; that language has the capacity to break free of social restrictions and through its own dynamics to undermine the power structure it seems to reflect; that political norms are inscribed in aesthetic judgment and therefore inherent in the process of interpretation; that aesthetic structures shape the way we understand history, so that tropes and narrative devices may be said to use historians to enforce certain views of the past; that the task of literary historians is not just to show how art transcends culture, but also to identify and explore the ideological limits of their time, and then to bring these to bear upon literary analysis in such a way as to make use of the categories of culture, rather than being used by them.[2]

Foucault, too, has attempted to reconceptualize the relationship between texts and their material referents through his concentration on discourses and practices rather than words and things.[3] An archaeological analysis of a painting, for example, would try to discover whether space, distance, depth, colour, light, proportions, volumes, and contours were not, at the period in question, considered, named, enunciated, and conceptualized in a discursive practice; and whether the knowledge that this discursive practice gives rise to was not embodied perhaps in theories and speculations, in forms of teaching and codes of practice, but also in processes, techniques, and even in the very gesture of the painter. . . . It would try to show that, at least in one of its dimensions, it is discursive practice that is embodied in techniques and effects.[4]

In this way, through the conjunctural analysis of social and cultural discourses, the shadows of the men and women whose lives were pulled this way and that by the swirl of textual and contextual artifacts begin to emerge.

The actual subject matter of Foucault's investigation—the various institutions within the human sciences, notably medicine and psychiatry—makes his project all the more useful as a reference point for my own.[5] As defined by Foucault, psychiatry is a publicly and legally recognized social authority, an institution with its own rules and etiquette and its own group of professional practitioners. He concentrates, therefore, not on "madness" per se but on the "unity of discourses on madness . . . the interplay of the rules that define the transformations of these different objects." This book follows Foucault's intellectual historical impulse "to discover that whole domain of institutions, economic processes, and social relations on which a discursive formation can be articulated."[6] It explores the intersection of psychiatric associations and treatments with wider notions of femininity, family, and women's roles; and it reads professional and popular psychiatric literature from a women's studies perspective. Where Foucault attempts to discover "how criminality could become an object of medical expertise or sexual deviation a possible object of psychiatric discourse,"[7] this study will attempt to describe how female deviance became an object of psychiatric expertise and how the interaction between psychiatry and female deviance became an object of fictional cinematic discourse.

Of course, postwar American psychiatry has already been subject to an exhaustive feminist critique, beginning perhaps with Betty Friedan's feminist classic, *The Feminine Mystique* (1963), and continuing with Phyllis Chesler's *Women and Madness* (1972), to cite what are by far the two most well-known texts on the subject. These books are the historical foundation of the feminist proposition that the institution of psychiatry, encompassing therapeutic practice and psychoanalytic theory both, is largely oppressive to women; that it works in concert

with patriarchal ideology to enforce restrictive sex roles legislating female passivity on the basis of theories that infantilize and secondarize
women in comparison with men. This book is written very much in the
wake of that tradition. The chapters that follow delineate some of the
specific discursive operations of what I will call "adjustment psychiatry," following social critic Russell Jacoby, who has used the term "conformist psychology" to characterize the orientation of neo-Freudian
and post-Freudian psychology, and following feminist film scholar Diane
Waldman, who has used the term "adjustment therapy" when characterizing the gender-specific ramifications of American psychoanalysis
and its thematic portrayal in certain Hollywood films.[8]

As a psychiatric term, "adaptation" means to fit "one's inner needs
to the environment, typically by a combination of autoplastic maneuvers (which involve a change in the self) and alloplastic maneuvers
(which involve alteration of the external environment)," while "adjustment" is glossed in psychiatry as the "functional, often transitory, alteration or accommodation by which one can adapt himself better to
the immediate environment."[9] Used as a feminist term, however, "adjustment" implies the imposition of socially legislated behavior on a resistant person by an authority figure—so that feminine adjustment is a
process of fitting a woman into a rigid gender stereotype. While not to
be conflated, the psychiatric and feminist meanings of "adjustment"
are related. It is precisely that conceptual interplay between the supposedly objective scientific definition and the partisan one that makes
up the terrain on which we will abide here.

At the same time and without departing, I trust, from an American
feminist perspective on the history of psychiatry, it is just as much the
aim of this book to show that the oppressive mantle of adjustment psychiatry was far from all-encompassing within postwar American
psychiatry's various institutions and practices. American psychiatry
did not by any means operate under a fully misogynist patriarchal consensus nor did it operate as a thoroughly effective cultural force. At the
very time of psychiatry's greatest authoritarianism, dissident psychiatrists were joined in their internal critique of the profession by feminist
and/or humanitarian nonanalysts, and debates on applications of
Freudian theory challenged psychoanalytic authority with interesting
implications for feminism. As the work of historian of psychology Ellen
Herman has begun to demonstrate,

> Psychological theory and practice offered women's liberation a
> number of significant ideas and organizational models that could be
> and were productively incorporated as well as angrily rejected.

Psychology helped mobilize feminist political activism even as
feminists were accusing it of instilling self-hatred and pacification.[10]

One of the hazards of feminist thought is that the justifiable effort to
communicate the depth and pain of patriarchal oppression can lead to
characterizations of patriarchy and its constituent institutions, including psychiatry, as monolithic and inescapable. This seems to me
largely untrue and ultimately unproductive. This project aims to characterize some of the contradictions in the social field inhabited by
psychiatry, women, and film; to argue, in short, that the discursive
practices and formations around psychiatry, women, and film couched
resistance as well as adjustment.[11]

Like the term "adjustment," the term "resistance" resonates variously in its different definitions and applications. Within Freudian psychoanalysis alone the concept enjoys a range of meanings. In one
sense, the term has to do with the resistance to or obstruction of psychoanalysis itself.[12] Freud used the term to describe the hostile reactions of his contemporaries to his discoveries, and in psychoanalytic
treatment he defined the term as "whatever interrupts the progress of
analytic work."[13] But in spite of this sense of resistance as operating
against the progress of the analysis, the concept is in fact fundamental
to the whole Freudian psychoanalytic framework as a practice and
metapsychology. Resistance in these terms is conceived as operating
through the very same forces as repression, so that analytic progress is
precisely the elucidation of resistance and its accurate interpretation.
As J. LaPlanche and J.-B. Pontalis have explained, "Resistance was
itself a means of reaching the repressed and unveiling the secret of
neurosis."[14] This notion of the elucidation of resistance informs my
analysis of filmic and other cultural texts in which alternative views of
feminine subjectivity and mental illness are articulated precisely as
textual repressions or resistances.

In its political and specifically feminist usage, too, the term "resistance" evokes various practices and meanings. "The Resistance," used
to name the American anti–Vietnam War movement of the late 1960s
and early 1970s, was perhaps the most overt and politically activist use
of the term. More common in the post–World War II period, or in describing the post–World War II period, is the use of "resistance" to indicate a kind of cultural resistance to dominant norms, a resistance
that was pervasive, ideological, and political, although not fully realized or recognized as effective political action. For example, the anthology *Resistance through Ritual: Youth Subcultures in Post-War
Britain* studies subcultural codes through which "the problematic of a
subordinate class experience can be 'lived through', negotiated or re-

sisted."[15] The authors represented in the anthology take various positions on the perceived effectivity of largely symbolic resistance: some suggest that the problematic cannot be resolved at the symbolic level, while others suggest that "meanings alternative to those preferred by the dominant culture, generated within the experience and consciousness of a suppressed social group, may be brought to the surface, and so transform the original discourse."[16] Following this precedent, "resistance" will be used here to characterize various ways psychiatrists, patients, and people concerned with the representation thereof sought to rethink ideas, actions, and lives at odds with a status quo according to which institutional psychiatry dictated normative and gender-allocated behavioral patterns.

As with "adjustment," my aim is not to consolidate but rather to link various uses of the term "resistance." For, whether contained in cinematic images or written texts, whether for popular or professional consumption, resistant representations stand in the cultural history of the period as distinct but related ways of revising or articulating dissatisfaction with the "original discourse."

Like postwar psychiatry, Hollywood cinema has been subject to considerable feminist analysis. And like the feminist critique of postwar psychiatry, which concentrated initially on delineating the patriarchal bias of the psychiatric institution, the feminist reading of Hollywood cinema has been concerned to delineate the patriarchal underpinnings of classical narrative representation. Contemporary film theory, in particular, has shown convincingly that Hollywood classical narrative cinema is a representational form determined by processes of structuration that resemble and engage psychic processes that are themselves put into place as an infant becomes a sexed subject under patriarchal family organization.

In the touchstone paper of contemporary psychoanalytically informed feminist film theory, "Visual Pleasure and Narrative Cinema" (1975),[17] Laura Mulvey argued that the significant psychic processes involved in film spectatorship are voyeuristic and narcissistic scopophilia, and that these processes engage and inscribe a male spectating position. The male spectator receives pleasure in viewing by gazing at the screen and by identifying with the gaze of the fictional male character and with the gaze of the camera.

Because Mulvey's article clarified the basic general operation of the classical Hollywood film, other authors as well as Mulvey herself have been able to take feminist theoretical inquiry in other directions, investigating different types of Hollywood films addressing correspondingly different spectators. Crucially, a number of authors and editors, including Mary Ann Doane, Christine Gledhill, and Diane Waldman, have taken the Hollywood women's film as their point of departure, examining films of this genre for evidence of textual disturbance around the position of the woman character and for evidence of the way female spectators were imagined, solicited, and hence envisioned textually by Hollywood's commercial complex.[18] The importance of this line of inquiry has been underscored recently by the appearance of a special issue of *Camera Obscura* edited by Janet Bergstrom and Mary Ann Doane on the female spectator, entitled "The Spectatrix" (1989).[19]

In fact the question of how and by whom attributed textual disturbances may be read has been a source of great debate in the field of feminist film studies. Some have argued that reading is primarily a function of gender-based psychological differences between the sexes, while others have stressed that overall cultural placement should be more carefully considered: a female spectator is not only gendered, but placed racially, economically, nationally, and ethnically as well.[20] Currently, as witnessed in the pages of the *Camera Obscura* special issue, feminist film theorists seem to have reached a kind of consensus in the critique of both essentialism (the reduction of mediations of spectatorship to innate biological, sexed "essence") and the empiricist bias of reception studies (the notion that every reader is unique and may be described quantitatively).[21] The problem for feminist film theory today is how to research and discuss a female spectator who must logically be both unconsciously and socially constructed.

Contemporary feminist film theory is not alone in having grasped the significance of textual bumpiness. Contemporary film theory in general, as influenced by the study of ideology and by its mutual exchange with feminist film theory, has also been centrally concerned with the question of whether and, if so, *how* classical narratives support textual contradiction. Stephen Heath's "Film and System: Terms of Analysis" (1975) exemplifies this study of the characteristic openness of the narrative form, a form he sees as animated by an endless conflictual process of structuration rather than by a discrete and finite structure.[22] Dana Polan's book *Power and Paranoia* represents a notable instance of a work that takes up the challenge of describing the contradictions of "history" and "narrative" in a specific and detailed way and with reference to actual films and historical events.[23] This book shares Polan's premise that textual contradiction may be elaborated most fruitfully not in purely formal or even formalist terms, but in terms, once again, of the sociocultural context for contradiction. It aims to open up what Foucault has called "the different *spaces of dissension* in the discursive history of ideas" that concern, in this case, psychiatry, cinema, and women.[24]

Ten Hollywood films on psychiatry and women will be examined closely in this vein and many others will be referred to. In the order of their analysis the ten films are *Whirlpool* (1949), *The Three Faces of Eve* (1957), *Tender Is the Night* (1962), *The Snake Pit* (1948), *The Cobweb* (1955), *Lilith* (1964), *Spellbound* (1945), *Knock on Wood* (1954), *Three on a Couch* (1966), and, by way of summary, *Freud* (1962). These films are representative of a list of over forty films that picture not just psychiatry but the very specific relation, psychiatry and female madness, under consideration here (see Filmography A). This group in turn is representative of an even larger corpus of several hundred Hollywood films on psychiatry and mental illness (studied in Gabbard's and Gabbard's *Psychiatry and the Cinema*),[25] which corpus includes films from the time periods preceding and following the period under analysis here, films primarily concerned with male madness, and films concerned with madness but not with psychiatry (see Selected Filmographies B and C).[26]

At first introduction, the list of films may not seem an august one. Contemporaneous reviewers called screen psychiatry pat, simplistic, jargon-ridden, and, in the words of psychoanalyst Lawrence Kubie, "Hollywooden."[27] Nor do those in film studies today hold these films in any high regard. Even *Spellbound*, directed by the celebrated Alfred Hitchcock, tends to be regarded as cumbersome, obvious, and disappointing. A good case might be made for the cinematic value of some (I would propose *Lilith* and possibly *Whirlpool*), but some of them would fit very well, indeed, into the category of treatises Mark Poster says Foucault would have the "archaeologist" examine; treatises that are "cramped and cranky, turgid, boring, and uninspired, written by proponents of fanciful projects, by seekers after hopeless delusions, by advocates of ridiculous proposals."[28] And yet, if these films are not taken as failed masterworks or as legitimate renditions of either Freudian theory or American psychiatry, they may be taken as texts that bear, individually and as a group, an interesting and rich ideological relation to nonfilm discursive practices and formations. We needn't assume, because these films literalize and trivialize mental illness and its curators, that they do not also derive their structure from basic psychoanalytic principles and in relation to specific historical patterns of institutional psychiatry.

The contemporaneous critical response to this group of films criticized them not only for being jargonistic, but for being unrealistic, as well. A number of the contemporaneous reviewers were in fact psychologists or psychiatrists, like Kubie, who assumed that ideally informative films about psychiatry could be produced given the right conditions, notably psychiatric advisers to the filmmaking process.

They leveled the complaint that the films overemphasized such sensational symptoms as kleptomania[29] and such dramatic curative methods as narcosynthesis and hypnosis.[30] The etiology of neurosis as well as its cure were often oversimplified, they asserted, the former commonly being depicted as a single traumatic incident, the latter as a cathartic flash(back). The formulaic "collapse-therapy-cure" plot design named by critic Manny Farber was simply not indicative of the way actual psychoanalysis worked.

Contemporary textual analytic studies of films on psychiatry have been able to make observations similar to those of earlier critics and develop them along different lines. For example, Marc Vernet broached an issue also noted by an earlier critic, psychologist Franklin Fearing. In 1946 Fearing made a backhanded attack on *Spellbound*'s treatment of the love affair of the "Beautiful Psychiatrist" (Ingrid Bergman): "It is perhaps kinder not to discuss a psychoanalysis which contains no reference to the patient's sex life."[31] Thirty years later, Vernet pointed out that the Oedipal scenario common to these films takes the shape of the *death of* the father, thus eliding the problem of the *desire for* the father and supporting the common wisdom that mental illness is born of the exceptional, pathetic family (rather than of social problems or the inherent problems of subjectivity).[32]

But instead of dismissing the collapse-therapy-cure narrative as improbable, it is useful to inquire into its ideological import. Dana Polan has linked the use of thematized Freudian psychoanalysis in films of the forties to a broader social-cultural dependence on science as "humanist rationality," as "the sense-filled journey through chaos to the stasis of an ending, the erection of a system."[33] And Marc Vernet, Diane Waldman, Mary Ann Doane, and Dana Polan have all argued that psychoanalysis operates in narratives about mental illness, in the words of Doane, "to validate socially constructed modes of sexual difference which are already in place."[34] In particular, the cathartic method rejected by Freud early on was adopted in the first place by Hollywood narratives precisely because it fit already existing narrative patterns that are themselves products and producers of patriarchal social organization. "Beyond the specific content of psychoanalytic precepts," writes Polan, "artists find in the new science a form whose narrativity seems ready-made and thus allows the construction of suspense and climax. . . . Psychoanalysis serves precisely as a force of narrative resolution."[35] Waldman further emphasizes the historical component of the filmic appropriation of psychoanalytic ideas, indicating that Hollywood not only picked and chose from psychoanalytic thought in ways consistent with its narrative imperative, but also drew

from existing contemporaneous American reworkings of Freudian psychoanalysis.

Here I will proffer some readings that are consistent with this argument that psychiatric subject matter did often work in with existing
patterns of narrative resolution and status quo ideology in Hollywood
films. For example, *Whirlpool*, *The Seventh Veil*, *The Dark Mirror*, *The
Three Faces of Eve*, *The Cobweb*, *The Snake Pit*, and *Lady in the Dark*
are read in these pages as films in which psychiatry (usually in a vague
form of psychoanalysis) colludes with heterosexual monogamy to provide the happy ending.

However, there is another facet of the recirculation of women and
psychiatry in filmic subject matter, one that is touched on but not developed by recent critical work on these films, and one on which I hope
to concentrate here. Prior authors generally concur in their view of the
ultimately conservative ideological import of psychoanalysis in Hollywood films, and yet each author suggests differently how particular
moments or aspects of certain films escape totalizing consistency with
the patriarchal status quo supported by psychiatry. Waldman, for example, points out that the gothic romance films she discusses, including some with psychological subject matter, do not only operate to
"normalize the experience of the heroine as part of the 'natural' conditions of marriage"; they also do the reverse. Through processes of
spectator identification with the subjectivity of the heroine, they make
"what the culture defines as 'natural' and 'normal' appear eerie, bizarre, and strange."[36] And although Doane argues that "by activating a
therapeutic mode, the films of the medical discourse become the most
fully recuperated form of the 'woman's film',"[37] she still describes textual passages that point up very precisely the "impossibility" of a
female point of view. Polan and Maureen Turim also suggest that patterns of narrative resolution enabled by popularized psychoanalysis
may be reread as less resolved through recourse to psychoanalytically
informed theoretical reading practices. Polan explains the case as
follows:

> Maureen Turim has argued that the flashback structure of some films
> about psychology—for example, *The Locket* (1946)—institutes a gap
> between discourse and story in which the forward progression of the
> story exists in a contradictory relation to a complicated structure that
> posits the inability of a story to offer fully or adequately an explana-
> tion of psychic processes.[38]

The films under study here do contain significant moments and
even passages where the smooth functioning of the phallocentric representational system is interrupted; and they contain even more such

passages than previous critics have indicated when dealing with some of the same films. But the gist of this project lies not so much in the delineation of film textual discord as in the insistence that the *ideological import of filmic representation is legible only in reference to a wider field of cultural representations*.[39] Furthermore, if Polan's "specific content of psychoanalytic precepts" must be looked beyond so that patterns of psychoanalysis-influenced narrativity may be examined, the content of these precepts are still key to ideological formulations of diverse cultural texts.

The organization of the book follows its overall aim to detail aspects of the relationship between the historically specific sociocultural debates and polemics of the period and the film textual discord through which those points of view were reexpressed. Chapters 1 and 2 are concerned with psychiatric texts and contexts and with developing various facets of the adjustment/resistance problematic in post–World War II American psychiatry vis-à-vis women. Chapters 3 through 6 examine film texts and contexts and suggest how the adjustment/resistance problematic was refigured narratively in a certain body of Hollywood films.

Chapter 1 presents the history of American psychiatry as one of institutional growth predicated on contemporaneous conceptions of femininity and female deviancy, and as one of eventual decline in the wake of rising antiauthoritarian social movements, including the women's movement of the 1960s. Chapter 2 moves in on historical processes of treatment and on the doctor-patient relationship itself as a privileged paradigm of the larger discursive crossovers between psychiatry and ideas about women. Chapter 3 analyzes the male doctor–female patient couple (in *Whirlpool*, *The Three Faces of Eve*, and *Tender Is the Night*) as a key way psychiatric concepts are introduced into Hollywood narratives. Here, especially, theoretical models of transference are interjected as a means of exploring both the fictional representation of analytic transference and the overdetermination of the couple in films where the doctor-patient duo doubles for Hollywood's traditional romantic couple. This chapter also initiates a central argument of this book: that the identity crisis of postwar American psychiatry is refigured in Hollywood films through the character of the troubled psychiatrist. This informs chapter 4, where the doctor-patient couple is found in an institutional setting (*The Snake Pit*, *The Cobweb*, *Lilith*), and chapter 5 (*Spellbound*, *Knock on Wood*, *Three on a Couch*), where the roles are reversed and the female is the psychiatrist. Chapter 6 moves to a different and more practical level of the correspondence between institutional psychiatry and psychiatric films to present a case study of how some psychiatrists were able to influence

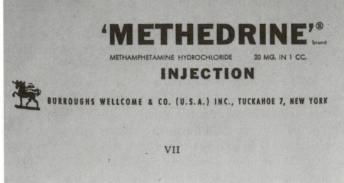

VII

Figure 1. Psychiatric pharmacology borrows the language of narrative fiction in this advertisement from *The American Journal of Psychiatry* 109, no. 2 (August 1952). Reproduced with permission of Burroughs Wellcome Co.

very directly the subject matter of three films about psychiatry and women: *Shock*, *The Snake Pit*, and *Freud*.

When one focuses specifically on psychiatry, in its social and cinematic manifestations, one sees far greater play in what might otherwise have appeared to be a monolithically and unproblematically patriarchal institution. The psychotherapeutic scenario might tend at times and in certain cases toward adjustment—toward, in the words of ad copy for the drug Methedrine, "help[ing] the patient to accept the psychiatrist's interpretation" (Figure 1).[40] And yet, because psychiatry could facilitate "a spontaneous free flow of speech," or, more suggestively, because it could "release the *story* for analysis," the institution of psychiatry in the context of Hollywood film as well as in the treatment setting could also present a more complex and very fertile ground for the exploration of some of the integral conflicts of feminine psychosexuality. Psychiatry, then, as I will attempt to argue, troubles the operation of patriarchal narratives at the same time that it enables them. With regard to women and psychiatry, it is precisely the wider cultural context of the critique of psychiatry that makes legible filmic explorations of the chilling effect of psychiatry on female expressivity.

1

Psychiatry after World War II
The Stake in Women

As revisionist social historians have argued, the "fabulous fifties" was a mythic construction laid on a foundation of simultaneous celebration and denial: celebration of progressive prosperity for all, desirable suburbanization, and family stability; and denial of the social inequities and oppression suffered by women and minorities and of the imperialist means of securing economic prosperity.[1] When acknowledged in this ideologically myopic atmosphere, social problems had to be contained and were indeed contained by their focalization onto the site of the family.[2] Juvenile delinquency, crime, and the failure of American soldiers, "our boys," to shoot to kill in battle were blamed on failed mothering, making the woman who was not living up to her supposed feminine potential a scapegoat for narrowly construed social malaise. As feminist social historian Lois Banner put it, "The anti-feminism of the postwar 1940s held women responsible for society's ills—either because they were failures as mothers or because they had left the home for work."[3] To carry through the popular logic, problems that might have been perceived as broadly social were either ignored or rewritten as narrowly familial, and since mothers were responsible for family life, it was at the feet of women that these problems were laid. The pervasiveness of these myths, along with their formulaic desirability and avoidance of real underlying problems, allowed them to be thoroughly marketed and packaged in popular formats, including film narratives, and it also made them a factor in thinking about and prescribing for women.

1

The purpose of this chapter, then, is twofold: to describe American psychiatry's increasing significance in the post–World War II years as a crucial architect of social activity and values, and to argue that this hegemonic status was in no insignificant part dependent upon psychiatry's perceived ability to address the "problem of women"—the projection of social problems onto the personal problems of individual women.[4] For such a projection enabled an otherwise unavailable expedient: individual therapeutic rehabilitation; and rehabilitation fell within the purview of psychiatry. Institutionalized psychiatry had a specific historical stake in the identification and treatment of the woman patient, which stake it is the project of this chapter to describe.

Psychiatry's turn toward women patients and questions of femininity is best seen in the context of the growth of American medicine and the psychiatric specialty overall, and in terms of the enthusiastic popular reception of psychiatry as a general panacea.[5] By the end of World War II psychiatry had taken its place in the heady atmosphere of economic expansion and prosperity characteristic of the age and enjoyed by medical practice in general. Where psychiatry had been focused initially on the care of the insane and the profession had been marginalized in accordance with the disenfranchised place of its patients,[6] the profession could now turn its attention to the ever more numerous and seemingly more deserving patients emerging from the wartime experience. Psychiatrists were called upon to examine recruits and treat soldiers returning from the battlefront suffering from "combat fatigue" or "shellshock," to use the terms carried over from World War I.[7] Over 1 million wartime recruits were rejected from military service on psychiatric grounds, and another 850,000 soldiers were hospitalized for psychoneurosis. To treat them, 2,400 army medical officers were added to the original 25 assigned to psychiatry.[8] As Dr. William Menninger (chief consultant in neuropsychiatry to the surgeon general of the army from 1943-46) indicated, writing at the time, the success of army psychiatry enhanced its perceived authority.[9]

The expansion of the mental health professions, most notably psychiatry, psychology, and social work, continued after the end of World War II. Created in 1949, the National Institute of Mental Health (NIMH) was the fastest-growing subdivision of the National Institutes of Health (NIH).[10] The number of psychiatrists increased from 5,500 in 1950 to 19,532 in 1966, the number of clinical psychologists from 3,500 to 18,430, and the number of psychiatric social workers from 3,000 to 12,000 over the same period.[11] Public attention to mental hospital conditions, as exemplified by the heavy sales of the novel *The Snake Pit* (1946), and the popularity of its filmic adaptation, added to the visibility of the profession.[12]

Postwar American psychoanalysis, like the larger medical specialty psychiatry,[13] underwent a tremendous organizational and clinical expansion, with long-term psychoanalytic therapy reaching its peak in the late 1950s.[14] In 1953 the first issue of the *Journal of the American Psychoanalytic Association* contained the text of a speech by outgoing president Robert P. Knight, noting that membership in this, the most powerful psychoanalytic society and training institution in the United States at the time, had been increasing by geometric progression each decade. In 1932, the American Psychoanalytic Association had only 92 members; in 1948, 343; and by 1952-53, it had 485 members. Knight pointed out that one-third of the membership in 1953 had joined since 1948. At the same time there were 900 candidates in training.[15]

Administratively, 1946 saw the reorganization of the American Psychoanalytic Association from a federation of constituent societies with just one training center for each region to a membership association of societies and institutes.[16] This meant that individuals could be members of more than one society and that each locale could have more than one training center. For example, the Los Angeles society of the American Psychoanalytic Association obtained approval for a training institute in 1946, and in 1950 the Society for Psychoanalytic Medicine of Southern California sought and subsequently obtained provisional approval for its institute.[17]

The strength of the American Psychoanalytic Association was further consolidated through its position in relation to the International Psychoanalytic Association (IPA). When the International Psychoanalytic Association, headed by Ernest Jones, was finally able to resume operations following the war in 1949, the independence of the American Association was made official. At the same time, American participation in the IPA had grown to over half of the total membership, and to 64 percent by 1952, whereas only 30 percent of the members of the IPA had been American before the war.[18] Moreover, Leo Bartemeier, an American, took over the presidency from Ernest Jones, an Englishman.

The immigration of European analysts to America slightly increased the ranks of American analysts, but greatly increased their prestige. Famous analysts, many of whom had been the esteemed teachers of young Americans who had gone abroad for training, came to the United States as political refugees. They came from Germany and Austria in 1933 and again in 1938, as well as from many other countries.

The increased prestige of American psychoanalysis due to the influx of the émigré analysts was somewhat paradoxical, since that prestige has traditionally been supported by its medicalization and the European analysts were more likely than their American counterparts to follow Freud's defense of nonmedical or "lay" psychoanalysis.[19] The fact was that in postwar America the vast majority of psychoanalysts were psychiatrists and therefore medical doctors. In 1952, 82 percent of the members of the American Psychoanalytic Association were also members of the American Psychiatric Association,[20] and a representative entry under "psychoanalysis" in the *Encyclopedia of Mental Health* (1963) praised the qualifications of psychoanalysts on the basis of their medical education.[21] Clarence Oberndorf, an analyst and contemporaneous historian of the period very appropriately called his field "psychoanalytic psychiatry."[22] In America up to the present day one may hardly speak of psychoanalysis without speaking of its medical umbrella, psychiatry, or, conversely, speak of psychiatry without speaking of its theoretical basis, psychoanalysis.

Although only 10 percent to 30 percent of psychiatric residents were actually applying to psychoanalytic institutes, all psychiatrists after World War II were being exposed to psychoanalytic ideas in the course of their psychiatric residencies, and psychoanalysis represented a theoretical core of psychiatric training.[23] As claimed by a survey of psychiatric residencies, "What analysts teach is so much a part of residency training that it is no longer identified as 'psychoanalytic,' but, rather, as 'dynamic'—and the sum and substance of psychiatry proper."[24]

Further work to enhance psychoanalytic authority by requiring medical credentials came in the form of a movement to *double* the medical credentials of American psychoanalysts. It was proposed that "certification in analysis" be made an accredited subspecialization within the American Psychiatric Association, analogous to the various specializations within the American Medical Association. Although the practice of certification was not finally adopted, its advocates argued that it would preserve and supplement the existing high standards in psychoanalytic practice.[25]

Interestingly, the arguments that opposed making psychoanalysis a speciality within psychiatry are themselves illustrative of psychiatry's perceived dependency on psychoanalysis. The victorious opponents of the proposal feared that certification would make psychoanalysis a dependent tool of medicine and psychiatry, and would therefore weaken it. They argued, in effect, that the creation of a subspecialty in psychoanalysis would actually undercut the mainstream status already enjoyed by psychoanalysis as compared with psychiatry.

For the individual practitioner, the crossover between psychiatric and psychoanalytic practice has interesting implications. He or she commonly would serve on the staff of a medical school or psychiatric hospital where psychoanalytic principles would not be the dominant strain of treatment (although they would be the core theoretical mod-

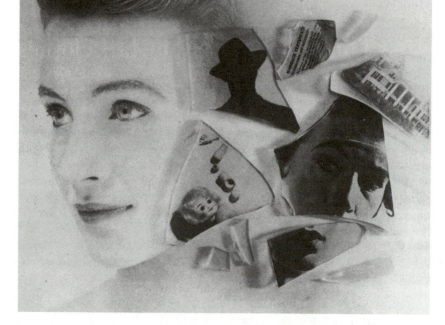

Should you be psychoanalyzed?

Illness, worry, deep depression
brought me to the analyst....
I stayed to work the
puzzle to its end

Figure 2. Magazine stories and their accompanying graphics aided the popularization of psychoanalytic treatment. *Mademoiselle,* October 1953, p. 100.

els studied by the psychiatrists during residency). Yet under the term "psychodynamics," psychoanalytic techniques and principles could be incorporated, especially in private mental institutions. It was in private practice, however, often a very limited practice on the side, that the psychiatrist would see most of his or her strictly analytic patients.[26]

Films on psychological subjects have a tendency to confuse medical doctors with hypnotists, psychologists, or other nonmedical specialists, or to portray psychoanalysts administering medication. For example, Dr. Kik in *The Snake Pit* combines shock treatment with psychoanalytic investigations of infancy as he tries to help his patient. One would be hard pressed to argue that these ofttimes confused representations are accurate, but they do evince, however unrealistically, the key characteristic of psychoanalysis in America being discussed: that is, its thorough imbrication with organized psychiatry.

American psychiatry and psychoanalysis, then, grew up together and each strengthened the supremely authoritative status of the other. Yet the Siamese twins made strange bedfellows. If, as I argue, the general tendency was complementarity, there were sources of conflict. One such conflict, especially strong in mental hospitals, was over the practice of psychoanalysis as long-term analytic therapy versus the tendency toward employing a physiological or pharmacological psychiatric approach, with or without psychotherapy. The ideological implications of this conflict will be discussed in chapter 2, and its filmic applications in chapter 4.

The growth and entrenchment of professional American psychiatry in the years following World War II were attended, as indicated previously, by an upsurge in popular accounts of the ideas and practice of the discipline. In fact, historian Nathan Hale calls the popularization itself a characteristic of the American scene.[27] Of course, psychiatry had been the subject of popular attention before World War II, showing up in fiction and nonfiction sources.[28] But it was during and after World War II that psychoanalysis came before the public through mass popular outlets at an unprecedented rate. Magazine articles and "spreads," such as *Life* magazine's 1957 series on psychology by Ernest Havemann and the *Atlantic* collection on psychiatry in education and religion, began to be ubiquitous (Figure 2). The blurb on the back cover of the book Ernest Havemann created from the *Life* series is typical of the glee with which psychology was marketed:

> We live in the Age of Psychology.
> Most of us are fully aware that a new science of human behavior has, within a few decades, completely changed the nature of modern life. Few of us are completely aware of how deeply its findings (often misinterpreted, often virtually turned upside down by untrained "middle men") have pervaded our lives, subtly changed our thinking, our actions, our very language.[29]

The book itself is also typical of the popular tendency mentioned above in relation to filmic depictions to conflate the various psychological disciplines without the careful specification of pertinent distinctions that would be underlined in the professional literature.

Books of psychology, psychiatry, and psychoanalysis written for the lay person often reached best-seller status. Lucy Freeman's *Fight against Fears* had sold 385,000 copies by 1957, and Robert Lindner's *The Fifty-Minute Hour* was an extremely popular collection of case histories. The specialized terminology of psychoanalysis was simply defined and entered colloquial speech. Even professional literature achieved high sales on the general market. *The Basic Writings of Sigmund Freud*, a Modern Library Giant, had sold over a quarter of a million copies by 1957.[30]

Sociologists claimed that the spread of psychoanalysis was indicative of and/or influenced the changing shape of American thought, society, and culture. Hendrick M. Ruitenbeek, for example, in *Freud and America* (1966), explained the diffusion of Freud's ideas in the United States, while *The Freudian Ethic* by Richard LaPiere mourned the replacement of the Protestant ethic, the source of American initiative and greatness, with the pervasive Freudian ethic, which he saw as socially corrosive.[31]

Threading consistently through the popular representation of psychiatry, psychoanalysis, and psychology is the discourse that heralds these therapeutic practices as general panaceas for the dimly perceived social problems construed as individual problems. Psychiatry was not only marketed as an interesting offshoot of the sciences, but as a domain with clear practical uses, as well. The work of Viennese psychologist Ernest Dichter illustrates the link between the economic imperatives of the postwar economy (which required the full-time wife) and popular psychiatry. In 1946, under the auspices of the Motivational Research Institute, Dichter and colleagues experimented with using a pop version of Freudian psychoanalysis to find out how to sell detergents, vacuum cleaners, creams, powders, cake mixes, and so on. Pop psychology was used here to develop the "professional housewife"—the housewife who could be encouraged by specialized cleaning products "to use at home all the faculties that she would [otherwise] display in an outside career."[32]

Book after book ended with the call for more mental health workers.[33] *The Age of Psychology* boasted of its project to describe "how this vast new body of knowledge is used to free the individual and to benefit society."[34] Nine out of ten of the major U.S. daily papers were carrying at least one help column dependent on psychology. "The Worry Clinic," a syndicated help column, claimed a circulation of 19 million; "Mirror of Your Mind," 20 million; and "Let's Explore Your Mind," 21 million.[35]

Psychiatry's application to the "problem of woman" focused and consolidated the profession's authority and redirected its social influence. From a popular perspective, psychiatry could be celebrated as a profession uniquely fit to deal with deviant women who were being blamed for social malaise. From the perspective of professional psychiatry, female psychology represented a fruitful area of study producing a tremendous body of literature and a lucrative source of income. And it was in this joint context that psychiatry's concentration on women as wives and mothers, though designed to be objective or neutral, often amounted to a prescription for exclusive domesticity.[36]

At the very moment when psychiatry seemed to be totally invested in the mostly male world of the military, it was in fact plunging through to the females behind those military men—their mothers. And once the war was over, psychiatry was able to expand its clientele from military men to civilian men and women. If the treatment of "emotional stress of war," "combat fatigue," and neurotic recruits had catapulted army psychiatry to professional and popular heights, the search for the causes of these ills in the psychology of women lent a new face to psychiatric authority. The rise of psychiatry in the post–World War II period, in short, was every bit as dependent on the figuration of the patient-mother (in both senses of the word patient) as on the illness of draftees.

If the role of women as a contributing factor to the increased prominence of the medical specialty is too often ignored in existing histories of psychiatry, these histories did discuss female psychology and the mother-child relationship, and so, reading between the lines, they can be used to demonstrate the importance of women to the rise and authoritative status of American psychiatry.[37] A chapter entitled "Mental Health in the Home" in William Menninger's *Psychiatry in a Troubled World: Yesterday's War and Today's Challenge* (1948) exemplifies psychiatry's concentration on home, family, parents, and hence, mothers. Here Menninger noted that the postwar family was in crisis, citing the increase in juvenile delinquency and divorce as evidence. He then went on to argue that since the "foundation for good or poor mental health is laid in childhood," the importance of the "healthy, happy home life" is immeasurable.[38] To his credit, Menninger acknowledged and even validated the working wife and mother. He was also one of the few to realize that the neurotic recruits in question were not the sons of the working women reaching child-bearing age after World War II, but rather they were the product of family life of the teens and twenties. Menninger called for "unlimited efforts" to study the family, and publicized wartime psychiatric observations as a source of clues about how to strengthen the family.

While Menninger did not blame women or proscribe women's work outside the home, two best-selling popular books written by psychiatrists did blame "bad" mothers for the ills of recruits and, by extension, for the ills of the world in general. These two popular books are typical of a more specific inflection given to "the problem of woman": the revelation that maladjusted women were actually *neurotic* and in need of psychiatric help. And they illustrate the way the original call to study the mother-child relationship got shifted and exaggerated, in popular literature (and in some professional literature), into a justification for reducing the advised role of the woman to exclusive maternity. They illustrate, that is, the historically current "essentialist" view that women's psychology could and should be defined by her "essential" (read exclusively) biological reproductive and nurturing capacities.[39]

The authors of *Modern Woman: The Lost Sex* (1947), sociologist Ferdinand Lundberg and psychoanalyst Marynia Farnham, decried the "destruction of the home," which they attributed to women working for pay outside of the home, and offered a typology of dangerous and prevalent patterns of mothering, including "the rejecting mother," "the overprotective mother," and "the dominating mother."[40] Edward Strecker's *Their Mothers' Sons* (1946) offered an argument along the same lines.[41] In the book's foreword, Eugene Meyer, chairman of the National Committee on Mental Hygiene, indicated that Strecker should have called the talk from which his book emerged "Psychiatry Speaks to the Neurotic Moms of Psychoneurotics." Enumerating the now familiar litany of the men who avoided the draft or were rejected or discharged from military service on the basis of psychiatric disorders, Meyer set the ground for Strecker's analysis. Strecker's work was to warn the nation of the root cause—psychologically inadequate moms:

> Our war experiences—the alarming number of so-called "psycho-
> neurotic" young Americans—point to and emphasize this threat to our
> survival. No one could view this huge test tube of man power, tried and
> found wanting, without realizing that an extremely important factor was
> the *inability or unwillingness of the American mom and her surrogates*
> *to grant the boon of emotional emancipation during childhood.*[42]
> (emphasis added)

Similarly, Lundberg and Farnham argued that, as neurotics, women consequently became carriers and disseminators of neurosis:

> The conclusion seems inescapable, therefore, that unhappiness not
> directly traceable to poverty, physical malformation or bereavement is
> increasing in our time. This subtly caused unhappiness is merely
> reinforced and intensified by such factors. The most precise
> expression of that unhappiness is neurosis. The bases for most of this

unhappiness, as we have shown, are laid in the childhood home. The principle instrument of their creation are women.[43]

Feminists were subject to particularly pointed attack by Lundberg and Farnham. For example, Mary Wollstonecraft, author of *A Vindication of the Rights of Woman* (1792), was denounced as an "extreme neurotic of compulsive type" who wanted to do injury to the world out of a misguided attempt to redress grievances against her parents.[44]

This derogatory identification of the neurotic mother was also the basis of Philip Wylie's *A Generation of Vipers* (1942), wherein the misogynist concept of "momism" was sensationalized.[45] Wylie blamed women not only for raising infantile sons unfit for war, but also blamed women for raising men who make war in the first place.

Lundberg and Farnham and Strecker, however, provided something that Wylie omitted: an *antidote* to the problem they identify. And that antidote was psychiatry. Psychiatry was heralded by both books as a crucial step to take in correcting the problem. Both books emphasized the shortage of medical professionals. *Modern Woman* called for government action to make psychotherapy available to those who otherwise couldn't afford it. Citing the program proposed by the eminent psychoanalyst Dr. Lawrence Kubie, the authors also called for government action to subsidize the training of practitioners.[46] *Their Mothers' Sons* ends with an epilogue entitled "Psychiatry Speaks to Democracy," promoting the social role of psychiatry.

If the history of psychiatry in this period is represented as a history of male doctors and the female patients who supported these doctors' practice,[47] it behooves us to ask whether women did indeed represent the most numerous patient group. The answer to this question is surprising. In the postwar period through the early sixties women did not significantly outnumber men either as psychiatric or as psychoanalytic patients. In the postwar period, especially the years immediately following the war, there were at least as many if not more male patients than female. Perhaps the reason for the mistaken assumption by psychoanalytic professionals and popularizers alike is the fact that today more psychoanalytic patients are women. Recall, however, the wartime uses for psychiatry and the consequential male patient constituency. This patient constituency remained in place for some years after the war and was supplemented by men undergoing analysis as part of their analytic training.[48]

In 1950, Lawrence S. Kubie published "A Pilot Study of Psychoanalytic Practice in the United States."[49] The results were obtained from a series of questionnaires sent to members of the American Psychoanalytic Association. Questionnaires inquired about fees and gross income of analysts, the age and sex of patients, and the distribution of patients in analytic centers. Kubie, aware that he was dispelling common misconceptions about the gender of analytic patients, found that although there were more females under the age of thirty in analysis, the overall percentage of men in analysis was higher.[50] By 1962, when Nathaniel H. Siegel presented his study, little progress had been made in determining the general characteristics of patients in analysis.[51] Querying 100 analyst members of the American Psychoanalytic Association, responsible for 476 patients, he too found slightly more male than female patients. The largest occupational group of psychoanalytic patients were physicians themselves, including psychiatrists and candidates in training, who were overwhelmingly male.[52] Summarizing past research and providing their own research based on a small number of questionnaires distributed in 1962-63, H. Aronson and Walter Weintraub concurred that most psychoanalytic patients were male.[53] In fact this study of the sex of patients found a larger differential in sex than other studies: 62.5 percent male and 37.5 percent female. It also made available the data of the Central Fact-Gathering Committee, which surveyed 10,000 patients. Although male patients did not outnumber female patients according to that survey, they were not a minority either. The survey discovered a 50-50 ratio of men to women.[54]

Studies of patients in mental institutions and studies of nonanalytic patients (patients of psychiatrists and clinical psychologists)[55] show the same results as studies of psychoanalytic patients in regard to gender. For example, a book-length study by Thomas Pugh and Brian MacMahon compiling various data for the first time in 1962 found that in 1950 admission rates for males were higher than for females and increasing at a faster rate.[56]

Mental Health in America,[57] a comparison of "help-seeking patterns" in 1957 with those in 1976, also finds that, although women turn to others for help with problems they define as mental-health related more than men do, the sources to which they turn tend to be informal—spouses, friends, and so on—rather than formal—health-care professionals. When women do seek help from formal sources, they tend to contact general physicians and clergymen. Men, on the other hand, turn to psychiatrists and psychologists.[58] The authors speculate that men turn to psychiatrists in greater numbers than women in part because the social taboo against admitting vulnerability causes men to wait to seek help until they are quite ill. At that point a mere friend will not serve. The exception is young women who turn to psychiatrists and psychologists in greater numbers than their older counterparts. But the relatively small number of young women in proportion to the female population as a whole is not enough to tip the balance of psychiatric and psychological patients toward females over males.

If it is true that until the early 1960s most, or at least as many, psychiatric patients were men, and men who were desperately ill, why was it the psychological problems of *women* that were identified as the root of social problems by a whole range of discourses in this period? Why were women's psychological problems receiving a balance (or rather imbalance) of popular attention unwarranted by sheer numbers? Part of the answer is that social attitudes about appropriate female roles accepted female vulnerability and illness, but did not so readily accept vulnerability or illness in men. The authors of *Mental Health* express this in psychological terms, speculating that "sex differences in professional help-seeking are primarily due to a greater psychological propensity among women to see themselves as vulnerable and needing help."[59]

But perhaps even more important, the overemphasis on the psychiatric problems and treatment of women, given their numbers, is evidence that the cultural urge to disavow problems other than those that could be viewed as "the problem of woman" was echoed in the psychiatric sphere. The status of the psychiatric institution was enhanced by reference to the seemingly manageable "problems" of neurotic and psychotic women.

This is *not* to deny the presence of mental illness in women. Clearly many women suffered from neurosis, depression, schizophrenia, and other diagnostic categories of illness, the causes of which are still partially unknown, but which seem to range from the organic to the environmental causes Phyllis Chesler identifies in *Women and Madness*. For example, one study from the period links marriage with the onset of mental illness in women requiring hospitalization. This book-length study reveals that although males in mental hospitals outnumbered females in general, there was one category where females outnumbered males: the "married" category. With insight thought by some to be absent from discourses of the period, the book's authors actually attribute the higher incidence of married institutionalized women to women's role in marriage: "The findings suggest that *factors associated with the role of women in marriage may be psychotogenic*, and indicate that these factors operate primarily within the reproductive age" (emphasis added).[60] Thus, my aim in the preceding discussion has not been to gloss over mental illness in women or the very real adverse psychological effects of women's social inequality, but rather to acknowledge that certain psychiatric discursive practices themselves were motivated by and even contributed to the attribution of illness to women.

Professional psychiatric literature reiterated at a theoretical level psychiatry's institutional and popular concentration on women as wives and mothers and the ideological import of this concentration. Freud's work has long been criticized by feminists for the greater attention paid to the boy child who often stands as a model for all children. From this perspective, Freud's emphasis would seem the reverse of that of American postwar popular and professional psychiatry. Yet as early as the 1920s and 1930s, a great deal of psychoanalytic theory was devoted precisely to the correction of this imbalance. The psychosexual development of the girl and of the woman was attended to by such luminaries as Karen Horney, Helene Deutsch, Clara Thompson, Gregory Zilboorg, Marie Bonaparte, Frieda Fromm-Reichmann, and of course, Freud himself. The question of feminine psychosexuality not only loomed large in the 1920s and 1930s, but was pursued as a heated *debate* (of which more later) within psychoanalytic theory rather than as an untroubled investigation.

But what about the postwar years? In *A Mote in Freud's Eye*, Hannah Lerman argues that the years between 1940 and 1965 amounted to "a latency period" in which "overt interest in the theoretical problems of the psychosexual development [of women] subsided."[61] She frames this as a coherent period for women and psychoanalysis based on the omission of such research. Horney and Deutsch, according to Lerman, had completed their dissenting work on female sexuality by 1945 and turned to other issues in the 1950s. Indeed, the publication history of Horney's essays on feminine psychology brackets the "latency period." Written in the 1920s and 1930s, these essays were only collected and published in book-length form in 1967 (as *Feminine Psychology*).[62] Citing an article by Nancy Chodorow,[63] Lerman claims that the number of women analysts declined after World War II as the result of the increased medicalization of the profession as it crossed the Atlantic, and that a climate of fewer women analysts meant less work on feminine psychology.

My own research does not completely support this characterization of a latency period for women's issues. In the 1940s and 1950s Judith S. Kestenberg and Therese Benedek were at the center of a dispute that emerged in American psychoanalysis but that was international in scope.[64] The dispute concerned the organic nature of feminine sexuality with reference to the question of early vaginal sensation. Around the same time, European analyst Marie Bonaparte published *Female Sexuality* (1953) out of New York, and the book was reviewed in the *Journal of the American Psychoanalytic Association*.[65] Male analysts, as well, took an active role in the investigation of feminine sexuality, focusing particularly on physiological and psychoanalytic responses in female reproduction and psychoanalytic studies of the child. René Spitz, Marcel Heiman, and Charles Sarlin were some of the many participants.[66]

Clara Thompson was also a notable contributor of numerous papers on feminine sexual development, publishing a series on the psychology of women between 1941 and 1950.[67] Lerman does not see the existence of Thompson's writing as undermining her thesis that there was a dearth of work on feminine sexuality in the 1940s and 1950s, because she characterizes Thompson as "outside the mainstream of psychoanalytic theorizing."[68] This is true in one sense. Thompson and Karen Horney did break away from the New York Psychoanalytic Society and Institute in 1941 to form their own institute, which was not accepted for membership in the American Psychoanalytic Association. However, the nonacceptance of Thompson's work by the psychoanalytic mainstream is not reason enough to discount its substantive significance in the debates on penis envy, the castration complex, and the Oedipus complex. This is especially true since the mainstream rejection of Thompson's and Horney's institute had a political as much as a theoretical basis.[69] From a historical perspective, this work represents a very significant contribution to psychoanalytic theories of feminine sexuality.

If not as a "latency period," how then might one characterize the postwar period as far as the study of women and psychology is concerned? In spite of some undeniable continuity between the work of prewar and postwar analysts, there were also some crucial shifts in the emphasis of the work that were characteristic of the postwar years. The postwar interest in feminine psychosexuality focused on the link between the physiology of reproduction and the mother-child relationship.

Theoretical literature of the postwar period reiterated popular and professional attempts to trace neuropsychiatric disabilities to the mother-child relationship. Reuben Fine indicates that "once the importance of mothering for the young infant was realized by the profession, a flood of publications poured forth."[70] These publications covered many areas of child analysis, among them the oral phase, childhood phobias, sleep disturbances in young children, psychosomatic diseases, childhood dreams, and learning difficulties. They tended to roll back concern to the earliest days of childhood, thus "naturally" emphasizing the central importance of the mother.

In this research climate it was particularly easy to describe feminine sexuality in terms of motherhood rather than sexual desire. Helene

Deutsch did so in *Psychology of Women* (1944-45),[71] where she extended Freud's claim that the shift from clitoral to vaginal orgasm was necessary for mature feminine sexuality. An equivalence was made between the girl child's (supposed) rush to replace the penis she lacks with a baby from the father (motherhood) and the (supposed) physiological transference of the orgasm from clitoral to vaginal.[72] Here, as in popular writing of the period, maturity for a woman implied maternity, thus reducing to one the number of acceptable adult female roles. *yes*

And yet if I take pains to describe the advantages to institutional psychiatry of taking a practical and theoretical adjustment orientation toward women, I do not intend this ideological sketch as the full story. This is not to say that psychiatry was not adjustment oriented, but rather that it was *and* it wasn't. In postwar American psychiatry relating to women we have an exemplary Foucauldian "space of dissension," a disciplinary purview that was the "meeting place of different discourses" on "the path from one contradiction to another."[73]

In spite of the considerable power of the undiscerning psychiatric discourses and practices described above, they failed to achieve a complete ideological stranglehold on the profession itself, much less on the wider social formation, that failure being especially noticeable in the latter years of the period under discussion. Moreover, if the authoritative status of psychiatry was thoroughly tied up with its figuration and solicitation of women, its status also fell in proportion to psychiatry's finally perceived inability to define femininity or the female role in the context of the social parity for which many had begun to call. In the mid-1960s the face of American psychiatry became less authoritarian, more self-critical, and less liable to dictate prescriptive roles for women, with these changes occurring in an atmosphere of political activism, including feminist activism.

In fact, the optimistic rhetoric was less all-encompassing than self-description would have it: large-scale social problems were in fact being reported and analyzed in newspapers and mass circulation magazines such as *Life* and *Look*. McCarthyism, above-ground nuclear testing, misogyny, and antifeminism were being discussed as the order of the day. They were documented, analyzed, and resisted by a courageous and committed cohort of individuals that grew larger every day. *The Lonely Crowd* by David Reisman, Nathan Glazer, and Reuel Denny (1950, 1953); William H. Whyte's *The Organization Man* (1956); *The Power Elite* (1956) by C. Wright Mills; and *A Preface to Democracy* (1956) by Robert Dahl all provided incisive contemporaneous critiques of the existing social arrangement.[74]

Recent social historians Marty Jezer and William Chafe also do more than simply acknowledge large-scale political problems and social repression; they delineate the discourses of cultural resistance emergent *at the time*. For example, Chafe's book, *Women in America*, includes a chapter titled "The Debate on Women's Place," presumably in order to emphasize that the dominant discourse on women was not the rhetoric of optimism at all, but the feminist/antifeminist debate itself, meaning the debate over the social roles of women. More nebulous and varied than the rhetoric of optimism, this "rhetoric of resistance" strove, through its very multiplicity, to characterize and ameliorate politically the myriad existing social problems.

The intelligent and lucid *Adam's Rib* (1948), by Ruth Herschberger, is direct evidence of feminist writing in an era commonly thought to be devoid of it.[75] The book was not as popular as *Modern Woman: The Lost Sex*, but it was not completely obscure either, having been reviewed in major metropolitan newspapers. Herschberger begins with a thorough refutation of a study by Robert M. Yerkes in which an experiment with male and female chimpanzees was used to "prove" the "natural" dominance of male *humans* and the natural tendency toward prostitution of female *humans*. Herschberger goes on, in successive chapters, to refute the claim that women want to be raped, to argue that clitoral sexuality is not infantile and that the clitoris is not a lesser imitation of the penis, to encourage active female sexuality, and to provide a clever and sophisticated analysis of the social myth of female inferiority. She calls for women to be regarded as human beings in general, instead of beings whose reproductive sexuality exhausts their human potential.

The sophistication and relevance of Herschberger's view is apparent in that it is strikingly similar to that of contemporary French feminist theorist Monique Plaza.[76] Whether purposefully or inadvertently, both studies follow an argument similar to the one Walter Lippmann made in 1922 when he observed that stereotypical personality traits of slaves were being used to justify their oppression, as if they were responsible for it.[77] Herschberger and Plaza both argue that a woman's ability to bear children was wrongly being used to justify her oppression as a being made solely for reproduction, and both Herschberger and Plaza called for the acknowledgment that women possess general human characteristics as well as gender-specific ones.

Adam's Rib was not unique in the views expressed. The year 1952 saw the American publication of Simone de Beauvoir's *The Second Sex*.[78] In addition, mass-circulation magazines and even women's magazines, though still lacking when it came to political issues not pertaining directly to women, did publish articles analyzing certain perceived conflicts of women's lives. A summer 1947 issue of *Life* magazine contained a feature spread titled "American Woman's Dilemma."[79] Here *Life*'s editors acknowledged the conflict between the traditional view of woman's place (in the home) and the reality of the postwar trend toward women working outside the home. The dissatisfaction of women with what they viewed as the overly narrow range of acceptable roles is also evidenced by the results of a poll published in *Fortune* magazine in 1946, according to which 25 percent of women polled answered that, given a choice, they would prefer to be men.[80]

Women Today (1953), a collection of magazine and book excerpts, is a conscious attempt to represent the widely different views of the "average woman," what she is and what she should be, that were current at the time of its publication.[81] The highly antifeminist "Marriage as a Career" is reprinted following the feminist "The Little Woman." "The Little Woman" traces the history of the suffragette movement and exhorts women to work outside the home. In the last section, "The Men's Corner," Abraham Myerson decried the scapegoating of women as practiced by Philip Wylie and the proponents of his "momism," aware of the misogyny behind such scapegoating:

> Mom thus is a victim of social pressure and its distortion, and this social pressure is mainly the creation of a long, confused and complicating line of directives issued by the male commanders.
>
> We have a long way to go in scientific understanding before we can find a real scapegoat for the maladjustments of human beings. We are our mothers' sons and daughters, likewise our fathers', but we are also the mental sons and daughters of all the institutions and of all the conflicting pressures of our confused and tensely disharmonious times.[82]

Interestingly, Myerson not only decried the scapegoating of women, but suggested a broader context for social analysis, which context is virtually Foucauldian in its designation of institutions and social dissonance as the motor of history.

Anthropologists Florence Kluckhohn and Margaret Mead (who often published articles on the family in popular magazines such as *Ladies' Home Journal* and *McCall's*), sociologists Elizabeth Nottingham and Mirra Komarovsky, among many other prolific social scientists, rejected the biological determinism of the misogynist and/or antifeminist spokespeople, emphasizing the importance of environmental and social factors on individual lives.[83] For example, in 1946, Komarovsky published the following summary of her sociological study: "[Women] college Seniors . . . commonly face mutually exclusive expectations of their adult sex roles. In particular, a girl's family and her male friends are the agencies through which she meets the inconsistency between the ideal of homemaker and that of 'career girl.' "[84] These social scientists, like the popular writers described earlier, argued that women's conflicts arose not out of misdirected departure from exclusive domesticity, but out of the context of the structural conflicts of modern society vis-à-vis prescribed roles for women.[85]

By the mid-1950s written social criticisms began to be backed up by the well-documented mass activism of "the sixties" in the form of the civil rights movement and then by demonstrations for women's rights and against the war in Vietnam.[86] By the early 1960s great numbers of women were discovering that "there ha[d] been a persistent decline in the relative status of women since 1940 as measured by occupation, income, and even education,"[87] and they were acting to rectify the inequity.

If one major theme may be said to subtend this feminist point of view it is the critique of the nuclear family. The symbiosis between monopoly capitalism and the nuclear family, always the subject of a certain amount of attention, was finally being addressed by great numbers of politically active men and women. The attempt to gloss over social problems that characterized the late 1940s and 1950s was replaced as early as the late 1950s and early 1960s with an active struggle for social justice, the activity of which extended beyond the written word to marches, demonstrations, consciousness-raising groups, and in general, the organization of political groups to effect legislative reform. On this basis, the period from World War II through the mid-1960s may be divided into two impulses that dovetail: the discursive repression and *resistance* that characterized the early postwar years on one hand, and the mass activism of the late 1950s on the other.

This was the context in which psychiatric hegemony was challenged by alternative views of what constituted appropriate femininity and suitable psychiatric authority. In fact, the growth of American psychoanalytic psychiatry was slowing anyway by the 1960s for other reasons than those having directly to do with social censure.[88] The current and future viability of psychoanalysis was being questioned, as underscored by the typical title of an article published in 1968 in the *American Journal of Psychiatry*: "Is the Unconscious Necessary?" Some causes to which this decline has been attributed include the departure of European analysts from practice as many of them reached retirement age; increased diagnostic ability leading to a decrease in patients for whom classical analytic treatment could be deemed appropriate; a phasing out of hospitals where analysts often practiced in favor of community medicine and antipsychotic medications; an increase in the involvement of analysts in emerging nonanalytic medical fields, such as sleep physiology and neuroanatomy; and finally the saturation of the analytic field.[89]

But despite the fact that there were many reasons for psychiatry's decline that did not have to do with either a humanitarian or a feminist critique of the institution, that latter critique did emerge by the early 1960s as both credible and influential. By the early 1960s, rigid psychiatric models of feminine psychosexuality were being challenged both from inside and outside the profession. In the field of psychoanalytic theory, Helene Deutsch herself ultimately revised her prior ideas about vaginal and clitoral orgasm. At a panel on frigidity in women sponsored by the American Psychoanalytic Association in 1960,[90] she questioned whether the vagina was actually created for the sexual as opposed to reproductive function, breaking out of the argument that mature feminine sexuality required the replacement of clitoral orgasm with vaginal. She came to see the vagina as primarily a reproductive organ that could be involved in orgasm originating with the clitoris.

The implication of this change for feminists is that maternity could now be posed as a choice rather than as the exclusive path to sexual maturity for women. Deutsch's about-face was probably stimulated by the huge volume of clinical data being gathered. According to the Kinsey study, *Sexual Behavior in the Human Female* (1953), vaginal orgasm is a "physical and physiological impossibility":

> It is difficult, however, in the light of our present understanding of the anatomy and physiology of sexual response, to understand what can be meant by a "vaginal orgasm." The literature usually implies that the vagina itself should be the center of sensory stimulation, and this itself as we have seen is a physical and physiological impossibility for nearly all females.[91]

Kinsey's study went even further to point out that if vaginal orgasm is actually impossible, then many psychoanalysts and other clinicians had been leading women in a futile exercise when encouraging them to learn vaginal responses.

The same findings appeared in the Masters and Johnson study of 1966,[92] and Mary Jane Sherfey used this research to emend psychoanalytic work on female sexuality.[93] Although her proposed alterations in psychoanalytic theory are quite tame from a contemporary feminist perspective, they were radical enough to provoke the ire of some members of the psychoanalytic community. Like Deutsch in her later work, Sherfey rejected clitoral-vaginal transfer theory and also rejected the "rigid dichotomy between masculine and feminine sexual behavior" contained in some psychoanalytic work.[94]

The major challenge to rigid psychiatric notions of femininity came, of course, from the women's movement of the 1960s. Here Betty Friedan's *Feminine Mystique* is notable once again, this time as one of the earliest feminist critiques of American psychology, anthropology, and sociology.[95] Simone de Beauvoir's feminist classic *The Second Sex* (English edition, 1952) also broached a challenge to what de Beauvoir identified as the second-class status of women perpetuated by aspects of psychoanalysis, and Phyllis Chesler's *Women and Madness* pointed out how mental institutions reproduced the female experience in the family where men are dominant.[96] Feminist work of the 1970s and 1980s furthered the founding challenge thrown down by de Beauvoir, Friedan, and Chesler. The recent book *Women and the Psychiatric Paradox* is exemplary in this respect, its thesis being that the very institution to which women are forced to turn for help (out of conventions and lack of alternatives) is itself an institution that oppresses women.[97]

Since the 1960s, Freudian psychoanalysis has come under far more thoroughgoing attack by American feminists than that brought to bear by Friedan. The most objectionable concepts have been penis envy, with its obvious implication that the girl feels and is inferior; the assertion that maternity is the final (and only) step to mature normal femininity; the female triad of passivity, narcissism, and masochism (highly undesirable characteristics in our society); the assertion of woman's inferiority and arrested childlike nature; and the psychoanalytic denial of the existence and/or importance of sexual seduction, or rather, in the terms of many feminists, the actual fact of abuse, rape, or molestation.[98] The status of psychiatry fell, then, in proportion to its ever-growing perceived inability to define femininity or the female role in the context of the social parity for which many had begun to call.

This feminist critique both contributed to and benefited from the general social critique of psychiatry. Historian Sanford Gifford discusses the decline of American psychiatry not only in terms of the number of practitioners, but in terms of its status as an ideological force, noting that American psychoanalysis was attacked in the 1960s as an agent of conformity. The attack affected the government's attitude toward the medical research establishment and resulted in a gradual reduction of research funds. This was ironic vis-à-vis psychoanalysts, as they more than any other medical specialists had tried to resist the authoritarian role and were the least directive, as will be seen in chapter 2. The question became that of whether it is ever possible for an institution such as psychiatry to avoid functioning as an authoritarian discourse of expertise supported by and supportive of "the establishment."

The Politics of Therapy (1971) by Seymour Halleck,[99] a book that was much discussed in educational psychology, summarized and extended views critical of psychiatry that had emerged in the early 1960s. He argued that psychiatry could not and should not be practiced as though it were a neutral medical model of healing: "Any kind of psychiatric intervention, even when treating a voluntary patient, will have an impact upon the distribution of power within the various social systems in which the patient moves."[100] Halleck attributed his own ability to see through the neutrality claims of psychiatry to 1960s activism. By contrast, he says, prior views of psychiatry had developed in an atmosphere of consensus:

> Until the past decade [the sixties] psychiatrists were allowed to pursue their work in a climate of relative calm and consensus, a climate in which most people who were able to voice their opinion approved of the basic institutions of their society. This consensus was especially strong in the years immediately following World War II and throughout the 1950s; during that time psychiatry gained considerable respectability and rapidly expanded its ranks.[101]

The acknowledgment of the "politics of therapy," or the concept that therapy is not neutral, goes hand in hand with a changing view of the relationship between society and the individual. In its American incarnation, psychoanalysis often held that the function of civilization was to regulate basic human instincts and drives that otherwise would be quite barbaric.[102]

But World War II and Nazism made it necessary to reconsider whether the nonconformists needed regulation or whether in fact the society needed to become less oppressive. It was becoming obvious to many that often it was the society and not the individual that was "sick."[103] Humanistic psychology, which Abraham Maslow named the Third Force (Freudianism represented the First Force, Behaviorism the Second Force) and which included psychologists Gordon Allport, Carl Rogers, Erich Fromm, Erik Erikson, Rollo May, and many others among its practitioners, seemed to many to be the psychology most able to help human beings realize their positive potential given the troubled state of society in general.[104]

In 1962 Maslow wrote:

> Adjusted to what? To a bad culture? To a dominating parent? What shall we think of a well-adjusted slave? . . . Clearly what will be called personality problems depends on who is doing the calling. The slave owner? The dictator? The patriarchal father? The husband who wants

his wife to remain a child? It seems quite clear that personality problems may sometimes be loud protests against the crushing of one's psychological bones, of one's true inner nature. What is sick then is *not* to protest while this crime is being committed.[105]

By the mid-1960s, then, the notions that social problems sprang from female maladjustment and that they could be stemmed by therapeutic attention to same, if not totally discredited, were at least being very seriously questioned and overhauled as a motivating ideological platform of postwar society.

2

Women and Psychiatric Technique

When individual psychiatrists, whether purposefully or inadvertently, used their treatments to adapt deviant women to traditional gender roles, they brought home to the doctor-patient relationship the institutionalized psychiatric gender-specific authoritarianism previously discussed. Conversely, when individual psychiatrists *questioned* that psychiatric prescription, whether they construed it as misapplied Freud or as being implicit to psychiatric foundations; when they abjured narrow prescriptions of appropriate femininity and supported wider notions of healthy feminine psychosexuality, they engaged in theoretical and/or practical *resistance* to adjustment therapy for women. This chapter will explore how the doctor-patient relationship, as the smallest unit of the relationship between psychiatry and women, embodied very specifically the larger institutional contradictions discussed in the previous chapter. Psychiatric technique, it will be argued, displayed both aspects of the adjustment/resistance paradigm.

Adjustment

There is no vagueness about the goals, functions, and needs of the
normal woman. Science in recent years has thrown a bright
light on her, and that is why we can be certain of many fundamental
details about her.

—Marie N. Robinson, M.D.
The Power of Sexual Surrender (1959)

23

In *Medicine and the Reign of Technology*, Stanley Reiser argues that over the last few centuries the techniques used by physicians to diagnose illness have changed.[1] Whereas in the seventeenth century doctors relied on patients' own accounts of their symptoms, even to the point of diagnosing through the post, in the twentieth century doctors rely on evidence gleaned from more objective and efficient new technologies such as the microscope and the X ray. Reiser interprets this trend as the substitution of one unsatisfactory form of evidence gathering (what the patient says) by another (what the machine says). According to Reiser, both diagnostic techniques undermine what he sees as a desirable personal *relationship* between doctor and patient, because neither requires the physical and conscious presence of the patient. That is, the patient may be present bodily, but he or she is not necessarily an active subject who relates his or her case history, but rather a passive object of manual palpitation and visual scrutiny.[2] Under this latter type of examination, the patient is not viewed as a whole person but as a collection of internal organs or systems to be penetrated by instruments.

Although Reiser does not dwell on psychiatry, his work reflects interestingly on this medical specialty, for the technological orientation Reiser bemoans was abundantly present in certain psychiatric practices that distanced doctor from patient and relied on a battery of instruments (drugs and electroshock therapy, for example) rather than personal communication, creating an aura of scientific efficiency that sought short-term solutions to psychological disorders. Furthermore, the social climate described above was one where this technological orientation could align itself with wider ideologies validating psychiatric authoritarianism in regard to women. Examples from the realms of psychosurgery, shock treatment, drug therapy, psychotherapy, and psychoanalysis will be used here to illustrate the presence and ideological import of the technological orientation in psychiatry as it relates to the treatment of women.

Psychosurgery was the most radical treatment for mental illness and represented the most extreme use of corrective apparati in the service of behavioral adjustment. Invented in its twentieth-century form in 1935 by a Portuguese neurosurgeon who called his procedure the prefrontal leucotomy, psychosurgery enjoyed its greatest popularity between 1948 and 1952.[3] Between those years, tens of thousands of patients were subjected to various mutilating brain operations. The transorbital lobotomy, a later development by preeminent American psychosurgeon Walter Freeman, was an operation in which the surgeon or psychiatrist entered the brain with a sharp instrument from under the eyelid rather than by drilling through the skull as in the original leucotomy or prefrontal lobotomy. Freeman first established this later type of lobotomy as an office procedure taking only minutes, done with an ice pick using electroconvulsive shock as the only anesthetic. In the late 1940s and 1950s, Freeman toured the country performing mass lobotomies to demonstrate this procedure. In West Virginia, for example, he spent one afternoon lobotomizing thirty-five women, one of whom is thought to have been the actress Frances Farmer.[4]

According to Elliot Valenstein, author of the definitive history of psychosurgery, in the best of cases lobotomy led to a "normalization of behavior;" in the worst of cases, the patient's impairment reached a devastating level.[5] Patients subjected to lobotomies frequently died or if they survived the operation, often suffered massive memory loss and extreme inability to function in even the most elementary of tasks, such as self-feeding and dressing or control of the bowels. Others descended into dementia that may or may not have been present prior to the psychosurgery.

Although Valenstein himself does not make this point, an examination of his sources confirms that the majority of lobotomy patients in the United States were women. In state hospitals, psychosurgery was performed on two females for every male.[6] The "normalization of behavior" that was a hoped-for result of psychosurgical procedures was actually normalization of behavior for women in particular. As was also the case in England, according to Elaine Showalter's discussion of gender and lobotomy in *The Female Malady: Women, Madness and English Culture, 1830-1980*, women in the United States were prime candidates for psychosurgery for reasons deeply involved with the ideologies of a culture that denigrated socialized feminine behaviors such as dependency and passivity even as it legislated these attitudes, and that treated women as less than adults, questioning female capacity for intellectual and moral development. Showalter argues that female madness in the postwar period was no longer linked to hysteria, as it had been, but to schizophrenia, which "offers a remarkable example of the cultural conflation between femininity and insanity":[7] "Schizophrenic symptoms of passivity, depersonalization, disembodiment, and fragmentation have parallels in the social situation of women."[8] In other words, in certain cases socialized female behavior may be construed as insanity.

But although psychosurgery was performed on schizophrenic women, the literature of psychosurgery stresses over and over again that the most important criterion for selection was not diagnosis, but rather the existence of a proper environment for care to which the patient could be returned.[9] In accordance with vestigial Victorian sentiments about women's dependency and patriarchal protective responsibility, it was thought that women could be sent home more easily than men "because of the greater protection afforded them in the home."[10] This variable also made women prime candidates for psychosurgery because if few postoperative lobotomy patients could ever return to outside jobs, lobotomized women could be returned to the routinized domestic duties that society often delegated to them. Freeman and his coauthor Watts admitted that after a prefrontal lobotomy "no physician, dentist, artist, musician, or writer has been able to make the grade," but they did think that a domestic worker might be able to carry on as usual after a prefrontal lobotomy.[11] The gender assignments implicit in this seemingly neutral enumeration of occupations become obvious in the following quote about the prefrontal lobotomy: "This procedure is always followed by more or less great alteration in character and defects in judgment. In a washer*woman* these results may be of little concern, but when a patient is a professional business *man*, who must make decisions affecting many people, these results may be disastrous" (emphasis added).[12] Indeed a description of the emotional impairment produced by lobotomy, for example Valenstein's statement that in a postlobotomy patient "there is less activity and more inertia; [t]he intellectual processes are simple, with attention to the immediate rather than to the remote, to the factual rather than the theoretical, with decisions that are simple rather than deliberative, and with a restriction of the intellectual range,"[13] reads strikingly like that of feminist descriptions of what housework does to the mind, or, alternatively, like sexist descriptions of the female psyche.[14] If women are not traditionally called upon for an opinion, neither are lobotomy patients: "When before has an educated man asked a woman how in her opinion war can be prevented?" asked Virginia Woolf in 1938, while Freeman and Watts were bemoaning the case of lobotomy patients, saying "[it] is almost impossible to call upon a person who has undergone operation on the frontal lobes for advice on any important matter."[15]

Psychosurgery shares its history, fields of application, and effects with two other somatic treatments developed around the same time: insulin shock therapy, which followed the historical course of psychosurgery most closely, peaking in the 1940s and early 1950s, and electroconvulsive shock therapy (ECT), still in use today on a much greater scale than psychosurgery.[16] And as with psychosurgery, the prime candidates for shock therapy in England and the United States were women, outnumbering men by a ratio of two or even three to one.[17]

As with psychosurgery, women received electroshock more often because they were "judged to have less need of their brains," and indeed were thought to be more fit and docile for the monotony of housework after ECT.[18] In keeping with the view that ascribes to women a lack of intellectual ability, the patient's own consent to the procedure in all the somatic treatments is often skirted. It is the family that gives its consent. Thus, should any disagreement between patient and family, wife and husband exist, it is the relative rather than the sick person who is deemed to know better. "With successful handling," says Lothar Kalinowsky, author of the period bible of shock treatment, "most patients can be persuaded."[19]

Professional literature often explains the patient's resistance to shock therapy as a symptom of his or her illness:

> Is treatment against a patient's wishes ever ethically permissible? At first glance there is something most distasteful about the idea of applying electric current to the brain of an unwilling patient. And yet it is a familiar paradox that the extreme guilt and self-punitiveness of a deeply depressed patient are likely to make him reject anything that could make him feel better. He may cling to his depression as an imagined punishment for past wrongdoings, or his pathological hopelessness might not let him believe that any treatment can possibly work in his case.[20]

In *Shock Treatment: And Other Somatic Procedures in Psychiatry*, Kalinowsky puts it this way:

> Some patients do not want the treatment [insulin shock] because it renders them unconscious and they expect to be experimented upon, or raped, or castrated during this period. Others refuse the treatment in the framework of their general negativism; they are against any form of therapy. With successful handling most patients can be persuaded.[21]

Unfortunately, the fears presented as delusional in this passage did sometimes have an all-too-real basis. Freeman did actually perform the experimental brain surgical technique, the transorbital lobotomy, on patients anesthetized by shock.

In 1953, a poem and letter to her male doctor from a female patient who had undergone ECT were printed in the *American Journal of Psychiatry*.[22] As the presenting doctor notes, the abbreviation "I.V." stands for the intraveneous injections of barbiturates routinely given to patients before treatment (he does *not* mention that the need for barbiturates was based on frequent injuries sustained by patients during shock treatments before the use of drugs to combat this). "Conv." stands for convulsion and "Consc." for consciousness:

Dear Dr. Bowman:

In appreciation for all the clinic has done for me, I turn over full ownership, rights, and privileges to verses called "Shock Treatments." I hope they might in some small way prove to others they need not fear these treatments.

Sincerely yours,
D. R. P.

ELECTROSHOCK THERAPY

I.V.
Oh ship ahoy! we're sailing high
Across the sea so wide and bare.
The breeze against the full-blown sail
Lends music to my fleeting prayer.

A moment's sleep upon the deck—
My back against the hard, white board;
Not ever dreams can enter here—
No haunting fear—no hanging sword.

Conv.
I know not when the lightning strikes
Nor how I'm beaten with its whip.
I know not when all hell lets loose
Its fury on this fearful trip.

But there's a captain at the helm.
In spite of storm, he will escort
This craft across the surging sea
And bring it safely into port.

Consc.
When I awake, I rest awhile—
The voyage done—and no regret
To mar the strangely quiet peace
Of safe return. I just—forget.

The stated purpose of the publication of the poem was to show that women appreciated the beneficial effects of shock therapy and to defend the psychiatrist from accusations of sadism. But the poem and letter are actually evidence of some rather different things: the romantic light in which the doctor himself would like to be regarded (he published the letter in a professional journal read by his colleagues), the distribution of power implicit in the depiction of doctor as "captain" and woman as damsel in distress, and the extent to which this woman

has internalized the hidden power relation as she gives up "full ownership" of her verses to be retitled by the doctor.

In the mid-1950s psychotropic drugs came into use. These drugs
could help shorten the hospital stay of seriously disturbed patients,
make the patient more tractable during his or her stay (reducing the
destruction of hospital property and significantly simplifying hospital
management), and make patients more receptive to psychotherapy by
reducing the need for restraint and seclusion.[23] Though I would agree
that drug therapy, unlike the procedure of lobotomy, has its legitimate
uses, its administration in this period was notably consistent with patterns of adjustment treatment. Drugs were often administered according to socially determined notions of sex roles and they furthered the
dependence on technological cure rather than self-directed analysis or
change.

The advertisements for these drugs in professional journals provide
a unique kind of evidence about how pharmacotherapy fit into existing
views of gender and psychiatry.[24] Obviously, these documents are ads
and cannot be understood as the equivalent of serious psychiatric research on diagnosis and treatment. However, precisely because they
are ads, they can be interpreted to reveal the ideological nature of the
images and scenarios of doctors, patients, and treatments of which
they are composed. By offering images in keeping with the psychiatrists' expectations and fantasies about the doctor-patient relationship,
the ads attempted to solicit the purchase power of the psychiatrists
who were in positions to prescribe the advertised drugs. These ads are
of further interest because their visual representations of doctors and
patients may be compared with the visual depictions of doctors and patients in fiction films of the period.

The candidates depicted and the nature of the desirable behaviors
the drugs promise to produce are consistent with wider social norms
being discussed. The male doctor as authority figure—a man among
male colleagues (I did not come across one female psychiatrist pictured in a drug ad)—the housewife overburdened by routinized tasks,
the working woman in women's service jobs such as secretary or
teacher, and the promise that with drug therapy she will better carry
out her appropriate role may all be found.

A representative ad from 1960 shows in six photodocumentary
frames the progress of a woman's treatment.[25] The first frame depicts
the kindly physician in white listening across his desk as the "tense,
nervous" patient discusses her "emotional problems." Her hands are
clasped together and her head is bowed. After taking a capsule in frame
two, the patient is able to stay calm "even under the pressure of busy,

Weight loss could improve her mental outlook

You will find 'Dexedrine' Spansule sustained release capsules facilitate weight reduction by providing daylong control of appetite. Improvement in mental outlook almost always follows.

For example, Settel[1] reports:
"Fifteen of 16 patients (94 per cent) reported excellent appetite control. . . . The resulting improvement in appearance and figure [following weight reduction] bolstered morale and raised the level of interpersonal relations."

Dexedrine* Spansule† capsules are available in three strengths: 5 mg., 10 mg. and 15 mg.

Smith Kline & French Laboratories, Philadelphia

Figure 3. The iconography of this ad echoes closely that of Gene Tierney's shoplifting trip at the opening of *Whirlpool.* From the *American Journal of Psychiatry* 114, no. 11 (May 1958).

crowded supermarket shopping." In frame four she enjoys her evening meal with her husband and two children, and in frame five "she is able to listen carefully to P.T.A. proposals." Frame six finds her "peacefully asleep." Here, then, is the woman's day—the goal of psychiatric prescription.

The appropriate role for women involves an appropriate physical appearance. Drugs for weight reduction capitalize on this. One striking ad shows a hefty woman in a long coat gazing into a store window through which we see her (Figure 3).[26] In the foreground and background slim mannequins (counterparts of those imitated so well but only superficially by the troubled Ann Sutton [Gene Tierney] in *Whirlpool* [see chapter 3]) model dresses, high heels, and pearls. "Weight loss could improve her mental outlook," claims the ad.

Notably, these drug ads do not deny real-world problems. They refer frequently to the pressures of modernity and to the monotony of household tasks. But it would be against the interest of the drug companies to admit any possibility that social change is what is required to relieve some of the symptoms depicted. The cure they promise is individual behavioral and cosmetic change. For example, Dexamyl may be prescribed "to help the depressed and anxiety-ridden housewife who is surrounded by a monotonous routine of daily problems, disappointments and responsibilities. . . . with 'Dexamyl' you [the prescribing psychiatrist] can often help her to face her problems" (Figure 4).[27] It cannot be suggested that the housewife get an outside job and spend less time on housework.

Men do not escape this prescription of drugs to ameliorate social problems. A ubiquitous image is that of the harried businessman. One ad picturing a man in a business suit, hat, and overcoat and carrying a portfolio claims that "in these times of accelerated activity, strife, and resulting mental tension, appropriate dosage of 'Seconal Sodium' fully answers the problem."[28] Another ad depicts a drawing of a man in hat and overcoat silhouetted against a lighted doorway. Superimposed over this image is a giant stethoscope and the words, "the patient who won't 'fit in' " (Figure 5).[29]

But if men and women alike are subject to rigidified representations in these ads, there is a significant difference in the depiction of men and women in relation to their (always male) doctors. The male patient is someone with whom we may identify as he seeks to verbalize his problems. We see almost his whole body, and, most often, the male patient is depicted seated next to rather than across the desk from his physician. With both garbed in business suits and glasses, in appearance, the male patient could almost *be* his physician (Figure 6).[30]

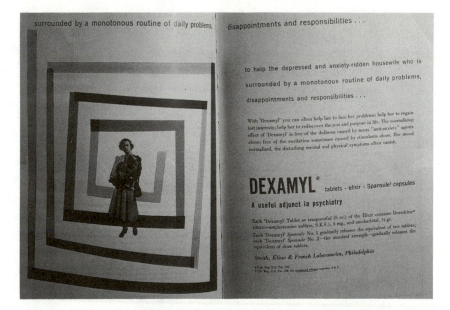

Figure 4. Gender-stereotyped conformity is encouraged in this ad from the *American Journal of Psychiatry* 112, no. 11 (May 1956).

Alternatively, in ad after ad figuring a woman patient, the point of view of the photograph or drawing is that of the male psychiatrist (with whom the psychiatrist subscribers to the *Journal* were presumably meant to identify): through his eyeglasses (Figure 7), over his shoulder, from behind his desk. In one ad we see, from a vantage point over his shoulder, a woman speaking to her doctor (Figure 8).[31] A beam of light is projected from behind the white-haired, white-coated doctor onto the anxious woman. The "goals, functions and needs of the normal woman" are enumerated by the ad copy, which recounts how "raging, combative, unsociable patients usually become more co-operative, friendlier, quieter, and much more amenable to psychotherapy and rehabilitation measures." Unacceptable angry behavior is replaced by socially acceptable docility. As in the epigraph at the start of this section, science throws a "bright light" on this woman and the women she represents, isolating her "fundamental details" or supposed essence as it isolates her figure, and presenting her for psychotherapy and the "rehabilitation" with which psychotherapy is here coupled.

The epigraph at the start of this section is taken from one of the popular, "modern" marriage manuals that were authored by highly trained physicians, psychiatrists, and psychoanalysts and that appeared in profusion in this period. Designed for a mass audience, these manuals

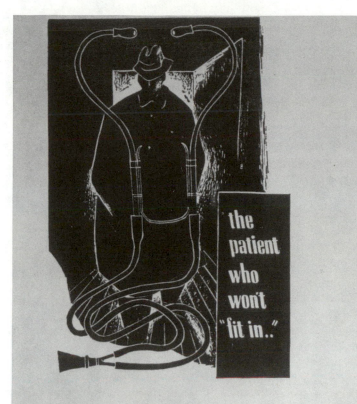

Figure 5. Men do not escape prescriptions for conformity, as illustrated in this ad from the *American Journal of Psychiatry* 109, no. 1 (July 1952). Reproduced with permission of Burroughs Wellcome Co.

Figure 6. The representation of the male psychiatric patient is illustrated in this ad from the *American Journal of Psychiatry* 115, no. 4 (October 1958).

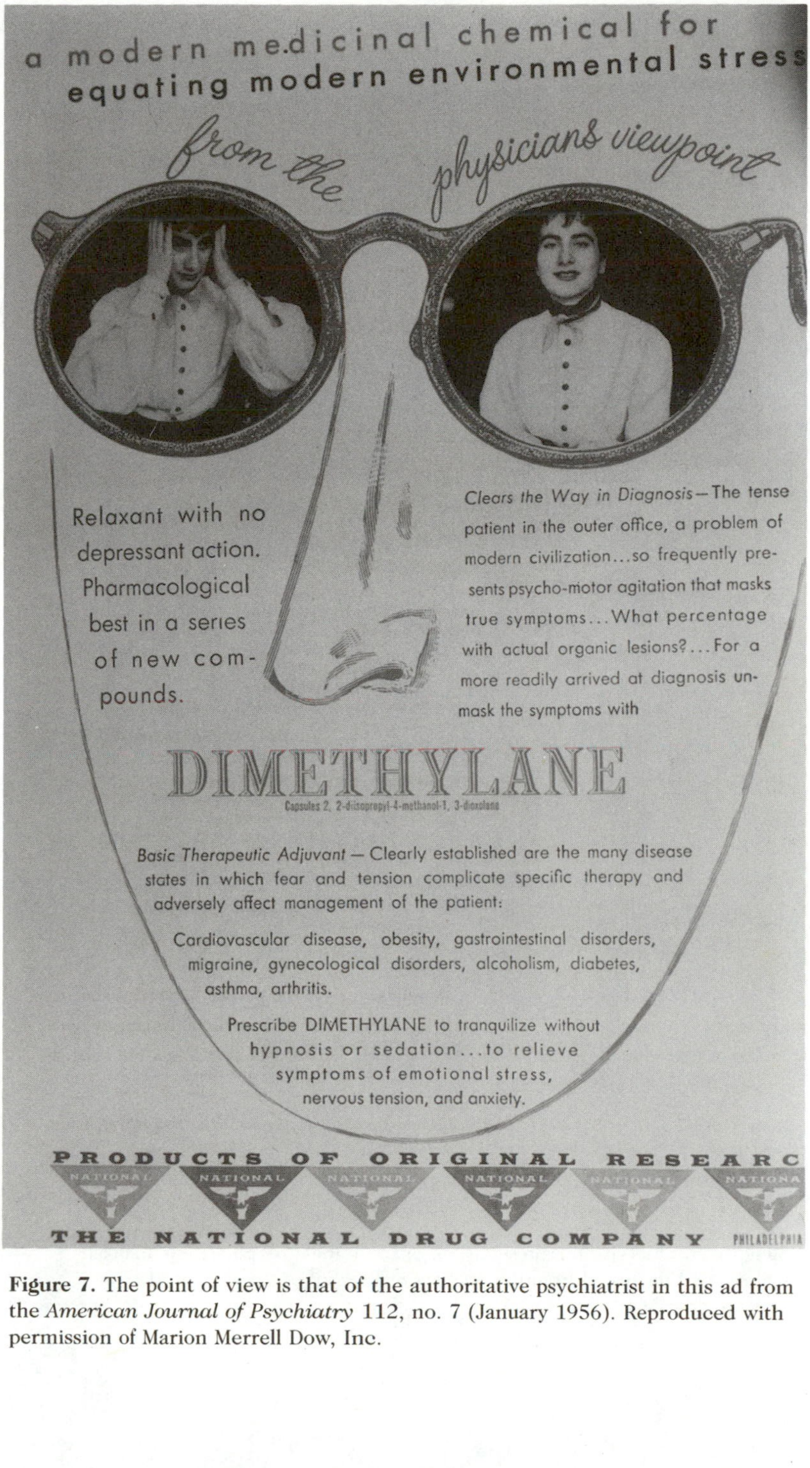

Figure 7. The point of view is that of the authoritative psychiatrist in this ad from the *American Journal of Psychiatry* 112, no. 7 (January 1956). Reproduced with permission of Marion Merrell Dow, Inc.

Figure 8. The typical representation of the female psychiatric patient is illustrated in this ad from the *American Journal of Psychiatry* 112, no. 7 (January 1956).

extended adjustment to individuals not otherwise in treatment.[32] Unlike the bible of marriage manuals, *Ideal Marriage* by Dutch gynecologist Th. H. van de Velde, which is encyclopedic in its description of male and female physiology and relations,[33] popular offshoots contained a paucity of information and a surfeit of moralizing. Psychoanalyst Marie Robinson spends a core chapter answering the questions, "What is the mature woman? Who is she? What are her characteristics? Her personality? Her role in Life?"[34] In answer, Robinson gives the case history of a "tragic" married woman whose mother had emphasized achievement in the "male world" and encouraged her to be tied down no more than a man. And Robinson congratulates herself for helping this woman decide to adopt two children. The shared philosophy of these manuals is that a woman should gain her personal satisfaction as a secondary product of satisfying her husband. To be a proper wife a woman must not only "learn something" about preparing appetizing meals, but she should also learn how to "*satisfy her husband sexually*" which in turn will result in her own greater happiness."[35] Book after book exhorts the woman to take a submissive position to her husband, to learn that "the excitement comes from the act of surrender,"[36] and to retire from the outside world, "brutal as it is," in order to "keep the flames of affection and tenderness burning."[37]

Almost twenty years after the case study of her treatment became a bestseller, Chris Sizemore, the subject of *The Three Faces of Eve* (1957), wrote her autobiography, *I'm Eve* (1973). Written from a feminist perspective, the book provides a fascinating account of common psychiatric discursive practices that were oppressive to women, many of which will be discussed in chapter 3 in conjunction with the film, *The Three Faces of Eve*. One particular passage is useful here as a kind of summary of a prevalent attitude in psychiatry. Near the end of her treatment, Sizemore's psychiatrist, in an attempt to be reassuring and congratulatory, instructed her to "sit back and live the life of happiness she so richly deserved, never forgetting that *the most important thing in her life was to make Don [her husband] happy and to devote the rest of her life toward that end*" (emphasis added).[38]

Resistance

But if the adjustment impetus has been explored here independently of its counterpart, psychiatric resistance to conformist and gender-normative psychiatric treatment, this has been done for heuristic reasons. In fact, authoritarian psychiatric techniques very often fell under criticism and certain areas of psychiatry were characterized much more by internal *debate* on the problems of psychiatry's conventionalist ten-

dencies and on its limitations and efficacy than by adjustment strategies pure and simple. At the same time, for example, that marriage
manuals were calling for "sexual surrender," Norman Reider, chief of
psychiatric service at San Francisco Hospital, was evaluating society's
bias toward marriage and calling for its reevaluation.[39] Reider viewed
the profamily prejudice as understandable in a society where the "importance of the family as a primary social unit has almost never been
questioned" and was not being loudly questioned at the time he was
writing (1956): "We live in an era wherein tightening and fortifying of
bonds and ties is the order of the day rather than any lessening of
them."[40] The therapist's or counselor's evaluation of each marriage
cannot escape the prevalent ideology on marriage, or, as Reider put it,
"those irrational elements, highly emotionally tinged, that make us au-
tomatically consider possible divorce or separation with a certain
amount of discomfort and anxiety."[41] Nevertheless, Reider called for a
more complex psychiatric view of the family that could be read as less
oppressive to women because it questioned family maintenance at all
costs. He urged psychiatrists to resist the limited view, asserting that
"to continue some marriages, given certain insoluable conditions, may
be a disservice to both the marital partners and to the children as
well."[42] Under Reider's conception, marriage is a nonhomogeneous institution in which individuals change, quest for security, repeat previous patterns of home life, and look for socially condoned outlets and
various other satisfactions. He believed that for these reasons marital
permanence need not be the primary goal of the researcher or therapist.

Even an individual's own work could harbor the contradictory aspects of the adjustment/resistance paradigm. On one hand, psychoanalyst Robert Lindner was the author of a famous case history from
the postwar period, which I read as implicitly adjustment oriented.[43]
The study is of Laura, a "fashionably thin," attractive woman, who
would eat to the point of falling unconscious. Lindner's successful analysis revealed that Laura was consuming food to fill the emptiness
within her in order to simulate pregnancy by her father. In the terms of
the narrative that Lindner weaves, his analysis makes perfect sense.
Yet we might also ask what psychoanalytic traditions are furthered by
its content and what implications for female roles are inherent. I do
not disbelieve the case history; I "merely" find it ideologically charged.
The extreme classicism of the analytic interpretation in which the patient is revealed to be acting out the little girl's fantasy, described by
Freud, of having a baby by her father strikes me as a convenient reaf-
firmation of a basic psychoanalytic explanation. The choice to popu-
larize this particular case history reveals that there was great stake in

this literal "proof" of theory, and conversely, that behind the theory being proved lay a perceived social need to see women as professional mothers. Perhaps unselfconsciously, but certainly revealingly, Lindner's study draws on the explanatory capacity of shared standards, such as "thin is beautiful," for example.[44] The key to Laura's illness was uncovered one day when Lindner burst into Laura's apartment during one of her eating binges and discovered the pillow apparatus she had fashioned to simulate pregnancy. Her successful treatment would lead, presumably, to marriage to her eligible boyfriend, Ben.[45] Lindner seems, here, to be subscribing to the view that a woman must be married to be happy. He titled this case history "Solitaire," implying not only the isolation of illness, but the isolation of being a single woman, as well. And yet, in spite of this ideologically complicit orientation in the case of Laura, Lindner was also the author of well-known and explicitly antiadjustment books by the suggestive titles *Must You Conform?* and *Prescription for Rebellion*.[46] Significantly, however, these books dealt with and were aimed at "mankind," rather than women per se, so their nonconformist attitudes were perhaps purchased at a lower price than they would have been had Lindner considered a woman's rebellion.

Challenges to the hidden ideologies of psychiatry's adjustment impulse were usually not so overtly articulated as that of Reider or even those of Lindner in his nonconformist books, nor were they clearly feminist in intent. But discursive practices in several areas did amount to a freer therapeutic environment for all patients, and particularly for the women patients often subject to oppressive social practices and adjustment treatments.

A central area of nonconventionalist possibility is precisely that of psychiatric and particularly psychoanalytic therapeutic technique as distinct from therapeutic treatments such as pharmacotherapy. In keeping with the larger adjustment/resistance paradigm under discussion, the specific attention paid to psychotherapeutic technique in the postwar period was characterized by the *debate* over the desirability and even possibility of what amounted to an adjustment orientation. Practically, psychoanalysis-based psychotherapies ran the gamut from the strictest Freudian analytic psychoanalysis to a substantially modified form of psychotherapy. Theoretically, the question of whether psychoanalysis was (or should be) nondirective or directive was a central theme returned to time and time again in core psychoanalytic journals in the 1950s.[47] Each postwar analyst who contributed to the debate on technique coined terms to describe the "classical" psychoanalytic process: "nondirective," "clarification," "uncovering," "working through," "insight therapy," "interpretive"; and words to describe the procedures less classical and more psychotherapeutically oriented: "supportive," "working out," "suggestion," "manipulation," "abreactive," "corrective experience."[48]

The result of this range was that some forms of psychotherapy lent themselves more easily than others to the work of adjusting women to traditional gender roles because the therapeutic technique itself involved conscious attempts on the part of the therapist to change the behavior of the patient. In the modified form of analytic psychotherapy, the psychiatrist would be likely to use any combination of "support, exhortation, argument, rewards and punishments, [or] education" to bring the patient to "general situational adjustment."[49] It is not surprising, then, given the nature of the "situation"—the social system to which the female patient would need to be fitted—that psychotherapeutic practice often encouraged the dominant model of normal femininity. In this case the therapeutic situation itself could be construed as a kind of discursive technology where what is administered is not an electroshock or a drug, but a formalized technique for raising, discussing, and correcting psychological problems.

Classical Freudian psychoanalysis was least reconcilable with this adjustment impulse because its goal was not to adjust the patient's behavior, but to help the analysand gain insight into his or her unconscious processes. Nevertheless, there were doctors in postwar America who considered themselves psychoanalysts rather than psychotherapists who used a technique that must be deemed more rather than less adjustment oriented.[50]

Franz Alexander was one important psychoanalyst who was for the unification of the profession and thus for the integration of "supportive" procedures into mainstream American psychoanalytic technique. In 1954, he noted five therapeutic forms of support of the patient by the psychotherapist: gratifying dependent needs through ego support; abreaction to reduce emotional stress; objective reviewing, in which the therapist reviews the patient's situation and assists the patient's judgment; aid to the ego's own neurotic defenses; and, finally, *manipulation of the life situation*.[51] According to Alexander, "*Supportive measures knowingly or inadvertently are used in all forms of psychotherapy*" (emphasis added).[52] In fact, Alexander went on to argue that transference, the principal psychoanalytic therapeutic tool, consisted precisely in a kind of support necessitated by the patient's regression to dependent attitudes of infancy and childhood.[53]

Analyst Phyllis Greenacre also points to a form of the transference relationship being practiced in which the analyst takes an active, directive stance toward current events in the patient's life.[54] This form of transference relies on the process of "working out," not on the process of "working through." It relies on "carrying into reality actively new behavior patterns under the suggestion and support of the analyst."[55]

Although it would be virtually impossible to prove that the majority of patients subjected to such an impulse were women, the following example suggests one interesting avenue whereby supportive technique might be advocated for the female patient in particular, thus corroborating the larger argument that the supportive impulse is consistent with the management of power in American society, which locates the female as dependent.

In the face of the relatively small number of patients for whom the treatment was deemed appropriate, analysts became interested in "widening [the] scope of indications for psychoanalysis."[56] Thus, Leo Stone undertook to explore "borderline cases."[57] The patients Stone discussed were allied as a diagnostic grouping by their narcissism. But narcissism and transference seem mutually exclusive. The incapacity for transference in narcissistic neurosis originally led Freud to deem such neurosis inaccessible to psychoanalysis. Yet, drawing on the work of Karl Abraham and others, Stone includes among his recommendations for the special management of these patients "prolonged preliminary periods of *supportive* therapy" (emphasis added).[58]

But who are these patients with narcissistic neurosis for whom supportive therapy is specially indicated? They are women. Freud associates narcissistic object-choice with women and anaclitic object-choice with men, yet he points out that his distinction is merely "schematic" and that "both kinds of object-choice are open to each individual."[59] Stone, however, mentions six of his own cases as examples of narcissistic transference and all six happen to be women. The most highly elaborated case involves a "gifted woman composer" who "in an atmosphere of a mildly friendly positive transference" was able to "swing for a time from a highly personal and recondite musical idiom, which brought her little of the recognition which she so desperately needed, into a routine but secure effort, quite remote in character from her original work." This career change "paralleled efforts to establish a genuine relationship with her husband."[60] One cannot overlook the similarity between this reported success with supportive analysis and the larger social impulse to discourage professional careers for women in favor of happy marriages to which women totally devote themselves.

In spite of the prevalence of this explicitly and implicitly adjustment-oriented impetus in psychoanalysis, there was an ongoing and extremely committed struggle on the part of other well-respected analysts to assert the importance of the interpretive model in the face of the seemingly more efficient model of adjustment. Probably the most significant area of psychiatric technique to challenge the simple adjustment model had to do with the advocacy of nondirective or "inter-pretive" technique over manipulative technique, and the increasing interest in the transference and especially countertransference rela-tionships, although, to be sure, this advocacy was part of a polemic.

These latter analysts drew on and took very seriously Freudian writ-ings admonishing them to resist the temptation to mold the patient to their own, the analysts', worldview: "The analyst reflects the patient's individuality and does not seek to remould him in accordance with his own—that is, according to the physician's—personal ideals; he is glad to avoid giving advice and instead to arouse the patient's power of ini-tiative."[61]

Later, in *Outline of Psychoanalysis* (1939), Freud expresses the sentiments as follows:

> However much the analyst may be tempted to act as teacher, model,
> and ideal to other people and to make men in his own image, he
> should not forget that that is not his task in the analytic relationship,
> and indeed that he will be disloyal to his task if he allows himself to
> be led on by his inclinations. He will only be repeating one of the
> mistakes of the parents, when they crushed their child's
> independence, and he will only be replacing one kind of dependence
> by another. In all his attempts at improving and educating the patient,
> the analyst must respect his individuality.[62]

In the pages of the *Journal of the American Psychoanalytic Associa-tion*, American analyst Merton Gill reasserted the importance of Freud's call for analytic neutrality: "Psychoanalysis is that technique which, employed by a neutral analyst, results in the development of a regressive transference neurosis and the ultimate resolution of this neurosis *by techniques of interpretation alone*" (emphasis added).[63] Of course, it is one thing to give lip service to pure analysis and quite another to put it into practice. However, the work of Gill and others displays great sensitivity to the disconcerting ease with which an ana-lyst can fall into advice giving, and sensitivity also to the nuances of the call for "interpretation alone." Significantly, Gill and others did not take "neutrality" to mean perfect, unproblematic objectivity. That was recognized as impossible. Rather, "neutrality" meant precisely that the analyst should attempt to refuse "supportive" or "directive" tech-niques[64] in favor of "explorative" or "interpretive" ones based on the transference relationship.[65] The emotional response of the analyst then comes into play through the countertransference, where the an-alyst is "alert for the development of patterns of emotional response in himself to the patient."[66] And since countertransference is the mech-anism through which we can conceptualize the analyst as an active participant without seeing him or her as an adviser, it is this aspect of technique that was pivotal both to the resistance of psychoanalysis to adjustment therapy and to its status relative to the prescription of female roles.

As J. LaPlanche and J.-B. Pontalis indicate in their definition of countertransference, Freud very rarely used the term.[67] Instead, countertransference received much more attention later in the United States, where psychoanalysis itself came more and more to be understood as a *relationship* and where the concept of countertransference could then come into its own in debates over the doctor's status in the doctor-patient relationship. A large number of articles on the subject, including the seminal overview, "Transference and Counter-Transference: A Historical Survey," by Douglas Orr, appeared in American journals of the 1950s, and in 1959 the book *Countertransference* was published.[68]

Of course countertransference is best regarded along with the concept of transference, much better developed in Freud's work. According to LaPlanche and Pontalis, Freudian transference developed from its conceptualization as a mode of displacement in connection with dreams to its conceptualization as the "transference-neurosis," the process of treatment where infantile conflicts are replayed in the doctor-patient relationship.[69] Countertransference in Freud's writing, then, is defined by LaPlanche and Pontalis as "the whole of the analyst's unconscious reactions to the individual analysand — especially to the analysand's own transference."[70]

In spite of some variations in interpretations of transference (was transference the whole doctor-patient relationship or a specific part of it?),[71] authors of the period regard the concept of transference as enjoying "some semblance of evolutionary progression to something commanding wide agreement."[72] Alternatively, the literature of the period recognizes wide *disagreement* as to what the term "countertransference" comprises. Is it the analyst's response to the patient's transference? If so, does this refer just to the analyst's unconscious response or to his or her conscious response as well? Or, should countertransference include *all* of the (conscious and unconscious) feelings or reactions to the patient, even those outside what may be provoked by the patient's transference? Does countertransference include the doctor's choice of couch and general decor? Should countertransference be revealed to the patient, seen as ubiquitous and necessary, inhibited as an undesirable factor, dealt with in private self-analysis, or seen as an indication of the analyst's need for reanalysis? The divergence of opinion itself is evidence of postwar analysts' need to reassess the role of the analyst as "human" or, alternatively, as "mirror," with particular reference to his or her position in the doctor-patient relationship.

In fact the increased interest in countertransference and the debate over its definition are evidence that the role of the analyst presented a theoretical problem with which the field was obsessed. For to pose one's own role, one's authoritative status, one's very livelihood as an open theoretical question is to undermine the discursive practice of rigid prescription and to open up more varied alternatives.

When countertransference was regarded as an abnormal and undesirable characteristic of the analytic relationship, as in the opinion that "counter-transference is the same as transference—it is then immediately obvious that counter-transference is undesirable and a hindrance," the radical potential of the concept could not be realized due to the implication that psychoanalysis could function without the doctor's emotional response.[73] The belief in this so-called "sterile" analysis reflects a desire to maintain a belief in the omnipotence and objectivity of the analyst, and a desire to disavow the real power imbalance of the analyst-analysand relationship. Countertransference can be used to advertise the importance of the analyst, shoring up rather than combating his dictatorial position.

Another viewpoint held that countertransference was *normal* and constantly present in analytic work, yet defined countertransference as desexualized and sublimated in nature. Here a tentative admission of the emotional role of the analyst is allowed, but only in the carefully controlled context of the absence of any implication that the analyst's response could be construed as at all erotic.[74]

The most progressive accounts of countertransference, however, assume it is an *inevitable* characteristic of psychoanalytic technique and admit of an emotional and even erotic response on the part of the analyst. Writing in France, and responding to what he saw as simplified and inappropriately desexualized American models of transference and countertransference, Jacques Lacan went a distance to question the authoritative role of the analyst.[75] He called the analyst "the subject [only] supposed to know," and suggested that to divide transference into transference and countertransference only served to avoid the "essence of the matter," which is that all transference is the desire of the *analyst and* of the analysand.[76]

Perhaps surprisingly, in light of the limited and self-serving accounts of countertransference that were being put forth in the United States, here too there was some work on psychoanalytic theory of technique that not only acknowledged infantile sexuality, but reflected on its centrality to the analytic relationship of the analyst's own Oedipal complex.[77] As Lucia Tower put it, "No analyst has ever been presumed to have been so perfectly analyzed that he no longer has an unconscious, or is without the susceptibility to the stirring up of instinctual impulses and defenses against them."[78] And Freud, of course, was consistently sensitive to his own neurotic symptoms. For Tower, the countertransference is specifically a response to the patient's transference made up of unconscious phenomena derived largely from the analyst's childhood, including sexual material. She pointed to the great number of writers who say that such libidinal material on the part of the analyst should not be tolerated as evidence that "temptations in this area are great, and perhaps ubiquitous,"[79] and noted the irony of selecting candidates for training on the basis of significant libidinal resources and then deriding every libidinal investment as inappropriate.[80]

Drawing on clinical material from her own practice, Tower described a technique in which countertransference elements, after being subjected to a process of self-analysis, may be used to further the analysis. This is not "acting out," but rather the analyst's use of examined emotional material that has emerged in the context of the ongoing intimate relationship of the doctor and patient. Understandably, she viewed the countertransference as more fleeting and more quickly resolved than the transference since, after all, the analyst has already been analyzed and is assumed to be the less neurotic of the two. Particularly in the work of Tower, but throughout the literature on countertransference as a whole, variations notwithstanding, psychoanalytic meditations on the concept share the possibility of at least imagining the role of the analyst as nondictatorial.

In view of the richness of the professional literature, many popular accounts of transference and countertransference were crazily askew in that they spoke of the terms as though they were synonymous with actual love affairs. Some popular accounts of the analyst's countertransference, for example, used the term to mean "falling in love with the patient." Describing transference, one article spoke of how the patient will "shower the analyst with hatred or love," based on how he comes to represent early figures in his life.[81] The article went on to hint at the possibility of an active response on the part of the analyst:

> This phase is potentially very dangerous, especially if the patient and analyst are of opposite sexes and if the patient demands that the love he feels be gratified. Teachers of psychoanalysis constantly warn their students of the dangers of responding to the lover's role in which their patients may cast them. *When the analyst fails to heed the warning and does respond to the patient, it is called countertransference.*[82]
> (emphasis added)

Marriages or love affairs between analysts and analysands are common

in popular cultural representations and are described as transference/
countertransference. It is unclear whether these fictional marriages
represent the patient's fantasy or the doctor's. Perhaps this popular
(and illegitimate, according to professional standards) version of countertransference is partially responsible for the professional assertions
of the undesirability of countertransference and for the oft-asserted
objectivity of the analyst. In any case, this peculiar narrative twist on
transference/countertransference has a significant ideological content
that will be discussed in chapters to follow in relation to the films.

Nevertheless, other popular accounts of psychoanalytic technique
did display some resistance to the adjustment model. In a discussion of
what psychoanalysis can do for "you" in *Are You Considering Psychoanalysis?*, Alexander Martin wrote that analysis draws back from advice giving:

> Analysis is not the kind of treatment one ordinarily associates with a
> doctor-patient relationship. A condition is treated, it is true, but it is
> not treated by a prescription, a formula, or a blueprint from the
> analyst. This must be understood very clearly, for many individuals
> expect the analyst to advise them, to tell them how to lead their lives.
> The experienced analyst does not set out to do this. His intention is
> to help the patient, through increasing self-expression and gradual
> opening up, to see and to feel for himself the kind of life he is really
> leading, and the analyst hopes to develop in him the capacity and
> willingness to change. To the question "What should I do?" the
> analyst would be inclined to say "First let us find out all of what you
> are doing."[83]

One way psychoanalysts could resist the impulse to advise is paradoxically by admitting that it is virtually impossible not to advise. As a
female resident analyst put it in *Mademoiselle* (1947), "Values? . . . I
decided during residency that I had better be clear on what I thought
the good life was because every word the analyst says to a patient carries a value judgment."[84] This viewpoint recognizes that the practitioner and the patient both operate within the context of the wider social
system held together by ideological glue that constantly constructs individuality, and with this in mind it attempts to obviate the power of
analysts' personal biases by acknowledging them. The acknowledgment itself is evidence that psychoanalysis can open itself to a critique
of its own authoritative status, and in so doing operate as other than
adjustment therapy.

Besides basic theoretical affinities for "interpretive" rather than dictatorial technique, psychoanalysts were also hesitant to dictate to patients because of the perceived limitations of their technique as a

cure-all. In fact, this particular self-critical discourse was endemic to psychoanalysis. Even at his most optimistic, when developing the ca-thartic method, Freud drew back from claims about the palliative pow-ers of psychoanalysis, saying in response to an imaginary patient, "No doubt fate would find it easier than I do to relieve you of your ill-ness."[85] American psychoanalysts also entertained doubts about the numbers of patients for whom psychoanalytic treatment would be ap-propriate. By the late 1950s, a trend was evident indicating that the number of patients with neuroses was declining in proportion to a rise in the number of patients with psychotic disorders.[86] Other more di-rect challenges to the avowed efficacy of psychoanalysis had to be reckoned with. In 1960, *Reader's Digest* printed an article by a British psychologist titled "What's the Truth about Psychoanalysis?" in which he argued that the truth was that the technique didn't work: "The suc-cess of the Freudian revolution seemed complete. Only one thing went wrong: *the patients did not get any better*."[87]

In public, psychoanalysts tended to express their doubts about the curative potential of psychoanalysis in the form of admonitions against "unrealistic expectations." In her introduction to *Are You Considering Psychoanalysis?* Karen Horney says that one of the goals of the book is to "help to dispel mysterious notions about analysis by removing un-realistic expectations of a magic cure."[88] Psychoanalysts, then, were put in the unstable position of having to mediate between the *promise* of the psychoanalytic cure (a promise that aided institutional en-trenchment) and the *qualification* of what psychoanalysis could do to transform patients.

And even the popular realm of marital advice giving and receiving reveals certain resistances to psychological adjustment. When some popular writers voiced the fear that psychoanalysis was too dictatorial about patient relationships, analysts responded, denying that psycho-analysis should either prescribe or proscribe marriage or divorce. Pre-dictably, the fear of psychoanalytic advising did not take the form of a feminist critique of psychoanalysis as an agent of marital adjustment, but rather the form of fear that psychoanalysis would *disrupt* existing marriages. A 1950 issue of the *Nation* published a testimony by a woman who began the article with the statement, "My husband and I were recently divorced upon the suggestion of his psychiatrist."[89] The next issue contained responses from two well-known psychiatrists. One of them, Gregory Zilboorg, asserted that "no true psychoanalyst ever advises marriage or divorce as part of the therapy."[90] A passage in Lucy Freeman's best-selling account of a patient's analysis, *Fight against Fears*, is also illustrative of psychoanalytic disinclination to advise marriage, even though, paradoxically, the analyst here *advises* inaction:

> I wanted to get married. No longer was I content to sell my birthright for a mess of anxiety.
>
> I told John [the analyst] I felt free enough to try marriage. He rarely offered counsel, no matter how fervently I begged. He would reply, "How do you feel about it?"
>
> But he suggested I delay decision on the marriage. "Why don't you wait a few months?" he said.[91]

Of course these defensive assertions, for popular audiences especially, that psychoanalysts do not give advice should be taken with a grain of salt, but they may still be regarded as evidence that many analysts *desired* to resist advice giving, even if they were not completely successful.

The final area of antiauthoritarian psychotherapy that must be mentioned is the work of the culturalist psychoanalysts concerning feminine sexuality.[92] In spite of the criticism leveled by some contemporary critical theorists, especially Juliet Mitchell and Russell Jacoby, that the cultural school departed overmuch and to its great detriment from various basic tenets of Freudian psychoanalysis, such as the theories of instinct and of infantile sexuality and of the biologic basis of both of these findings, the fact remains that this psychoanalytic school did actually oppose authoritarian models and advocate equality for women.[93]

Like researchers in countertransference, American culturalists of the 1940s and 1950s were interested in the doctor-patient relationship, focusing on that relationship as a current manifestation of past infantile experiences. The interpersonal therapeutic relationship was thus contextualized within the large intellectual framework adopted by culturalists, a framework that drew on sociology and anthropology, as well as psychoanalysis itself, for theory of technique.[94]

Several eminent analysts of the American cultural school were explicitly interested in challenging Freud's views of female sexual development, which they took to be suffering from cultural bias and an exclusively masculine point of view. The work of Karen Horney and Clara Thompson exemplified this critique of Freud's views and the attempt to contextualize feminine sexuality with regard to sociocultural practices.[95] They saw Freud's work on female psychosexuality as tantamount to an accusation of biological inferiority for females, and responded by proposing female physiological attributes as objects worthy of male envy but denigrated by the prejudices of male-dominated society. Both Horney and Thompson were concerned with the way in which the real restrictions imposed on women by patriarchal culture were affecting their experience of sexual difference. Thompson distinguished psychologically produced neurosis from the difficulties of women's real social inequality.[96] For example, she separated the masculinity complex from the problems of an independent woman. She also observed that biological feminine fulfillment in reproduction may not add up to an affirmative attitude at all when considered in a cultural context, but rather a submissive or resigned one, and that female narcissism may not be innate but rather provoked by forced economic dependency.[97]

Horney's work with patients, along with that of her culturalist colleague Harry Stack Sullivan, very clearly opposed adjustment therapy and its implications for women. Two cases handled by Harry Stack Sullivan and Karen Horney, respectively, and published in a best-selling collection serve as an illustration.[98] Harry Stack Sullivan's case history involved a woman patient whose presenting complaint was that she was an inefficient housekeeper who "lazed" her day away. The patient, who had a Ph.D. in economics, had dropped her work to become a housewife. At the time she entered treatment, the patient had been married for ten years and had two children. Her husband was threatening divorce and devoting more and more time to his work so that the wife was becoming increasingly isolated.

Sullivan was not necessarily against the dissolution of this marriage: he noticed the problems of the husband ("The husband sounds more like an insecure tyrant than anything else. Maybe he is also schizoid."),[99] and attempted to figure out how the patient could raise her sights to a life more in keeping with her exceptional abilities, suggesting at one point that she look at events in her life as a research problem. He took for granted the feminist premise that women need not be housewives and might exercise other ideas:

> I would go on by saying that her training seems to be rather exceptional for a person who has accepted a purely domestic role all these years and that, under the circumstances, her feelings of helplessness to get going in the morning rather encourage me than otherwise. *Has she never heard of a woman who preferred something else to domestic preoccupation?*[100] (emphasis added)

Like Sullivan's work, Horney's work with one of her patients used early childhood material to illuminate current consequences of prior events and, like Sullivan, she acknowledged the importance of a career for women. The case study is quite beautiful in its intricacy, interweaving past and present structures and the analytic process of interpretation. Horney's patient entered therapy at age thirty, complaining of overwhelming fatigue that interfered with her work and social life, and a dramatic lack of self-confidence. Horney writes that the analysis could be divided into three phases: "the discovery of the patient's compulsive modesty; the discovery of her compulsive dependence on a partner; and finally, the discovery of her compulsive need to force others to recognize her superiority."[101] According to Horney, each of these compulsions handicapped the patient's enjoyment of life, but also her use of her *intelligence*. Clare, the patient, had dropped her earlier ambition to achieve in college. Summarizing why Clare could no longer make her formerly great achievement-oriented efforts, Horney says that Clare had to fight against constant doubts as to her intelligence because of compulsive modesty. Indeed, the free use of her intelligence was actually impaired by the repression of her critical faculties, and she couldn't risk failure because the need to excel was too compulsive.

The neuroses identified by Horney are those that inhibit worldly success and encourage personal dependency. The model of health toward which Horney shepherded her patient—the model that seemed most appropriate to this patient—is one of personal, career, and economic achievement, a far cry from the personal and economic dependency legislated for the housewife in adjustment therapy.

The feminist social critique provided by Horney in this case history is not surprising in that she drew for creative inspiration on her personal experiences as a professional woman. "Clare," struggling against psychological problems, was actually Horney herself.[102] Thus this case illustrates (if in an exaggerated manner) the way an analyst's view of his or her patient could be colored by a worldview in contradistinction from one that advocates exclusive domesticity for women.

In all, it seems a limited view to construe the psychiatrist-patient relationship in the postwar era as a relationship that admitted only of techniques to adjust the patient to the dominant ideology, or for that matter only of techniques that resisted "adjustment therapy." Like the wider field of psychiatric discursive practices discussed in chapter 1, the therapeutic discourses through which the doctor-patient relationship was articulated aligned themselves with *both* impulses and so represented a contradictory discursive field. It is this contradictory discursive field that will be pursued in relation to Hollywood films in the following chapters of this book.

3

Marriage and Psychiatry; or, Transference-Countertransference as a Love Affair

My chief objection is still that I do not believe that satisfactory plastic representation of our abstractions is at all possible. We do not want to give our consent to anything insipid. Mr. Goldwyn was at any rate clever enough to stick to the aspect of our subject that can be plastically represented very well, that is to say, love.
— Sigmund Freud in a letter to Karl Abraham regarding *Secrets of a Soul*, 1925

With these words about cinema, Freud intimates that to treat of love is to treat of psychoanalysis. But what he might not have foreseen was the literal extent to which fictional psychoanalysts in Hollywood films would be involved as counselors or even romantic partners in the love affairs and marriages of their fictional patients. If the doctor-patient relationship is the smallest unit where therapeutic technique is realized, it is also the smallest unit where its dynamics are personified, and thus altered in the service of fiction. This chapter concentrates on films portraying a male psychiatrist and a female patient.

A number of film plots reveal that the relationship between psychiatry and traditional views of femininity and marriage is a congenial one. In other words, the reciprocity between psychiatry and the institution of marriage, previously discussed in relation to the social formation, may also be observed transposed to narrative form in the films of this study.

The doctor-patient relationship represents a central vehicle for this collusion. In *Now, Voyager*, for example, Dr. Jacquith's treatment of Charlotte's (Bette Davis) "illness" leads her to assume the standards of female attractiveness. From a dowdy, solitary girl who doesn't pluck her eyebrows, she is transformed into a mysterious femme fatale ripe for romance.[1] In *Lady in a Jam*, a psychiatrist (Patrick Knowles) is called in for consultation by a woman's trustee. The woman's "problem," as her trustee expresses it, is that money doesn't mean anything to her; she has it, she spends it, and most significantly, it makes her independent of men. As the woman herself (Irene Dunne) puts it to her psychiatrist, "Women with money don't have to marry. My father used to say that poor people were the only ones who could afford to have families." Here the psychiatrist's job is actually to regulate the woman's views of money and hence of marriage. By the end of the film the woman has given up her fortune presumably to marry her psychiatrist. In *The Seventh Veil* a psychiatrist promises that "narcosis" will help a woman reveal the conflicts buried in her mind. "The human mind is like Salome—hidden by a series of veils," he says. "With friends she lets down three or four, with a lover, five, but never the seventh . . . five minutes under narcosis and down comes the seventh veil." Psychiatry thus becomes a woman's most intimate partner in her quest for a mate. By the end of the film the woman has been freed to choose "the one she loves . . . the one she's been happiest with" from among several suitors. In each of these films, the psychiatrist has the position of authority in the woman's life, guiding deviant femininity toward the path of marriage, whether or not he himself is the prospective spouse.

Other films of particular interest in this regard are *Cat People*, where the psychiatrist attempts to redirect a woman's sexuality by making love to her, but dies in the process; *The Dark Mirror*, where a psychologist's instincts and amorous attraction to the "good" twin help him solve a murder committed by the "bad" twin; *The Locket*, where a woman collapses on the way to the altar, but a psychiatrist promises her fiancé that love and time will prevail; and *The Chapman Report*, where a woman awakens sexually in a romance with a research psychologist who presents her with a questionnaire on female sexuality.

Sometimes the woman is not actually the doctor's patient, but the plot still turns on her troubled psychosexuality and requires its regulation for the film's resolution. In *Oh, Men! Oh, Women!*, a psychoanalyst (David Niven) learns that his fiancée (Barbara Rush) has had a past affair with one of his disturbed patients (Tony Randall) and with the husband of a woman patient, as well (Dan Dailey and Ginger Rogers). The fiancée is not technically a patient, but she is carefully established as utterly "batty" (à la such television counterparts as Gracie in *Burns and Allen* or Lucy in *I Love Lucy*) and compared on this basis with her fiancé-psychoanalyst's actual patients. She loses things and functions according to an illogical logic, posed in the film as female. In the psychiatrist-fiancé's words, "You are the most irritating, frustrating, exasperating woman I've ever met or even treated, bar none." After a series of misunderstandings and farcical narrative devices, the analyst and his fiancée end up together at the rail of the ship on which they are to be married and spend their honeymoon cruise. *The Cobweb*, to be discussed further in chapter 4, presents a rather clear-cut example of how the woman's sexuality may be the crux of the narrative conflict without her literally being a patient.

But though important, these scenarios of adjustment do not in fact exhaust the narrative operations of the films under analysis. Taken as formally complex visual and sound narratives, these films ensure marriage and mental health, but they also *bring up* the inherent problems of female and male adjustment. Our viewing pleasure seems marked as much by a fascination with deviant male and female psychosexuality, with unresolved sexual difference itself, as by the desire for resolution. For example, *The Dark Mirror* presents deviant femininity as the "twin" of the maternal ideal. The dangerous feline sexuality of the Simone Simon character in *Cat People* is otherworldly but "real" in the terms of that narrative. *The Locket* ends as a woman interrupts her own wedding ceremony by screaming and fainting, actions shown as the reasonable response to her psychobiography, which is the subject of the film. As the psychoanalyst's own training analyst puts it in *Oh, Men! Oh, Women!*, "The difference between the library [the man's domain] and the bedroom [the woman's domain] is astronomical . . . but the trip, everyone seems to agree, is worth it." The films of this corpus, then, are about the trip as much as the arrival.

Moreover, the very plot device that often enables psychiatry to collude with traditional marriage, the device of making the psychiatrist and husband one and the same, also enables a critique of psychiatric authority. As lovers themselves, the psychiatrist characters cannot remain omnipotent, objective professionals, but become vulnerable to mental instability.[2] And in the context of dubious male authority and identity, questions of female psychosexuality refuse easy answers.

Oh, Men! Oh, Women! undermines the authority of the psychoanalyst by bringing him from behind the couch to center stage where he struggles vainly to maintain order and his sanity in the face of his batty fiancée and a film comedy. At the start of the film, a woman patient calls him a god. But in her view he is a god not because he is rational, as he would like to believe, but because psychoanalysis opens the world of emotional conflicts — a world he would like to stave off but one in which he instead gets hopelessly involved:

DR. COLES: A psychoanalyst is simply a doctor who is trained in the complexities of human behavior, and it's his business to try to bring about some harmony between the intellect and the emotion.

PATIENT: Oh, you have for me, doctor. Before I came to you you've no idea how dull my dreams were.

DR. COLES: . . . and above all to remain rational and objective in the face of emotional conflicts.

PATIENT: I wasn't even *in* some of them.

In the final scene, after he has bumbled and stumbled but landed with his engagement intact, his fiancée gushes admiringly of his foresight. But the work of the film has been at least in part to undermine his authority and to present the outcome as incredible felicity rather than psychiatric competence.

The comedic disarming of male psychiatric authority is also seen in *Lady in a Jam*. Dr. Enright's confident boast that he can cure his patient and be back in time for a four o'clock appointment is thoroughly overwhelmed by her topsy-turvy world, and he abandons all appointments for a lengthy adventure in love and incomprehension. In the final scene the roles have been reversed. In place of the confident, controlling paragon of professionalism, we see a man who looks more like a patient. He wears a white lab coat rather than the dark suit he wore before. His former patient, June, is now charged by his superior with the duty of "curing" him:

JUNE: He can be cured, can't he?

SUPERIOR: He's half cured. Now you'll have to do the rest.

In a parody of the talking cure, June sits on Dr. Enright's lap and soothes him, saying, "I know," and, "Keep talking." His lament of the wasted "four years in college, four years in medical school, two years as an intern" finally ends in a frustrated scream. June approves of this release, asks if he feels better for it, and answers for him. "That's better. Don't you feel better now? Of course you do." He groans with his eyes closed and the film ends.

My point is that the explicit filmic incorporation of psychoanalysis or psychoanalytic psychiatry can raise the issue of psychiatric adjustment precisely to explore its authoritarian aspects and the weaknesses they mask, including an inability to account for feminine sexuality. Paradoxically, the theme of psychiatric adjustment may also be the pretext for the exploration of incipient feminist ideas that challenge its normative modes. If the films construct female deviance as an eminently correctable lifestyle irregularity, if, in other words, female neurosis is broached in order to be regulated, feminine psychosexuality is also broached in the films as something more, as a term that is problematic not because of individual women who refuse to conform but because of the oppressive nature of marriage and psychiatry. In this sense *Whirlpool*, *The Three Faces of Eve*, and *Tender Is the Night* all bear the marks of discursive resistance. The films' portrayal of feminine sexuality as a problematic term reiterates the heated social debate that refused an essentialist model of femininity by refusing to reduce social problems to the "problem of woman," and by attesting that it was not femininity itself that was a problem, but rather femininity under patriarchal social formation and theorizations of femininity as anything other than a contested domain.

The doctor/patient dyad, or more particularly the doctor-husband/patient-wife dyad may be characterized as a relation in which the male doctor is dominant, but it may also be regarded as the venue where prior, unconscious conflicts are represented precisely as unresolved conflicts. The combination of fictionalized transference and marriage can act to surface as much as to control the psychosexual problems of femininity. A comparison may be made with Freud's case history of Katharina (1893-95).[3] Vacationing on a mountain in the eastern Alps, Freud encountered a girl, the niece of an innkeeper (or in Freud's term, landlady), who begged to be cured of hysterical symptoms. In the resulting case history, Freud links marriage (or in less puritanical terms, sexual activity) and neurosis: "I had found often enough that in girls anxiety was a consequence of the horror by which the virginal mind is overcome when it is faced for the first time with the world of sexuality." Freud also complained in a footnote that another patient refused to admit the truth, which was that "her illness arose from her married life."[4] Here, as in many of the films being considered, psychoanalysis critiques the neurotogenic properties of marriage as well as enforcing the institution.

The body of this chapter will analyze the thematic content, narrative structure, and visual style of three films, including one film from each of the three decades represented in this study. The analyses of *Whirlpool* (1949), *The Three Faces of Eve* (1957), and *Tender Is the Night* (1962) are intended to illustrate the way films about male psychiatrists and their female patients function, crack apart, and develop over time as they figure the divergent impulses of adjustment and resistance that characterize the relationship between psychiatry and marriage.

In black letters on an off-white background patterned with the grey silhouettes of turn-of-the-century women, *Whirlpool* (20th Century–Fox, 1949) presents its authorial group from stars to producer-director Otto Preminger.[5] The roll stops as expected after Preminger's credit and a hidden cut initiates a quick reversal. Like a window shade refusing to remain in the lowered position, the roll snaps back and whirls in place—a blurred cylinder. But there is a difference. Title and credits disappear and the credit roll is transformed into a sheet of department-store wrapping paper being rolled up by a saleswoman. The Victorian silhouettes, now transferred from credits to wrapping paper, mark the high fashion pretensions of the "Wilshire Store–Los Angeles." They are the mark of the handcrafted in the postwar period of the ready-made; the mark of silent, corsetted, proper but unpropertied women. Without a cut the camera dollies back and pans up to reveal a scene in progress. As the clerk finishes rolling up the wrapping paper, a customer carries a pile of boxes away from the counter. The camera follows, then allows the male customer to leave the frame as Ann Sutton (Gene Tierney) enters and walks into a medium close-up. The relay is complete, from the presentation by 20th Century–Fox, through the man's purchase of what must be ladies' luxury items, to our purchase on the star in medium close-up.

But there has been a theft. Unbeknownst to us, Ann Sutton approaches the exit of the Wilshire Store with a swiped mermaid pin in her handbag. The swinging glass doors are open, providing Ann with a presumably clear path and us with a clear view from our vantage point outside the store. Without a cut, the camera captures Ann's exit and her glance at a store mannequin modeling mink. Her look is mastery tempered by irony. In her physical appearance she has achieved the glamorous perfection of the store mannequin, the ideal on which the pharmaceutical ads for weight reduction bank. But far from being the true master of her gaze she is instead a pawn in the masquerade of femininity, desirous of its trappings and sacrificed to its price. The store detective has been surreptitiously watching and following Ann. Now he demands her handbag, accuses her of shoplifting, and forces her to re-enter the store under the threat of causing a scene and attracting onlookers (as if she were not already the object of a different, more powerful "scene"—the filmic one). The doorman is called over as the detective pulls the shoplifted pin out of Ann's handbag: "Harry . . . I just want you to *witness* this." Now the camera's look, carrying on from the detective, proves its prescience and control as it retraces Ann's path, backing through the swinging doors. The sequence ends as the camera backs the captured Ann into an elevator already prefigured in the composition of the shot of Ann's attempted exit as the space to which she would inevitably be returned. The camera pins her down as she collapses in a faint. In the scene that follows, Ann is taken to the department store offices where she is interrogated by store personnel but extricated from her predicament by a party, unknown to her but clearly interested: Dr. David Korvo (José Ferrer), hypnotist, charlatan, and quack psychologist. Ann Sutton is a "poor, sick, woman," he tells her interrogators, a kleptomaniac who requires his ministrations to recover. And on this basis, ironically, Ann is free to go.

The logic of vision and control introduced in this opening scene is repeated later at the police station where Ann is again being held and questioned, this time for the murder of a woman. Matching the roll of department store wrapping paper with which the film opened, an official form rolls out of a typewriter platten. As in the first scene, Ann's statement is witnessed by a ring of gazing male officials, including a psychiatrist, and it is the statement of an act, which, if committed, must have been committed outside of her own volition. "I couldn't have done it . . . unless . . . unless I'm *crazy*," wails Ann. This piece of paper, matched with the earlier one, suggests that a woman is ill and places her illness on display. Here, and in *Whirlpool* as a whole, the conventional Hollywood rhetoric of vision is played out as an investigation of female mental illness and psychiatric control.[6]

Whirlpool does not so much ask "Who killed Terry Randolph?"—the traditional hermeneutic of a film noir–melodrama like *Mildred Pierce*—as ask "What is *wrong* with Ann Sutton?" It is a story of kleptomania and capture articulated as the case history of a neurotic woman. But *Mildred Pierce* itself slides from the story of crime detection to the stuff of female biography.[7] Neither the "confession" Mildred Pierce makes to the police detective nor the one Ann Sutton makes to the detective, her lawyer, and the police psychiatrist is purely a legal confession. Neither confession pertains to the murder being investigated as much as to the woman's past familial relationships. *Whirlpool* furthers the presentation of psychoanalytic retrospection suggested in *Mildred Pierce*.

In *Whirlpool*, the symptoms of Ann Sutton's adolescent conflict with her father reemerge from latency to mount an involuntary rebellion on the field of her marriage. As she describes it in her "confession" at the police station:

> ANN SUTTON: I did it before. I stole in school. When my father wouldn't
> let me spend money. And even after he died he tied it all up in a trust
> fund. Thousands and thousands of dollars but I could never have a
> new dress or have anything I wanted. That's how I fooled my father
> . . . by stealing. He didn't love me. He thought he did but he didn't.
> Nobody ever caught me. I thought it was over when I left school and
> met Bill. I wanted to tell him but I was afraid he couldn't love
> anybody who'd done that. I didn't tell him. It came back because he
> was like my father. He treated me like my father did and I had to do
> it again. I tried not to. I couldn't sleep and got a pain and had to do it
> again. I stole a pin from a store.

This retrospective psychoanalytic scenario is familiar. In the case history of Katharina, Freud demonstrates how two sets of sexually traumatic experiences—one from the past, the "traumatic" moment, and one from the present, the "auxiliary" moment—may jointly engage the neurosis. In fact, it is only the sexual knowledge of the mature woman that allows the prior events to be reexperienced as sexual and traumatic. In the case of Katharina, only moderate neurotic symptoms resulted from an early trauma in which she "felt her uncle's body" in his attempt to sexually molest her. A few years later, when she was more sexually knowledgeable, she caught sight of that uncle in bed with her cousin. Her symptoms increased to the point of great discomfort. As in Freud's case study, the woman's neurosis in *Whirlpool* informs both past and present so that narrative resolution and the concomitant cure imply a retrospective regulation of the path toward normal femininity. In this film, furthermore, cure and resolution also imply the reconstruction of feminine psychosexuality along lines more conducive to a woman's marriage to her psychoanalyst-husband.

The emphasis on individual feminine psychology as the crux of the narrative enigma involves a displacement of materialist explanations of conflict and trauma that are present but downplayed. The rejected explanations are of two related types: references to "the war" and references to economic deprivation. The war is carefully bracketed as no longer current in one of the film's opening scenes. In this scene Ann Sutton and her psychoanalyst husband, Dr. William Sutton (Richard Conte), assure one another that their marriage is a happy one:

> DR. SUTTON: I'm a busy doctor and a happy husband—an enviable combination. I wouldn't trade it for a dozen books. Just stay as you are. As you've always been. Healthy and adorable.

But in the course of the ostensible discussion of their marriage, an allusion is made that is glossed over and displaced—an allusion to the war. Ann expresses worry over having interrupted her husband's analytic session with a "veteran who won't talk." Her husband assures her that no harm will be done, going on to describe his projection of the patient's future progress:

> DR. SUTTON: He will [let me help him] eventually. It's just that it's difficult to begin unloading fears and secrets and guilts. Poor fellow. *The war was an easier conflict than the one he's in now.*

The unspecified war is characterized as an "easier conflict" than the unspecified psychological trauma of the film's present. With current psychological trauma the issue, it is but a small step to shift the terrain from the veteran's psychological problems to those of the woman. The veteran patient (never actually seen in the film) is "replaced" by Dr. Sutton's wife when his analytic session is interrupted, and he is completely forgotten in the rest of the film as Dr. Sutton's work becomes more and more involved with his wife's acquittal and related treatment. This relay set up between the war, general emotional trauma, and marital happiness, this relocation of psychopathology from soldier to wife, is in fact the narrative trace of the shift in psychiatric attention from military recruits to their supposedly neurotic mothers and, to the extent that maternity was regarded as a sufficient description of femininity, to women in general.

Like the war, economic disadvantage is figured but then displaced. Besides linking past and present traumas, Ann's confession links the control of money by her parsimonious father to the inequitable economics of marriage. In the scenario of the confession, the scenario of a woman prohibited from spending her own money, a "new dress" stands as the cipher for female desire, for the "anything" she wanted but couldn't have. Continuing the iconographic theme of fashion and appearance that runs throughout the film (recall that the opening scene is set in a department store decorated with mannequins dressed in mink), the privileged example of the dress represents both purchase power and the desire to please. It may be read as a profound mark of female economic and emotional powerlessness. Plotwise, however, the film downplays the issue of a woman's need for economic independence from men (fathers and husbands) and plays up her need for male love and protection. This obviates altogether the necessity of economic independence, since security lies in the love of a man.

Given Ann Sutton's psychological problems, her psychiatrist-husband's job is to reconstruct her along lines he determines. She must be made worthy to bear the name "Mrs. William Sutton," the name through which she secures credit at the department store, and worthy to live in a house the front door of which announces that it is the property and domicile of "William Sutton, M.D." As object of marital and medical attention, Ann Sutton is placed on display for the enhancement of her doctor-husband's public image and, coincidentally, the enhancement of his sexual pleasure expressed in the dialog as his "greatest kick:"

> DR. SUTTON: You know the greatest kick I get when we go to a party together is when people stare at you and say, "Who is that lovely girl?" "Why, that's Dr. Sutton's wife. She's very devoted to him."

As emissary of the narrative, the psychoanalyst banishes deviance hinted at in the desire for access to money and partially explored through the semisexual relationship that develops between Ann Sutton and the evil hypnotist, David Korvo.

In this sense, the imbrication of romance and psychoanalysis in *Whirlpool* works to propose a cinematic solution to social, economic, and political issues posed as an individual psychological problem. An-

a

b

Figure 9. In relation to male doctors and female patients, the representation of hypnosis as a form of psychological control in *Whirlpool* (*a, b, c*) may be compared to the commercial representation of the effects of psychotropic drugs (*d; American Journal of Psychiatry* 116, no. 9 [March 1960]).

c

d

other way to put it would be to say that the psychiatric institution, anthropomorphized, is married to the socioeconomic demand for heterosexual, monogamous womanhood. And if the doctor-husband/patient-wife relationship resonates with the pop version of the transference relationship crucial to psychoanalytic theory of technique, it is a version of transference that relies even more overtly on the analyst's ability to advise or manipulate his patient.

Another emissary of popular psychology in the shape of Dr. David Korvo *as hypnotist* asserts an even more thorough mastery over Ann. As Korvo himself puts it, "The fact that I know of your kleptomania, the fact that I know that your mind is sick and threatening to get out of hand gives me a medical position in your life."

Hypnosis represented, in fact, an exaggerated way to conceptualize the adjustment impetus in postwar psychotherapeutic technique.[8] Theoretical work on the hypnotic process from the period emphasized the importance of the dominant role of the hypnotist and the dependency of the subject: "The hypnotist becomes for a time the sole representative of or bridge to the outer world. The paradigm of this condition is the infant who is crooned to sleep in his mother's arms."[9] The article quoted, by Lawrence Kubie and Sydney Margolin, continues by describing a process through which the voice of the hypnotist is actually accepted as if from *inside* the subject's ego boundaries: "Once the subject is going 'under,' it is only in a purely geographical sense that the voice of the hypnotist is an influence from the outside. Subjectively it is experienced rather as an extension of the subject's own psychic process."[10] Popular fears of hypnosis as a form of brainwashing and mind control extended even further its status as a metaphor for the authoritarian relation of doctor to patient.

Thus, the choice to portray hypnosis in *Whirlpool* is a choice to emphasize Korvo's mastery over Ann. Moreover, hypnosis is particularly felicitous in its filmic incarnation for its dependence on the visual register, for hypnosis requires the subject to stare into the eyes of the hypnotist until falling into a trance, during which the regulation of the subject's vision and any independent consciousness is given over to the hypnotist. The process is figured cinematically as an ever-tightening exchange of close-ups, and it echoes the iconography of the female patient and the male doctor portrayed in the drug advertisements discussed in the previous chapter (Figure 9).

And yet, neither Korvo's control of Ann nor her husband's control of her is complete. The fictionalized transference used in *Whirlpool* to align deviant femininity with essentialist views of femininity allows what could be described as a fictionalized transference-*resistance*. According to Freud, transference is always bound up with resistance. In other words, though it is crucial to a successful analysis, transference also functions simultaneously as an *obstacle* to treatment, because it is always triggered precisely at the moment when the most important repressed material is in danger of being revealed to the very person the repressed material concerns: the analyst himself (or herself).[11] And since marriage and transference in *Whirlpool* are one and the same, transference-resistance is expressed in the film as resistance to marriage.

Overall, the film's articulation of female resistance occurs through a rhetoric of vision at odds with Hollywood convention. In *Whirlpool*, the domination of the male gaze is resisted by a marked absence of point-of-view shots or shots approximating character point of view,[12] despite the presence of hypnosis with its characteristic "look into my eyes" imperative. When present, such shots articulate a scenario *explicitly about the control* of feminine sexuality, thereby calling it into question. The cumulative effect of such an abnormal use of point of view is to resist the male objectifying gaze at the female—to throw the look back in the face of he who would look.

At the two interrogation locales, the department store and the police station, Ann Sutton is surrounded by men who seek to understand her actions and motives and perhaps to punish her. Many of the shots are crowded with men gazing down at Sutton in the center of the shot, demanding to know what she knows so that they may pass judgment, futilely trying to pierce her masklike exterior (Figure 10). But, with the exception of one shot of Korvo looking at the group, there is no individual inquisitor, no individual male point of view to provoke spectator identification and further the narrative. Instead, the collective gaze constitutes an institutionally supported attempt to get and record her history.

The frame crowded with male experts gazing at a female object of inquiry is a fairly common compositional device in psychological films of this period. In *The Seventh Veil* a psychiatrist demonstrates his technique on the Ann Todd character before a group of colleagues who crowd the frame to gaze at her. Near the start of *Possessed* there are several shots from Joan Crawford's point of view as she stares up (from a "nontraumatic stupor") at two doctors attempting to diagnose her case and who conclude with "Take her up to 'Psycho.' " The reverse shot of her face against the white of the examining table (cf. the famous shot of Barbara Bel Geddes' head framed against her hospital room pillow in *Caught*)[13] becomes the object of the joint gazes of the doctors leaning in to shine a light into her eyes.

The point of spectator identification in all of these scenes is not the male protagonist, as in *Morocco*, *Marnie*, or *Gilda*.[14] Instead the enunciator of the point of view is the woman. But her look is not an objec-

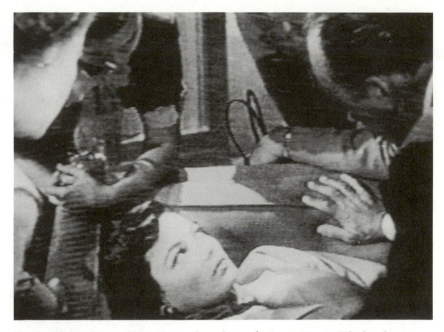

Figure 10. Ann Sutton (Gene Tierney) as object of interrogation in *Whirlpool*.

tifying look at a male, the possible reverse alternative to the patriarchal structure of the gaze for which some have tried to argue (e.g., close-ups of Gary Cooper in *Morocco*). Instead her look is a look *back* at a collective, inquiring gaze. Her view, whether marked by an actual point-of-view shot or by a glance around the room, points up the controlling presence of the medical, corporate, or legal collective gaze at the woman.

Specifically, in the relationship between Ann and Dr. Sutton and in that between Ann and Dr. Korvo, the classical structure of the controlling gaze is extended hyperbolically so that its relation to patriarchal power, now exaggerated, is also denaturalized. What might be a romantic exchange of glances between Ann and her husband is presented as a threat. Take, for example, the introduction of Dr. Sutton. After returning from her interrogation at the department store, Ann goes to her bedroom. Agitated, she sits down at her desk and picks up a photo of her husband and herself (barely visible in the film but described in the script as a girl sitting on a rock flanked by an adoring young man gazing down at her). As she stares at this symbol of the expectation of marital bliss, she hears her husband approach the closed bedroom door. Panicky at being caught with anxiety in her eyes, she leaps up and runs to her vanity area—the proper place to assure her wifely appearance. But before she runs for cover, there is a significant shot. The camera executes a slight dolly-in to a close-up of Ann Sutton as she leans forward, wide-eyed and frightened. As she runs to her dressing room, there is a cut to Dr. Sutton in medium close-up as he enters the bedroom calling her name. What would be a classical exchange of romantic glances is interrupted by the ultimate failure of the glances to meet.

Resistance to marriage is also depicted as the nefarious plot of David Korvo, who works to win control of Ann Sutton's psyche away from her psychoanalyst-husband, and hence to undermine her marriage. In this incarnation, antimarriage sentiment is coded as the improper product of brainwashing techniques.

But at the same time that the character Korvo lords it over Ann, he may also be read as her double, as the representative, therefore, of Ann's own antimarriage sentiment.[15] Both Ann and Korvo cast aspersions on Dr. Sutton's "twisted" patients, and both are drawn as being overly concerned with personal appearance. Ann gazes into a mirror ostensibly to check her hair and makeup frequently throughout the film, and especially when she has something to hide, when she is concerned to let appearances deceive. Korvo, too, gives his hair a last touch-up as he prepares to frame Ann for murder. Even the film's first introduction of Korvo suggests a comparison with Ann. Just prior to our first view of Korvo, Ann has walked out of the Wilshire Store and then been walked back in, through the swinging doors. In that same doorway, we first catch sight of Korvo as he exits, sees Ann, and turns to echo her progress back through the doors. Stylistically here, as well as thematically overall, his actions are the opposite of hers, or, more suggestively, his actions are the mirror image of hers. In short, the film has it both ways. It presents the woman as ostensibly innocent of antimarriage sentiments by letting the malevolent Korvo mouth them, yet it also uses Korvo as a mouthpiece for Ann's resistance to her marriage of false pretenses. As Korvo puts it to Ann:

You've locked yourself away in a characterization—the serene and devoted wife. That playacting is destroying you.

You mustn't be afraid of what you want. It's better than stealing. Better than exploding with neuroses.

I can release you from *a torture chamber called Mrs. William Sutton.*

The hypnosis scenes make the psychic identification between Ann and Korvo even more explicit, for through hypnosis Korvo enters Ann's very ego boundaries. Ann Sutton's hypnosis "frees" her to break off a love note to her husband, to act out against his interests, and to an extent the film's logic figures this as "being herself."

The spatial and narrative relationship between Ann and Korvo, like that between Ann and her husband, also connects the device of a character's gaze to the focalization of cinepsychoanalytic control, and to the film's stylistic subversion of that control. Near the end of the film, Ann's place as hypnotic subject is taken by Korvo himself as he conducts his self-hypnosis (Figure 11). The camera dollies in on Korvo's face, illuminated by a light he shines into his own eyes, as he tells himself, "I'm getting stronger, stronger, there's no pain." The film then cuts to his own reflection in huge close-up in a round hand mirror he holds. Korvo's eyes alone fill the whole surface of the mirror which in turn fills most of the screen. He intones, "I'm able to do what I want." The commands he gave Ann, to sleep and forget, are replaced by the auto-commands to get stronger and feel no pain. But the shot–reverse shot that accomplishes Korvo's self-hypnosis also inaugurates his downfall. He overestimates his physical strength and undergoes a fatal collapse. The fact that Korvo's self-hypnotic gaze proves fatal suggests the real power of the gaze and thus the potential threat it poses to the woman who is its most frequent object.

Interestingly, Korvo is not only doubled with Ann, but doubled too with Dr. Sutton; they are competitors vying for control of Ann's loyalty and for her very psyche. And, if Korvo and Sutton are flip sides of the same coin, then Sutton's analytic technique, by implication, is as suspect as Korvo's overtly authoritarian brainwashing tactics. At its most limited, Dr. Sutton's analytic technique with regard to his wife is reduced to that of crude suggestion. In the only scene in which we see him practice, he orders his wife to resist Korvo's order to forget. But to command her not to obey Korvo is virtually to command her to obey Sutton himself:

> Korvo gave you an order to forget. He placed it in your mind while you were under hypnosis.

> You're obeying his order. Don't obey him anymore, Ann.

The film concludes as Ann "remembers" the action she performed while in a trance and embraces her husband. Ostensibly a happy ending, this scene seems to me a nightmarish version of the wedding ceremony with its vow to "obey."

In fact, Korvo and Dr. Sutton are not so much *equated* as *compared* and found similar. They do not stand in the fiction for purely authoritarian psychoanalysis as much as they stand for its dueling aspects. Dana Polan has used "the crazed Dr. Korvo" and "the orthodox psycho-

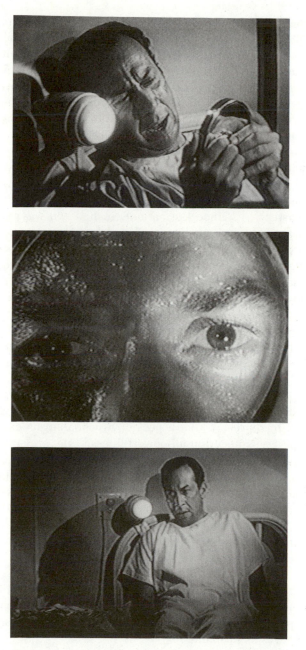

Figure 11. Dr. Korvo (José Ferrer) takes the positions of doctor *and* patient as he conducts his self-hypnosis in *Whirlpool*.

analyst" in *Whirlpool* to exemplify how "one way that narratives will resolve doubt about psychoanalysis will be to split the scientist into two figures: one authoritative and good, and one insane and bad."[16] This possibility is illuminated with reference to François Roustang's book, *Psychoanalysis Never Lets Go*, which presents a close analysis of the avowed and intrinsic differences between Freudian psychoanalysis and prior techniques of suggestion and hypnosis against which Freud elaborated his theories.[17] For Roustang, those distinctions are in some senses and cases quite evident. Psychoanalysis leaves the realm of suggestion as it follows the circuitous path of free association away from the explanation of symptoms toward the investigation of complexes, resistances, and repetitions. Here, says Roustang, "The analyst loses all mastery . . . since the patient, in his own way, at his own rhythm, meanders through his story and lets his fantasies and his drives appear, all of which permanently drifts in connection with everything that could be constituted as the analyst's expectations."[18] On the other hand, argues Roustang, the distinctions between suggestion and psychoanalysis may only be maintained by forgetting the transference, for the "center and motive force" of the transference "resides in the subjection-all-powerfulness that results . . . in the loss of subjectivity."[19] As Freud himself stated, "It must dawn on us that in our technique we have abandoned hypnosis only to rediscover suggestion in the form of the transference."[20] Freudian psychoanalysis, then, for Roustang, "finds itself inhabited by two contradictory tendencies": subjection and the circuitous path of analysis.[21] In this light, Korvo may be said to represent that aspect of psychoanalysis expressed in transference as "subjection-all-powerfulness." He seeks to control Ann's perspective on her marriage, her actions, and her fate. Dr. Sutton, on the other hand, practices the productive detours of psychoanalysis that distinguish it from suggestion. He gives access to Ann's past by affirming Ann's own contention that her mental health went awry when he, her husband, followed her father's pattern of denying access to Ann's own money. He encourages, in Roustang's terms, "the random ideas that structure or restructure the subject's uniqueness."[22]

And yet the film provides for Dr. Sutton's construction but not for Ann's reconstruction in analysis. Ann's psychoanalyst-husband as analyst does propose an explanation for Ann's problems, a solution in which he figures as husband:

> When you married me I insisted that you start with me as a poor
> doctor's wife; that you don't spend your own money. That brought
> back the neurosis. My acting like your father made you steal again.

However, Ann's reconstruction, the opportunity she would presumably have in classical Freudian analysis to accept or qualify or even to reject the analyst's interpretation, is cut off, ostensibly by the pressure of time: Lieutenant Colton has promised the Suttons only one hour at the scene of the crime to come up with the evidence. Under these circumstances, what Ann remembers is not past family conflicts, but rather, where she had put the recordings of the murdered woman's analytic session with Dr. Sutton. The end of the film engenders a shift away from the terrain of woman's biography to that of the mystery plot, amounting, therefore, to a reversal of the shift from film noir enigma to woman's biography with which the film began.

The Three Faces of Eve initially gives a very different impression than the melodrama of *Whirlpool*, for it presents itself as a serious psychological case study of a woman with three different personalities. Yet *The Three Faces of Eve* is actually constructed around the same thematic matrix of elements: the problem of female neurosis or psychosis, the repression of the social dimension of the film's fictional world in the concentration on the individual psychological cure, and the final presentation of ideal femininity. In the course of the conscientious psychiatric treatment performed by Dr. Luther, Eve White ("the defeated wife" of the poor and struggling rube, Ralph) and Eve Black ("the rollicking and irresponsible playgirl" who denies all connection to Ralph) "die" so that Jane ("What . . . nature intended this young woman to be") may be born (Figure 12). Maternal, exemplary femininity is proposed in Jane, whose insertion into the nuclear family is pictured as a *tableau vivant*, with which the film ends. In this final image we see Jane, her new husband Earl, and her daughter, Bonnie, driving off together to start anew: the reunited family. Earl is in the driver's seat, Bonnie in the back, and all are happily licking ice cream cones—the perfect resolution to the Freudian distinction between infantile oral sexuality and adult family roles. Here, then, is fulfilled the postwar dream of prosperity and togetherness.

The film links healthy femininity to the ideal of middle-class life, reiterating the treatment of these issues in other mass cultural outlets. In contrast to Eve's early marriage to Ralph, Jane's final marriage to Earl represents a step up in class. Among the signs that construct this class distinction is the contrast between Ralph's pickup truck, pictured in the first diegetic image of the film, and Earl's sedan, with which the film ends. Even the manner and etiquette of Jane herself, now a dignified, articulate, cultured wife and mother, associate her with the upper middle or upper classes—"culture" being a Hollywood code for class.

a

b

Figure 12. Dr. Luther (Lee J. Cobb) in *The Three Faces of Eve,* with the retiring Eve White (Joanne Woodward) and her husband (David Wayne) (*a*), and with the sexual Eve Black (*b*). Production stills.

But in spite of this ideological complicity, or perhaps because of it, *The Three Faces of Eve* displaces any real investigation of the socio-economic dimension of human life onto the realm of the individual psyche. This shift is obvious in comparing the fiction film and the psychological study of the same title on which the film was based with the autobiographical account by the woman who was the real subject of the famous case study.[23] *I'm Eve* (1978), written by Elen Sain Pittillo for her cousin Chris Costner Sizemore ("Eve"), emphasizes the part played in the precipitation of Chris's illness by the hardships of the Depression and the poverty of the small southern town in which she spent her childhood.[24] Also absent from case history and film but included in Sizemore's autobiography is an early marriage in which "Eve" was sexually and physically abused.

If, as suggested, the final synthesis of roles represents the film's most reductive account of femininity, the deviant alternatives themselves also conform to accepted conservative notions of femininity. The female roles presented by the film version correspond fairly closely to those described in the book *The Three Faces of Eve* (1957), by psychiatrists Corbett Thigpen and Hervey Cleckley.[25] The book in turn was expanded from an article that appeared in the *Journal of Abnormal and Social Psychology*, founded by Morton Prince. It is not surprising, then, that Morton Prince's own book, *The Dissociation of a Personality* (1905),[26] is prominent in the short bibliography provided by the authors of *The Three Faces of Eve*, nor that the 1957 case study relies on Prince's precedent for the description of the split personalities. As Thigpen and Cleckley note, Eve White resembles Miss Beauchamp, the cultured prude; Eve Black resembles Sally, the mischievous imp; and Jane may be compared to what Prince termed "BIV," the tabula rasa artifact personality. I read these similarities as a rhetorical technique used by Thigpen and Cleckley to enhance the credibility of their amazing findings.

Prince's own lengthy work seems to have an important precedent of a different sort—wider cultural archetypes. To quote from the preface, "If this were not a serious psychological study, I might feel tempted to entitle this volume, 'The Saint, the Woman, and the Devil.' " This passage in particular indicates the extent to which Prince relies on cultural mythology, where the flip sides of the coin of essential femininity (or The Woman) are the mother and the whore. He reworks this conceptualization through the Judeo-Christian tradition, so that mother and whore become Saint and Devil.

The archaeology of *The Three Faces of Eve*, where the relay of archetypes may be traced from cultural mythology through Prince's work through Thigpen's and Cleckley's into the Hollywood text, pro-

Figure 13. The advertising campaign for *The Three Faces of Eve* also capitalized on familiar and stereotypical views of women as saints or sexual teases.

vides a good example of how a model takes on historical specificity as it gets focused by postwar American culturewide notions of femininity. The archetypal roles described in the account of Eve's symptomology bear striking similarities to one of the historically specific ways of characterizing women's roles in popular books discussed in chapter 1, where women are described as inadequate mothers, neurotic sexual teases, or cured and exclusively maternal beings (Figure 13).

That these postwar texts and their precursors work to limit the range of female roles is especially suggested by another discrepancy between *The Three Faces of Eve* and *I'm Eve*. The discrepancy consists in the number of personalities reported. Whereas the film presents three distinctive archetypal personalities and the book delineates three personalities plus a vague synthetic personality (who is written up as sort of Jane but not Jane), *I'm Eve* identifies twenty-two separate personalities. The smaller the number of personalities, the more manageable they become in terms of narrative exposition and closure, and in terms of their exposition in professional literature. Given that current research on multiple personality disorder lists the average number of personalities, or "alters," in a case of multiple personality disorder as ranging from 8 to 13.8,[27] we might surmise that Thigpen and Cleckley's account of three personalities was influenced either by their therapeutic limitations or by the constraints of the documentation process itself.

There is also a crucial difference in the *kind* of personalities described. The eponymous connotations of Eve White and Eve Black include the biblical Eve and reach into the archetypal arsenal of descriptions of femininity so that Eve Black is characterized as sexual and mischievous (though not really evil), while Eve White is characterized as religious, good, and too tired to be sexual. The twenty-two separate personalities of *I'm Eve* substantially broaden the range of possibilities so that the personalities—the lying girl, the purple lady, the big-eyed girl, the freckle girl, and the turtle lady, among others (similarly named by Pittillo and Sizemore)—are not reducible to archetypes nor solely to sexual considerations. The film, then, requires a more controlled account of the possible personalities than the later *I'm Eve*, and that control itself seems to emerge from wider social configurations.

This control is important structurally as well as thematically. In its use of the flashback structure, *The Three Faces of Eve* partakes of an established convention for focusing investigation on the past. Films of the noir, crime-detective, or mystery genre were often structured around a past enigma revealed in a flashback denouement, a structure Marc Vernet and others have identified as strikingly similar to that of Freud's cathartic model.[28] In *The Locket*, a woman suffers from kleptomania due to a childhood incident in which she was forced to confess to a petty crime she did not commit, the theft of a gold locket. The film employs a series of flashback accounts by different people to unearth the past trauma, virtually equating the revelation of the trauma with the woman's cure. Interestingly, the trauma is bound to other visual and aural mnemonic cues besides those provided by the locket itself: notably the cues provided by a musical cigarette box and the tune it played after falling to the ground when the child was being violently questioned. The hermeneutic of *Lady in the Dark* also employs the device of a musical cue to evoke an original trauma revealed by psychoanalysis. In this film a little girl is caught playing dress-up in her dead mother's clothes in an attempt to please her father. Far from being pleased, he is horrified and angry. The psychoanalytic explanation provided by the film poses this event as the one that later caused the repression of the true femininity of the grown woman. The cure in *The Three Faces of Eve* is also enabled by a final flashback to a traumatic event. Here, personality integration is provoked when Eve recalls a past incident in which her mother forced her to kiss the face of her dead grandmother.

In all of these films, the original trauma revealed by the flashback is both key to the narrative and key to the enigmatic femininity of the woman. Since the original trauma itself is presented as a single event, its discovery stands as the unitary hub of the narrative, and since discovery equals cure under the cathartic method here adopted, cinematic representation of the event is allied with the correction of deviant femininity. The speed of the cure and the film's dependence on the cinematic technique of the flashback link this narrative fictional version of psychotherapeutic technique and cure with the social impulse toward adjustment therapy, where the desired rapid cure was encouraged by a range of physiological techniques.

The content of the past traumatic event in *The Three Faces of Eve* is also such as to air repressed feminine desire in alignment with conservative postwar familial patterns. In the past trauma revealed by the two flashbacks that resolve the drama, little Evie's mother, not seen elsewhere in the film, drags Evie out from under the house and leads her to her grandmother who is lying in state. Evie tries to run to safety in the arms of her father who stands at the deep apex of the frame, but he gives Evie to her mother. The final shot of this flashback is a medium shot of Evie's father, who closes his eyes as he hears the off-screen scream of this child. He is pained by but still guarantees the act the family forces on his daughter.

Not only is little Evie forced to do her familial duty, but at another level one could say that this scene also works to reinscribe the heretofore deviant adult Eve within a properly familial context. Earlier in the film the choices open to women were expressed in terms of broad social roles. Although these roles were limited as discussed, they did at least represent a number of choices encompassing familial and nonfamilial options. With the final flashback, however, the range and number of choices have been reduced to the familial sphere, here depicted as a sphere in which a woman's path is clear: girlhood, motherhood, death.

Embedded in a flashback narrated by Jane, little Evie, her mother, and her grandmother become structural representations of one woman's psyche. This familialization and psychologization of choices open to women reiterates Freudian work on femininity, where discussions of the girl child commonly include assumptions of inevitable maternity, unlike Freudian discussions of the boy child, which omit discussions of the boy's future paternity, and where discussions of the boy child explore his relationship to his mother while discussions of the girl child conflate her with her mother.[29] The flashback that precipitates narrative closure, then, may be read as a structure that unites a cinematic device (the flashback), a social and cultural tendency (the 1950s reduction of social problems to female psychical problems), and a psychoanalytic justification for the control of femininity.

The ideological import of the narrowing and psychologization of female roles may again be highlighted with reference to the different chronicle presented in *I'm Eve*. *I'm Eve*'s refusal to follow *The Three Faces of Eve* by speaking only of three or four personalities is attended by a refusal to portray past trauma as a single original event and by a refusal of final personality integration. Chapter 1 of *I'm Eve* opens with an account of a traumatic incident remembered from childhood in which a man, presumably drunk, had fallen into an irrigation ditch and drowned. Sizemore also describes frightening childhood experiences involving a kitchen accident, the horrific sight of a man who had been severed in a sawmill accident, and her complicated feelings about the death of her infant cousin when she herself was ten months old. It is another one hundred pages before she describes having been forced as a child to kiss her dead grandmother, and yet that single event is central to *The Three Faces of Eve*.

Once dissociated, three personalities merge neatly into one in *The Three Faces of Eve*. It is not surprising that twenty-two cannot and do not merge easily, according to the account in *I'm Eve*. On the issue of final integration, Sizemore and Pittillo are clear. Jane was by no means the final personality to emerge. Following the termination of treatment by Thigpen and Cleckley, new personalities continued to form. In the early 1970s, Strawberry Girl and Retrace Lady went in and out of one another, and Andrea appeared as late as 1975.

With amazing insight into the abstract connection between pronouncements of integration and loss of personal autonomy to psychiatric authority, Sizemore and Pittillo resist closure in *I'm Eve*. They even write self-reflexively of the struggle to reach a decision about whether to end their own book with a claim of integration. According to Sizemore, Thigpen defended his own exclusion of material that would have indicated that Eve was not cured by saying, "A book cannot be written with a 'lady or the tiger' conclusion, it ha[s] to have a resolved ending."[30] Alternatively, Sizemore and Pittillo end their book with a meditation on the impossibility of closure:

> And Chris' story? Which door would she choose? Elen did not know; only Chris could answer this all-important question.
> "Chris," she asked, "how does the story end? Tell me how you feel, and I'll write."
> "Elen," she whispered, "I loosed the tiger."[31]

The flashback that enables the realignment of deviant femininity in *The Three Faces of Eve* is but one of an arsenal of cinematic devices

functioning in concert to master "the problem of woman." Another
such device has to do with the way the case of "Eve" was presented to
professionals and to the public, as a serious, responsible, truthful, and
even *nonfiction* psychiatric case study. After the credits, where Nunnally Johnson's name is prominent as writer and producer-director,
but before the diegetic portion of the narrative, there is an introductory monologue delivered by Alistair Cooke, who is billed as a "distinguished journalist and commentator." He begins with the phrase "This
is a true story," and goes on to say that although we may have seen
such a statement many times about many films, in this case, "this is a
true story." Cooke goes on explaining about multiple personality, what
it is and how rare it is. Giving their credentials, he tells how Drs. Thigpen and Cleckley encountered this woman "who had one personality
more than Dr. Jekyl," how they presented the case to a meeting of the
American Psychiatric Association, and how it's "already a classic of
psychiatric literature." Finally, even though *The Three Faces of Eve*
was written by Nunnally Johnson, one of the most well-established
screenwriters of the day and one who had strong literary credentials,
Cooke claims that "this movie needed no help from the imagination of
a fiction writer. The truth itself was fabulous enough." Thus, the film's
opening establishes an authoritative relay from the psychiatric professional world of Thigpen and Cleckley through Nunnally Johnson
through the journalistic and commentative sphere of Alistair Cooke
through to the fictional world in which Eve White's husband delivers
her from her family physician to her new psychiatrist. In its amassing
of authorial agencies and authoritative physicians, this film multiplies
the principle that Polan has described in relation to *Now, Voyager*
(1941) of "the doctor work[ing] as a kind of relay between narration
and narrated event."[32]

Visually, *The Three Faces of Eve* is an even more specialized case
than that of *Whirlpool*. In *The Three Faces of Eve*, Dr. Luther's gaze at
Eve motivates the initial arrival of each of her various personalities and
governs the moments of transition from one to another, moments integral to the film's subject matter and structure. The film presents
nearly twenty transitions among the various personalities of Eve, most
of which occur in the office of her psychiatrist (and even those that
occur outside the therapeutic setting remain circumscribed by the
therapeutic process motivating the film's entire plot). The first emergence of Eve Black in the presence of Dr. Luther occurs when Eve
White is seated in his office. In despair, she covers her face with her
hands and purse. The film cuts to a close-up of Dr. Luther, who asks,
"Feeling better now?" When we return to the shot of Eve, she is no
longer Eve White but Eve Black . . . who feels fine. Thus, the cutaway

to Dr. Luther's point of view serves as a point of identification for the spectator, who sees the transition through the incredulity of the doctor's gaze.

By now Dr. Luther has gotten the idea that he may "call" to the dormant personality, who will then appear on demand. He calls his colleague, Dr. Day, to witness the spectacle. Although this time there is no insert of the doctor at the actual point of transition, the visual paradigm remains in force, since the transition occurs across a cut and in response to a verbal suggestion from Dr. Day. In a three-shot, Eve Black slouches on the couch as the two doctors look on. Dr. Day mentions Mrs. White's name and the film cuts to a close-up of her lifting her head. Four shots follow, alternating between the staring doctors and Eve White. Later, when he attempts to explain the rare situation to Eve White's husband, Ralph, Dr. Luther opts for a visual demonstration: the transition to Eve Black and back to Eve White is repeated with cutaways to dumbstruck close-ups of Ralph. The power of Drs. Luther and Day is here figured as superior even to Eve's own powers of self-determination, and moreover, Dr. Luther's psychiatric abilities, proposed by the plot, link up with the visual levels of filmic narration. His control over the woman is that of a narrator—a narrator of personality and cure.[33]

And yet, as with *Whirlpool*, there is a competing discourse in *The Three Faces of Eve*, one that is seen thematically and visually. The antimarriage sentiment is personified in the facet of Eve's personality who is Eve Black. She vociferously reviles Eve White's husband Ralph and wishes to enjoy her own sexuality (expressed as love of dancing). Eve Black refuses to conform to the social principle put crudely by one sailor who complains that he doesn't pay for drinks all night without expecting the sexual favors of his date.

Although *The Three Faces of Eve* is not the feminist text that *I'm Eve* is, and although illness and feminist resistance must not be conflated, there is room to read multiple personality as a particularly resonant symptom. At a time when women's roles were being widely discussed and challenged, multiple personality may have been read as an unconscious and expansive rendition of career and behavioral choices open to women.

In fact, many of the films of this group use the camouflage of illness to allow characters to "try on" alternative sexual dispositions. In *Lady in the Dark* the Ginger Rogers character must distinguish her own sexuality against that of three men among whom she must choose. In *Oh, Men! Oh, Women!* a psychiatrist's fiancée is confronted by prior boyfriends on the eve of her marriage. The "trying on" of roles here seems just as crucial an exercise as the ultimate selection among them.

The Three Faces of Eve also encompasses a disturbance of classical point of view. Firmly installed in the early transitions between personalities, the classical system is later replaced by a different editorial regime. The early transitions between "Eve's" different personalities occur across the cut, motivated by the psychiatrist's call and accompanied by nondiegetic music used to identify each personality. But as the film proceeds, the transitions are handled more frequently by the body language and acting of Joanne Woodward. In a marked example of this later trend, the film's cinemascope aspect ratio helps minimize Dr. Luther's role in the transformations. Having hypnotized Eve White, who sits to the right of the frame, he sits at his desk, frame left, turned away, making notes. When the transition occurs, not only is there no cutaway, but it is clear to the audience that Dr. Luther, who is visible on screen, has not participated in the emergence of Jane. Of course the mere foregrounding of the performance of a female actress by a film need not undermine patriarchal storytelling agencies. In this case, however, the pointed and increasing reliance on Joanne Woodward's performance over the traditional editorial scheme of point of view does attach a kind of discursive power to the female character.[34]

Tender Is the Night (1962) bears great resemblance to its precursors *Whirlpool* (1949) and *The Three Faces of Eve* (1957). It too tells a story of female psychological breakdown and recovery, and here too the woman's illness has its point of origin in a traumatic past event. As in *Whirlpool*, the psychiatrist is a psychoanalyst and he is the woman's husband. But precisely because *Tender Is the Night* does resemble the earlier films, the various ways in which it also *differs* are crucial.[35]

Tender Is the Night thoroughly disturbs the thematic matrix that at least partially held the element of ideal femininity in place in earlier films of the cycle. This film moves beyond female pathology, makes manifest the issue of social class, and questions psychiatric authority. It is a film in which the impulse of resistance to psychiatric adjustment is very strong. From this perspective *Tender Is the Night* may be read as a very apt cinematic representative of the later part of the period in question, during which time the wider social discourses resisting gender-specific and psychiatric-insured conformity gained strength.

A past event forms the structural center of *Whirlpool* and *The Three Faces of Eve*. It is the original moment to which the backward investigatory course of each narrative leads; it initiates both illness and narrative. In *Whirlpool* and *The Three Faces of Eve*, the discovery of the traumatic past event with its etiological connection to present illness provokes the films' resolution—the woman's cure. In contrast, the past traumatic event in *Tender Is the Night* is revealed early on but the revelation does not produce resolution. Instead, the narrative proceeds with its story of illness and problems now shifted to a different matter.

Comparing the three films, one realizes that the woman's trajectory of illness and cure remains, but that something has been *added* to *Tender Is the Night*, the latest film of the three. What has been added is *male neurosis* and its consequences in the scheme of mental health and sexuality. *Tender Is the Night* explores what happens when the psychiatrist isn't only a pristine guide to proper living, but rather subject to the same narrative investigation of his psychology as the woman patient. As Dr. Diver puts it, "Perhaps I'm going crazy myself." Significantly, the book he can't finish writing is "Psychiatry for Psychiatrists," a title that implies a treatise *on* psychiatrists as well as one for use by psychiatrists. The difficulty of this text, then, is not solely the woman, but the woman and the man or the doctor-husband/patient-wife relationship itself. There is an element of male self-reflection in *Whirlpool*. In the second half of the narrative, Dr. Sutton becomes the protagonist. In a series of encounters with the police detective on the case, he is forced to rethink the basis of trust in his marriage. *Tender Is the Night* takes such issues further. In the later film, the husband-psychoanalyst fails to work through his own psychopathology.

There are two problems the narrative must deal with: (1) Nicole Warren Diver (Jennifer Jones), the patient-wife, is richer than her husband, Dr. Dick Diver (Jason Robards), and (2) their relationship consists in a hydraulic economy wherein the mental health of one member of the couple is purchased only at the expense of the mental health of the other.

Direct negative consequences accrue to a previously respected male professional as the result of economic strength left in the hands of a woman. Because Nicole Warren has inherited from her father a huge fortune, "so big as the Morgan's Bank and Rockefeller," she is not totally dependent on her husband-psychoanalyst. What results is a conflict between Nicole's money and Dr. Diver's expert status as analyst and researcher. According to the initial ground rules of the marriage, Nicole should allow Dick to support her financially as well as in every other way. But Nicole's wealth—and illness—contribute to the Divers' ultimate tendency to live as she would live (in extreme luxury), and where she would live (the Villa Diana on the French Riviera). Dr. Diver drops his clinical practice to be with Nicole, and, although he establishes a study in the Villa Diana, he does not continue his work.

A similar conflict between a woman's financial resources and her husband's analytic expertise is present in *Whirlpool*. As noted before, the earlier film begins to question the ability of women to function in a

society based on familial patriarchy under which they are disenfranchised from the economic sphere. Both films clearly link female sexuality, money, and paternal dominance. But *Whirlpool* more effectively
neutralizes the seeds of its own social critique by categorizing the child
Ann Sutton's nuclear family as pathological and abnormal, absolving
the grown Ann's husband of any wrongdoing when he repeats her father's act of withholding money. His past actions are ultimately viewed
by the film as just and normal since they are in line with the terms of
the gender roles and social relations of the day, and it was only the personal circumstances of the character Ann that caused the problem.
Tender Is the Night refuses to explain Nicole's desire for pleasurable
spending as quirky pathology. In a revealing shift, Nicole is ill because
her father molested her as a child, not because he withheld money.
The film's plot explains that her father can never repay her for this
wrong, but his fortune, which she inherits, stands as partial reparation.
Her husband's attempt to make her live on his small salary is clearly
marked as self-interested. This film explores the fearsome consequences for the husband of a wife's control of funds and consequent
power.

Dr. Diver's descent into alcoholism, illness, and failure is presented
as a result of his loss of professional identity, a loss exacerbated by
Nicole's increasing mental health as well as her fortune. While she was
ill, at least he could rationalize cutting down on this practice because
he was giving so much attention to Nicole. When the American *vedette*
asks, "Are you still practicing?" Dick can roll his eyes to the upper
floors of the Villa Diana, where presumably his intimate relations with
Nicole are lived out, and answer, "Never stopped." But as Nicole mends
she removes his last pretense of professionalism.

According to the narrative, it is possible for a male psychiatrist to
maintain a good marriage with his female patient-wife only so long as
the distribution of power in the husband-wife coupling is congruent to
that of the doctor-patient relation. Once the roles are reversed in male
illness or female economic power, the resonance between the marital
and analytic situations ceases and both fall apart. In *Tender Is the
Night* this cessation of viability is predicted by Dr. Dohmler, Diver's
mentor:

> Dohmler: When she finds out that she married a human being, a
> fallible human being and not a God . . .
>
> Diver: Well you may smile, professor, but I think it possible that
> Nicole will love me as a human being.
>
> Dohmler: Of course all things are possible, but what will you be by
> that time? Will you be still what she wants or what you want? What

has already happened to you? Ours is a strange profession. Many of us come into it because we ourselves are a little broken up, a little bit crippled. We've become clinical before we can fight our own battles with life.

DIVER: That's another reason I want to come back. It's not only the work, not only Nicole. I need help for myself.

DOHMLER: Nicole could be helped were it not for you. You could be helped were it not for Nicole.

Whirlpool, like its classical 1940s counterparts, ends with the embrace of the reunited couple. *Tender Is the Night*, however, begins with the idealized couple and ends with its disintegration, or, if the events of the plot were reordered chronologically, the story would begin with the doctor-patient relationship, find their romance at the center, and end, again, with the dissolution of the couple in the dissipation of Dr. Diver. What is cured is not the woman or the troubled marriage, but the diegetic world itself, now purged of the trouble presented by marriage and psychiatry. The alternative narrative organization in *Tender Is the Night* draws attention to the supportive mechanisms of psychiatric authority, among which mechanisms traditional marriage is primary.

It is not only at the narrative level that this film questions the expert status of psychiatry, but at the stylistic level as well. *Tender Is the Night* departs even more dramatically from the construction of character identification through classical point of view than the earlier two films. In so doing it corrodes the hegemony of classical style and structure and its consistency with patriarchal social arrangement. It is not clear that Laura Mulvey's account of spectator identification with the male characters through a shared scopophilic drive would apply to this text. In fact, I would submit that *Tender Is the Night* is able to represent male mental illness precisely because it *withholds* from the male character the power of the objectifying gaze.

The film presents its own rhetorical system for the presentation of power relations, one that is not dependent on gender. There is a very clear association, in *Tender Is the Night*, of enclosed space with illness and unhappiness, and of open spaces and physical action with health and happiness. For example, the first shot of the film is of psychoanalyst Dick Diver (Jason Robards) aquaplaning with his son on his shoulders. It is a wide shot emphasizing the sun, the wind, and the beautiful surroundings of the French Riviera. Dick Diver is at the peak of health. At the Fourth of July party in the following scene, his wife and former patient, Nicole (Jennifer Jones), has one of her relapses. In contrast to the happy, open-air waterskiing scene, the site of Nicole's breakdown is a windowless upstairs bathroom decorated with large mirrors that reflect the image of her delusions and fury.[36]

Through this carefully coded spatial system of panoramic and enclosed spaces, the increasing health of Nicole may be charted in conjunction with the declining health of Dick. Near the end of the film, Dick goes aquaplaning again, but this time he has to be pulled onto the boat and dispatched to a hot shower after his tour around the lake. Once in the bathroom in the hold of the boat, Dick drinks a highball and showers. Through the ventilator shaft he overhears Nicole and her old friend, Tommy, up on the wide space of open deck discussing the end of Nicole's and Dick's love. Thus, Dick suffers his first realization of imminent expulsion from Nicole's life in a space that evokes the space of Nicole's earlier breakdown. This time Nicole is the one who is "up on deck."

The repetition of spaces where the couple meet to discuss their relationship also aids the representation of the rise and decline of the marriage. There is a small stone lakefront terrace in Zurich where Nicole and Dick meet, once near the beginning of the film and once near the end. The first time they meet Dick announces that he's going away, but it is clear that their romance is just beginning. The second scene that takes place on the lakefront terrace establishes Dick's decline and presages their separation. To cite another example, on the terrace of the Villa Diana, high above the sea, the Divers express their passion for one another and Nicole's concomitant dependency: "Don't ever leave me—without you I'm not alive." It is on this same balcony much later that they admit that their relationship is over, and it is across the expanse of the terrace that a shattered Dick departs at the end of the film.

The imputation of discursive authority is also nonclassical in *Tender Is the Night*. Throughout the film multiple characters utter predictive statements, yet authority constantly shifts from character to character. Characters turn out in the end to be partially correct, or correct at the expense of their lives, or correct because they are absolutely antipsychoanalytic. After her bathroom relapse (which occurs near the start of the film), Nicole despairs, "I'll never be all right. . . . I'll always be like this, no good for thee my darling, no good for thee." Dick answers by swearing on his life that Nicole won't always be ill: "On my life I swear it. Remember who I love, what I swore, what I promised." Nicole is correct in the end that she's "no good" for Dick, but she is wrong in her earlier self-prognosis. She does regain her health. Dick is correct regarding Nicole, but her health costs him his. In the flashback of their first excursion together into downtown Zurich from the clinic on the outskirts of town, a similar exchange transpires, in which Nicole asks Dick to predict her fate:

> NICOLE: There's something else. Something at the back of my head that keeps asking a terrible question. I want to know whether I'll ever be at ease with other men the way I am with you.
>
> DICK: You certainly will. After I discharge you.
>
> NICOLE: Discharge me? It sounds so cold, like divorce me or something. You don't think I'll be fit to marry anybody for a long time, do you?
>
> DICK: I don't see why not. You're attractive, bright, charming . . .

It develops that Nicole is not, in fact, fit to marry anyone else until after Dick divorces her. Dick's predictions were correct with a twist—the substitution of divorce for discharge. The morning after the Fourth of July party Dick finds has-been composer Abe North (Tom Ewell) still at the piano on the terrace from the night before. Abe predicts to Dick, "I can't finish a tune and you can't finish . . . ," and Abe's predictions are correct. However, his narrative sagacity doesn't save his life. He dies in a race-related incident after a run-in with a black piano player who finishes Abe's song to perfection. An early wish expressed by Nicole's old friend Tommy Barban comes true: "Why don't you go out there [on the water] again, Dick. . . . You might just drown and Nicole might just remarry." The substitution of "drowning" in alcohol for "drowning" in the sea seems ironic in that Tommy is one of the characters least invested in any kind of psychoanalytic insight.

Nicole's older sister, the wealthy, unmarried Baby Warren (Joan Fontaine), is also given a certain amount of narrative authority, although the film's view of her is highly ambivalent. While she is provided with the attributes of power, that power is also undermined. The best example of the narrative ambivalence around the character Baby concerns Nicole's childhood trauma. Although it was Baby who held the key to that trauma, she recounts it only with the authorization of Dr. Dohmler and within a flashback narrated by Dick Diver. Dr. Dohmler asks her to tell him and Dr. Diver of any event, "however trivial," that occurred before her father's death that might shed light on Nicole's illness. Baby replies, "It was not trivial," and continues by quoting her father to the effect that only God could forgive [him] for the wrong he'd done Nicole.[37] On the other hand, however, Baby Warren is presented as unfeeling and self-interested. In the character Baby may be read the culture's fear of powerful women (she is the castrating female par excellence), but also the inexorable attraction of ideas and images of female power.

Perhaps the greatest amount of narrative veracity is assigned to the character of the wise Dr. Dohmler (Paul Lukas). He warns Dick in his suitably Viennese accent against getting romantically involved with Nicole, asking, "How can a first-class brain with a brilliant future fall in love so-called with a broken mind that is healed?" After Dick's protest, Dohmler goes on to claim that in such cases it is "the tyranny of the weak, the tyranny of the sick. First you learn to live life their way and then later on to like their way." It turns out that Dr. Dohmler is correct. But he is also a harbinger of doom; a helpless teacher who watches his favorite pupil destroy himself before his own death.

Dr. Dohmler's role is particularly interesting in comparison with the wise old (usually) European psychoanalysts of earlier films, for example, Dr. Bruloff in *Spellbound* and the analyst's teacher in *Oh, Men! Oh, Women!* or *Knock on Wood*. In all of these films the older analyst is portrayed as someone who has left active practice and trained a younger analyst to take his place. In *Tender Is the Night* not only is Dr. Dohmler old but he actually dies of old age in the course of the narrative. There is a certain sense of verisimilitude in the death of the wise old European analyst, for by the early sixties many psychoanalytic pioneers were indeed yielding the ground to younger colleagues or passing away. But one could make a less obvious association with the social formation by saying that what the death of Dohmler evokes is the very same "death" of psychoanalytic authority in the face of social changes evoked by Dr. Diver's breakdown.

The film's plot has its own vocabulary for describing the rise and fall of Dick Diver's mental health, calling it a movement from "transference" to "countertransference." The following dialogue between Dr. Franz Gregorovius and Dr. Diver is presented as a correct explanation of the state of affairs near the end of the film, even though Dick is reluctant to admit the truth:

GREGOROVIUS: Wonderful, Nicole is cured, there's no doubt about that.

DIVER: Oh, I'm very happy to have your diagnosis, Dr. Gregorovius. And to what do you attribute this cure?

GREGOROVIUS: You know from where comes her new ego strength.

DIVER: Ah, you think it's anaclitic, do you? Transference of strength between doctor and patient?

GREGOROVIUS: Why are you so bitter, Dick?

DIVER: Ah, come now, Franz, you can tell me. What you also mean is that it has worked in reverse.

GREGOROVIUS: What I mean is that Nicole is no longer dependent on you.

DIVER: You imply the transference is over, the countertransference has begun, and I am the weak one.

Here countertransference is presented as a morass into which Dr. Diver, regardless of having been forewarned, must fall. Having fallen, he loses his effectivity as an analyst, his sanity, and his desirability as a mate.

In chapter 2 it was pointed out that Freud tended to shy away from explicit discussions of countertransference,[38] and the concept really only began to show up in American professional literature as late as the mid-1950s.[39] Its significance seemed to be as a way to broach the psychology of the analyst himself or herself. Countertransference represented a semicovert way for the psychiatric profession to admit that analysts have human vulnerabilities and that analytic authority could not be construed as objective or omniscient. Its use in *Tender Is the Night* transposes similar issues to narrative terms. In its general narrative trajectory, and in using the term "countertransference" to describe that trajectory, the film bears the marks of a challenge to narrative models of psychiatric authority much stronger than that seen in earlier films.

The narrative trajectory in the single film *Tender Is the Night* and the film's deviation from the narrative models presented in *Whirlpool* and *The Three Faces of Eve* make *Tender Is the Night* a good specific example of a general trend in the development of the whole cycle of films as they came to bear more and more the marks of a growing challenge to psychiatric authority. All share the dual impulses of adjustment and resistance, but in the later films the impulse of resistance to narrative modalities of adjustment psychiatry comes eventually to dominate.

The nature of the traumatic past event may be taken as a final point of comparison between earlier and later films. The Hollywood depiction of original traumas in films of the 1940s was often surprising in view of their importance in the narrative. There is a sanitized banality inherent in traumas such as being denied a new dress (*Whirlpool*), being accused of stealing a locket (*The Locket*), being scolded for wearing mother's best dress (*Lady in the Dark*).

The banality of these melodramatic traumas is especially apparent in comparison with the shocking nature of common past traumas in later films: little Marnie stabbing her mother's john in *Marnie* (1964), father-daughter incest in *Tender Is the Night* (1962), a gruesome attack by a gang of kids in *Suddenly Last Summer* (1959), and even later a mother who tortures her pre-teenaged daughter with "gynecological exams" in *Sybil* (1976) (where the mise-en-scène evokes a nightmarish cross between Nazi surgical experimentation and back-alley abortion).[40]

If the distinction seems abundantly clear, there is one important objection to be raised and answered. Read as fantasy scenarios rather than as literal renditions of childhood horror, the *import* of these traumas would be more in keeping with their weight in the narrative. Perhaps their semi-inanity covers but hints at, indeed *represses*, the volatile issue of female bonding and paternal abuse. For example, Maureen Turim interprets intimations of childhood homosexuality in *The Locket* when "two girls, almost identical in looks, are shown embracing in a closet, binding their exchange [of the locket] with a promise of eternal fidelity."[41] From this perspective, 1940s traumas and 1960s traumas have the same emotional charge.

But while the psychical charge may be the same, the nature of the trauma itself is also important, and here there is a difference. Twenty-five years later, in 1924, Freud added the following footnote to his case history of Katharina:

> I venture after the lapse of so many years to lift the veil of discretion and reveal the fact that Katharina was not the niece but the daughter of the landlady. *The girl fell ill, therefore, as a result of sexual attempts on the part of her own father. Distortions like the one which I introduced in the present instance should be altogether avoided in reporting a case history.* From the point of view of understanding a case, a distortion of this kind is not, of course, a matter of such indifference as would be shifting the scene from one mountain to another.[42] (emphasis added)

Similarly, the use of incest as the childhood trauma in *Tender Is the Night* instead of the loss of a locket is not a matter of indifference, but a matter of historical difference. The changing nature of depicted childhood traumas, as they became more obviously traumatic and less accessible to easy resolution, seems to me a narrative trace of the changing social discourses around women and psychiatry, as feminist thought and challenges to normalizing psychiatry came to the fore, and as a move toward a more comprehensive ego psychology established itself.

In summary, the pervasive tendency of American psychiatry, including psychoanalytic theory and practice, to authorize and publicize itself with recourse to a model of adjustment therapy for women affects the narrative and textual strategies of Hollywood films that overtly depict psychiatry and women. The adjustment impulse of the wider social formation embeds itself in the authoritative and authoritarian relationship of male psychiatrist to female patient. Yet this cultural complex is not a monolithic but a hegemonic and historical process. The contents of the debates within American psychoanalysis, as well as their very existence, reveal currents of resistance to normalizing models of femininity—currents of resistance whose strength increased as the period aged, and currents whose drift was surely transferred to filmic representation.

4

The Institutional Edifice

I'll tell you where it's going to end, Miss Summerville. When there are
more sick ones than well ones, the sick ones will lock the well ones up.
　　　—Virginia Cunningham in *The Snake Pit* (1948)

The apparatus of control present in classical Hollywood narrative film,
and specifically represented by the institution of psychiatry in the
films of this study, is overdetermined in films with mental hospital settings. These latter films translate the thematics of authority to the
physical presence of the asylum, hospital, state institution, or clinic.
The institution of psychiatry, in Foucault's sense of the term "institution," is expressed here literally as institutional psychiatry.

The rigors of confinement are evoked by the concrete structure of
the hospital building itself in *Bedlam*, *The Snake Pit*, *The Cobweb*, and
Lilith, among other films that show the outside of the inevitably large
and imposing institutional building within the first few shots of the
film. The institutions in *Bedlam* and *The Snake Pit*, in particular, are
brick fortresses, daunting from the outside and fitted on the inside
with a labyrinth of vacant corridors, dark cells, and strange devices of
restraint and torture. These literal images of locks, keys, doors, and
windows represent the tangible counterpart to the metaphoric use of
the devices in Hollywoodian psychoanalytic explanation. For example,
the metaphorical "locked doors of [the] mind" in *Spellbound* are expressed in *The Snake Pit* and *Bedlam*, and elsewhere in *Spellbound*
itself, as real locked doors.

But the psychiatric mastery embodied by the sets and art direction
of the institutional physical plant is no more totalizing than that of the
contemporaneous psychiatric literature. The cinematic institutional
edifice, too, is tempered by the possibility of resistance to its authori-

tarian impulse: the function of the iconography of confinement is not only to restrain but also to introduce the very problems of the psychiatry of restraint. The films are not so much blueprints for successful institutional treatment as they are meditations upon the delicacy and *+ 91* transcience of sanity.

Inside and Outside

Because the films under discussion are set in institutions, they add the physical boundary itself as a new component to the problem of the boundaries between health and illness previously described in films with family settings. In *Bedlam* (1946), *Spellbound* (1945), *The Snake Pit* (1948), *The Cobweb* (1955), and *Lilith* (1964), among others, the psychic states "mad" and "sane" are reexpressed in physical terms as "inside" and "outside" the institution. But the institution is not so much a dictatorial signifier where inside equals mad and outside equals sane; rather it is a spatial signifier of the two available options and their inevitable relation.

Doctors and patients are constantly changing positions with regard to the cell door. Mad with power, Master Sims (Boris Karloff), the head of St. Mary's Bethlehem Asylum (nicknamed "Bedlam"), imprisons a woman because she protests hospital conditions. Since she had been employed to amuse a wealthy lord, her protestations take the form of jokes. But in the Shakespearean sense the court fool or jester is the sanest of all, and in *Bedlam* (1946) the woman is clearly sane. It is a case of the sick locking up the well. Interestingly, this incarceration of a sane person is consistent with the history upon which this film draws. In London's Bethlem Hospital (also nicknamed "Bedlam"), confinement was often a police matter and the "hospital" was really a prison.[1]

A common theme is the person who comes to work at or to investigate the mental institution, only to be forced to remain as an inmate. *Bedlam*'s Master Sims is captured by the inmates for threatening the incarcerated "fool," Nell Bowen (Anna Lee), who has befriended them. He is placed on trial by inmates more humane than himself and deemed partly mad but worthy of release. But he is attacked by a mute girl with an angelic face, and the inmates, afraid of the consequences of the attack, drag his unconscious body behind a stone wall under construction. He is walled up alive, to be forever a physical inmate of his own confine. The outgoing director of Green Manors (Leo G. Carroll) in *Spellbound* also ends up a mental case, for he has killed his prospective replacement. In *The Snake Pit*, Miss Summerville, formerly head nurse on Ward 1, is driven mad by the constant influx of patients for whom there is no room.

Shock Corridor (1963) provides perhaps the prototypical example of the investigatory plot device. A newspaperman, anxious for a good story, arranges his own commitment to a mental institution so that he may investigate a murder. He discovers that patient abuse and poor hospital conditions are behind the murder, which was committed to cover up those problems. The reporter is released and his exposé is published. But he has suffered a mental breakdown and has to be re-admitted as a true patient.

The case of the sane outsider who enters the institution only to fall ill or be driven mad has a common counterpart: the case of the insider who imagines himself or herself sane. At the opening of *The Snake Pit*, the heroine, Virginia (Olivia de Havilland), invents a story to explain why she is incarcerated if she is really sane: "Why, yes, of course, I'm writing a novel about prisons and I've come to study conditions and take notes." In *Bedlam* a group of patients fancy themselves well and superior to the other patients. Indeed, this characterization of patients who believe themselves to be well is extended in drama and literature through the notion of the mental institution as a microcosm of the so-cial hierarchies of the real world.[2]

Accompanying this role reversibility between sane and insane is a kind of reversibility in the films' view of confinement. One might imag-ine that the idea of escape from the bonds of confinement would be unreservedly associated with the idea of freedom. This is broadly true of *Bedlam* and *The Snake Pit*, set in a state institution, in which the happy endings depend on the heroine's discharge. Nevertheless, these two films, along with other films set in private or state institutions, are equivocal on this issue.

Both *The Cobweb* and *Lilith* have attractive supporting characters who prefer to remain within the clinic walls. "I'm phobic" explains Su-san (Susan Strasberg) in *The Cobweb* when Stevie (John Kerr) invites her to a movie in town. Mrs. Meaghan (Anne Meacham) in *Lilith* is afraid to leave the building because her "enemies" lurk outside. Of course, the desire to avoid the outside world is portrayed as a symptom of illness, but at the same time the films render understandable that desire by representing the institution as a peaceful haven where incar-ceration may be equated with retreat. The sanitariums and clinics in *The Cobweb*, *Lilith*, *Spellbound*, and *Tender Is the Night* are expen-sive private ones (the director of the private clinic in *Lilith* explains that some of the patients' families pay seven thousand dollars per month for their keep), and, as their names suggest (Poplar Lodge, Green Manors), their buildings and grounds are spacious and peaceful.

In fact, the lack of regimentation in the private clinics seems exactly to embody the ideal advocated by those who saw or created *The Snake Pit* as an exposé of improper institutional conditions.

Even the narrative trajectories of these films present an ambivalent view of confinement by simultaneously figuring release and return trajectories and by alternating between them. *Bedlam* and *The Cobweb* begin with inmates breaking out, but these opening escape gambits present a difficult if not impossible narrative premise, for the thrust of the plot is precisely to allow the audience to explore the life of the institution. Thus, the escapee in *Bedlam* merely touches off the events of the film, he doesn't participate in them. The story is really the confinement of Nell Bowen. Similarly in *The Cobweb*, a dissolve between the film's fifth and sixth shots replaces Stevie's flight from the clinic with his return to the clinic. In shot five (part of the film's opening credit sequence) Stevie crashes through a cornfield fleeing the clinic. In shot six (the start of the diegetic portion of the film), Stevie emerges onto a road where he calmly hitches a ride back up to the clinic to attend a scheduled analytic hour. In a temporal reversal, the events begun in shot six are actually events that occurred at an earlier point than Stevie's flight. In fact they are the very events leading up to his flight. Interestingly, the screen direction in the five shots under the opening credits also participates in this departure-return pattern. In the first two shots, Stevie runs away from the clinic from left to right. In the third shot he runs directly away from the camera. In shots four and five he runs from frame right to frame left. Thus, even though he is still supposed to be fleeing the clinic, his direction has reversed itself in preparation for the start of the flashback, which begins with his ride up the road to the clinic.

Bedlam's structure unfolds via an outside-inside-outside pattern. It begins with the failed escape and ends with Nell Bowen's successful escape. In this it bears great similarity to the structure of *The Snake Pit*. The latter film opens with Virginia seated on a bench on the grounds of the institution. Although technically a patient, aspects of the narrative and mise-en-scène suggest Virginia's mental freedom. For example, a bird takes flight from a tree branch seen in the foreground of the walls and rooftops of the institution. After this prologue, the major events of the film are set within the walls of the institution and concern Virginia's attempts to get well. The film ends with her release.

The Cobweb retains this flight-incarceration-release structure of *The Snake Pit* but goes one step further. The film doesn't end with Stevie's escape, but rather with his subsequent return to his psychiatrist. Other films, too, including *Shock Corridor* and *Shock Treatment*, reverse the outside-inside-outside structure, ending pessimistically with the main character's descent into madness.

Here I would extend Shoshana Felman's notion of the ambiguous place of madness across the permeable boundaries of the institutional topography. For Felman, writing in the introduction to *Writing and Madness*:

> To say that madness has indeed become our commonplace is thus to say that madness in the contemporary world points to the radical ambiguity of the inside and the outside, insofar as this ambiguity escapes the speaking subjects (who speak only to have it escape them). A madness that has become a *common place* can no longer be thought of as a simple place (topos) inside our era; it is rather our entire era that has become subsumed within the space of madness.[3]

Likewise, for the films of this chapter, the reversibility of the narrative trajectories and the role reversibility between the sane and the mad suggest that the films are not structured according to a curative prescription, but rather structured to foreground the various possibilities themselves. In all of these films, to a greater or lesser extent, the narrative oscillation between inside and outside, illness and health, reveals these terms to be highly unstable.

The Psychosis

Besides intensifying the problem of the boundary between health and illness by making it a physical one, films set in mental institutions intensify the degree of illness depicted. In these films, the border and the *burden* of normalcy recede even further into the distance with the depiction of *psychotic* rather than neurotic disturbances.

The depiction of illnesses serious enough to require inpatient care might seem to encourage the depiction of treatment regimes more in keeping with the adjustment impulse native to the short-term physiological techniques described in chapter 2 than with less authoritarian long-term analytic approaches also described. And yet the physical apparatuses of psychiatry can incarnate an ideology of control, simultaneously taken up and subverted by the narrative. Precisely because these films are set in institutions they allow the depiction of serious, sometimes frightening, often excessive mental disturbances that cannot be fully contained. Because the promise of institutional control in these films is so great, the depiction of female deviance, in particular, may be allowed to threaten its traditional parameters.

The neuroses of the women in the films discussed in chapter 3 are relatively glamorous and endearing compared with the more extreme symptoms of institutionalized women. *Whirlpool*, *Lady in the Dark*, *Lady in a Jam*, *Tender Is the Night*, and even *The Three Faces of Eve* all provide the audience with the spectacle of a woman whose sexuality is temporarily unfurled due to a mental disturbance that proves relatively controllable with just a bit of psychological nudging. In *The Snake Pit*, *Lilith*, and other films set in institutions, however, a main female character evinces a psychotic complaint that is addressed but not necessarily corrected. Moreover, these films demand the presence of numerous supporting and bit characters, a chorus of psychotic women and men, who can no more be attended to individually within the parameters of classical narrative than they can within the depersonalized institutional setting. Their symptomatic disconnection with reality persists as a sobering backdrop to any possibility of cure. In *The Snake Pit* one patient attempts to brag to Virginia about her wealthy husband who has supposedly given her the Hope diamond. Another misapplies lipstick to her cheeks in preparation for her date with a man she represents variously as her husband and as her boyfriend. The symptoms of other patients show that they are removed from even this oblique connection to reality. One patient dances about in her own world; another is mute and violent; others shriek incessantly, repeat gibberish, and issue sexual invitations to doctors and orderlies. In *Lilith* some of the patients go on outings, but others laugh hysterically or, conversely, sit immobile in catatonic stupors.

Perhaps the greatest distinction between the neurotic heroines of the films of chapter 3 and the psychotic supporting cast of these institutional films is the visual distinction especially marked by the film image. In the former group, mental illness is indicated by certain noticeable alterations in the normal makeup and wardrobe with which a star is fitted. For example, mental illness is often coded as a lack of makeup, bushy eyebrows, or loose-fitting, shapeless clothing (*Now, Voyager*, *Johnny Belinda*, *Possessed*, Virginia in *The Snake Pit*).[4] As Mary Ann Doane writes, it is coded as "a marked lack of narcissism on the part of the sick woman. The illness of the woman is signalled by the fact that she no longer cares about her appearance."[5] Doane calls this the "despecularization" of women and argues that it accompanies the substitution of the "medical gaze." The reverse may also hold true. According to Doane, the illness of the woman may be coded alternatively as an *excess* of narcissism, as is the case in *Whirlpool* and *Tender Is the Night*. *The Three Faces of Eve* illustrates both cases. Where Eve White is dowdy and wears no makeup, Eve Black overdresses for her evening exploits. But over or under made-up, the "unattractiveness" of these heroines requires our suspension of disbelief, for the actress is still Bette Davis, Jane Wyman, Gene Tierney, Jennifer Jones, Joan Crawford, or Joanne Woodward.

The madness of the peripheral characters of *The Snake Pit* or *Lilith*, on the other hand, is marked by the outright violation of socially acceptable codes of female attractiveness and behavior. Many of the roles in *The Snake Pit* are played by old or fat or otherwise "undesirable" women. The sexual behavior these women act out appears particularly inappropriate in its disengagement from standards of youth and beauty given in the context of the Hollywood image factory.

The analysis of *The Snake Pit*, *The Cobweb*, and *Lilith* is intended to examine closely various instances of restraint in three films set in institutions, with emphasis on how that institutional restraint figures the ambiguities that abide in and in fact define determinations of social authority attached to madness or sanity. As Shoshana Felman puts it, "No discourse of madness can now know whether it is inside or outside of the madness it discusses."[6]

The Snake Pit

The Snake Pit (1948) has generally been regarded as a socially conscious critique of the inhumane nature of mental hospital conditions.[7] Given this reception and the project here to locate filmic challenges to the hegemony of the adjustment impulse, one might expect a celebration of *The Snake Pit* as a clear-cut example of this challenge. Indeed, a contingent case along those lines will be made in the second part of the discussion of *The Snake Pit*. It is necessary, however, to begin by showing that, in spite of the film's obvious intent and reception, its actual indictment of the American mental institution is quite limited, evidencing a strong tendency to support authoritarian psychiatric practice. Like the films of chapter 3, *The Snake Pit* is structured by a kind of textual dissociation in its ideological stance toward authoritarian psychiatry.

On the surface, regimentation, straitjacket restraint, electroconvulsive therapy, and hydrotherapy seem initially to be depicted as cruel and undesirable methods of treatment, as opposed to the positive treatment that psychoanalytic psychiatry receives. In this sense the film appears to enter the heated professional debate on the side of anti–adjustment psychoanalysis. Virginia waits terrified, not knowing what to expect, on the bench outside the room where the shock treatments are administered. Her name is called and she is ushered inside. She is forced onto the table and held down by three nurses, and her protests are cut off by a gag in the shape of a phallus. She is given three more shock treatments, each of which is shown in a systematic montage of three shots. The first shot is always of the dials of the ECT machine, the second is of Virginia just after treatment lying on the gurney with the gag still in place, and the third is of a typewriter rolling out the record of the treatment and its result. The mechanical trappings of restraint and the technique of visual repetition underline the horrific nature of the treatment and so indict it as inhumane.

However, the indictment of the physiological procedures is qualified in certain ways so that these procedures appear, on another level, as acceptable manifestations of similarly acceptable psychiatric mastery. Firstly, it is the wise and paternal Dr. Kik (Leo Genn) who prescribes shock treatment for Virginia in order to "reach her" for psychoanalytic psychotherapy. He justifies his use of ECT, and later of narcosynthesis, as necessary procedures given the time constraints of the institutional setting. Furthermore, time is money. Dr. Gifford wants to free Virginia's spot for other patients by releasing her to an out-of-state farm. The film's point of view is that ECT may be advisable in certain cases.

Indeed, an interesting enunciative device affirms the film's positive identification with the apparatus of shock treatment. The results of Virginia's final shock treatment are slightly different. She is not shown on the gurney, but up walking, and this improvement is reported on a chart that rolls out of the typewriter: "patient more alert but still confused in surroundings." But surprisingly, another line is added to the chart: "On the following evening, about . . . " After the word "about" there is a dissolve to a clock and then another dissolve to Virginia's face framed on her pillow. Thus, the film has introduced a narrational device that links shock treatment with visual storytelling. In other words, this succinct series of three shots organically connects ECT, cinematic narration, and the look at an immobile woman.

The potential indictment of ECT and of the hospital's regimentation in general is also undercut by the film's tendency to blame existing inhumane conditions on aberrant individuals. Nurse Davis employs shock treatment on Virginia as a punitive measure because she is secretly in love with Dr. Kik and jealous of the attention he lavishes on Virginia. We recognize her as a "bad" character by her severe hair style and through the comments of another nurse who implies that Nurse Davis's rules are overly strict. Nurse Davis fits within the Hollywood convention of the "masculinized" (unfulfilled) woman (like the female curator of the Thatcher library in *Citizen Kane*). Another nurse shown in the process of administering hydrotherapy against Virginia's will is also portrayed as unfulfilled and so inordinately harsh. Virginia asks whether she is single and the nurse replies ruefully, "Don't rub it in." The implication is that if only the personnel were kind, caring, and *fulfilled as women* through marriage, they would administer kindlier electroconvulsive shocks. And just as the indictment of authoritarian psychiatry is transformed into necessary adjustment therapy, psychoanalysis is reduced to its adjustment orientation. Psychoanalyst Dr. Kik is really the emissary of the institution, or its prodigal son, rather than its resident dissident.

The hybridized psychoanalytic therapy practiced on Virginia by Dr. Kik unfolds as a review of her past relationships with men. According to Kik, Virginia's "main problem happens to be complete inability to accept his [her husband's] love." The sign of the cure will be her acceptance of the therapeutically affirmed spouse, Robert, whom Virginia no longer recognizes. As Mary Ann Doane explains, "Her symptom is the erasure of the male figure but not of the social situation entailed":[8]

> DR. KIK: You've told me many times you were married, and how can you be married without having a husband?
>
> VIRGINIA: Yes, that's strange, isn't it?
>
> (*Dr. Kik then gets Virginia to repeat after him her married name.*)
>
> DR. KIK: Virginia Stuart Cunningham.
>
> VIRGINIA: Cunningham.
>
> DR. KIK: Mrs. Robert Cunningham.
>
> VIRGINIA: Robert.
>
> DR. KIK: Your husband.
>
> VIRGINIA: My husband.
>
> DR. KIK: Isn't it better to know?

Here again, the goals of psychoanalytic psychiatry are consistent both with those of traditional marriage and with cinematic storytelling conventions.

Virginia's own account of her past is bracketed between that of her husband and that of her analyst, and husband and analyst work in concert. It is Robert who delivers his wife into treatment with Dr. Kik by narrating the story of their courtship, our first glimpse of Virginia's past. "She needed me like a child needing protection," asserts Robert. Dr. Kik then interprets the elements of Robert's story as a means of Virginia's correction. For example, in one scene from the story Robert narrates, Robert and Virginia are in the kitchen arguing over her mental state. The mise-en-scène draws our attention to a knife lying on the kitchen counter. We notice that Virginia stares at it as if to take it up and threaten her husband, but he himself does not notice. Later, in Dr. Kik's office, Virginia glances down at a letter opener as if to menace Dr. Kik. He does notice, saying, "You want to hurt me, why? You'd want to hurt anybody who tried to stop you from doing away with a very important day in your life. Wouldn't it be better to try to face it?" The scenario, then, is one in which a woman's behavior toward her spouse is regulated by psychoanalysis.

When Virginia does narrate a sequence of events from her past, her story is authorized by Dr. Kik and his psychological interpretation of her case (and once it is even elicited by an injection he gives her). Virginia's account of her childhood relationship with her father is provoked by Dr. Kik's inquiry when he finds her cradling a doll. "Are you a good mother?" he asks. Virginia replies that "every woman wants to have [a baby]." She then recounts her childhood flirtations with her father, her jealousy of her pregnant mother, and the death of her father. Her father died on the heels of an angry act in which she crushed a doll dressed in a soldier's uniform that had been previously established as representative of him. According to the analysis provided by the film, Virginia unconsciously believes that she is responsible for the death of her father.

The film weaves still another layer of enunciative control in the form of Dr. Kik's flashback to Virginia's past. Dr. Kik's account begins as far back as Virginia's infancy, at a part of her story even she cannot relate. We see a crying baby, and hear Dr. Kik's voice describing how babies need love. Dr. Kik's narration later repeats the image of Virginia crushing the little soldier doll, and Kik explains that "children are afraid to grow up because they're afraid to let go of the love they felt for their father." Finally, Dr. Kik explains how Virginia's love for her husband developed out of her love for the kind and thoughtful parts of her father's character. In the course of the analysis, Dr. Kik teaches Virginia a proper reading of the events of her past. He teaches her to stop blaming herself for the death of her father, and to transfer her love for her father to the appropriate spousal object. She learns to crave the baby of her husband, not the baby of her father.

Like the stories of the women in *Possessed*, *The Three Faces of Eve*, *The Seventh Veil*, *The Locket*, and *Whirlpool*, this account conforms to an aspect of classical psychoanalytic theories of female psychosexual development in which the path to proper femininity converges with the path to maternity. Interestingly, in *The Snake Pit* the fictional analyst assumes an especially universalizing authority in that Dr. Kik was not even present at the events from Virginia's infancy that he narrates over on-screen images. He simply knows they occurred as part of a psychoanalytic generalization about human development. Dr. Kik asks Virginia if she understands his interpretation, and she replies that she knows what *he* thinks. Finally, in her successful prerelease interview, another doctor asks if she is "aware of the origin of [her] illness." She replies modestly, disclaiming her own authority to speak in the very act of accepting psychoanalytic authority: "I'd have to be a doctor to put it into the right words," she starts, and then continues with the account she has been taught.

To speak, then, is not to control one's own subjectivity, but to parrot the proper words one has been taught. In this light, a supposedly happy event near the end of the film must be qualified. Ready to leave Juniper Hill, Virginia goes to say good-bye to Hester, a mute girl she has befriended. She does so, but as she leaves, Hester grabs her arm. "Goodbye, Virginia," says Hester hesitantly. Virginia exclaims, "Oh, Hester, you've talked. I knew you would. You're going to get well now, I know you will." In the context of the reading I have been proposing, this pat link between speech and cure is not that of liberating analysis, but that of the adjustment impulse, for to speak is only to speak the words of patriarchal authority.

Virginia's psychosis itself opens the way for yet another figure of psychiatric control in the form of auditory hallucinations: Virginia hears voices. In the opening scene of the film an unseen man's voice is heard asking, "Do you know where you are, Mrs. Cunningham?" A close-up captures Virginia looking startled, and on the sound track in a nonsynchronous voice-over, we hear her speak: "Where is he? It's as if he were crouching behind me." At the end of this opening sequence we learn that the voice is that of Dr. Kik, whose face Virginia later fails to place but whose voice carries an eerie familiarity. The fact that in this case the cinematic manifestation of the male speaking voice is coterminous with the fictional Virginia's imagination of a male voice of authority implies a unique collusion of cinema and psychoanalysis through which the voice of psychoanalytic inquiry and control is injected into a woman's subjective process.

The deployment of authority in this sequence and in *The Snake Pit* as a whole may be described with reference to Foucault's *Madness and Civilization*. According to Foucault, the Quaker Samuel Tuke did not really liberate the insane when he unchained them. What he did to create the nineteenth-century asylum from the prison was to substitute "the stifling anguish of responsibility" for the stifling anguish of physical restraint.[9] Corporeal restraint imposed by chains and bars was displaced by self-restraint, the *internal*, moral version of the prison cell. In Foucault's terms: "Instead of submitting to a simple negative operation that loosened bonds and delivered one's deepest nature from madness, it must be recognized that one was in the grip of a positive operation that confined madness in a system of rewards and punishments, and included it in the movement of moral consciousness."[10]

Likewise in *The Snake Pit*, the straps and wires of the ECT machine and the seamless immobilizing embrace of the straitjacket give way to the moral confines of a male voice in the patient's head. The voice Virginia hears is simultaneously that of her analyst, that of her superego, and that of her moral consciousness: psychiatry, the family, and society. After all, the word "confinement" refers both to imprisonment and to "lying in," to being jailed and to giving birth—the double prescription of the feminine mystique.

Another way to describe *The Snake Pit*'s adjustment impulse would be to say that Juniper Hill is perhaps the most upright institution on film. It is not necessarily upright in the sense of being run without a hitch, but it is eminently upright in its adherence to a traditional hierarchy of power. Doctors, nurses and orderlies observe strict hierarchical positions. Dr. Kik is "above" Nurse Davis and so holds the power to monitor her performance. As she is about to administer a shock treatment to Virginia, he snaps, "Didn't you check her chart?" Even doctors themselves wield power at different levels. Dr. Gifford, who is described by Virginia's husband as being "over Kik," interferes with Kik's treatment of Virginia. At the bottom of the heap are the patients to whom the hospital personnel dispense rigorous treatment and bodily maintenance. Significantly these patients are primarily women; we do see male patients but not on the wards. Thus the whole hierarchical structure of the institution organizes an effort to treat women, and, given the nature of patriarchal social formation to which the mental hospital conforms, it is not surprising that the treatment itself is far from ideologically neutral.

At Juniper Hill women are treated according to a social definition of "normality" that enforces attitudes of obedience and passivity. One patient, Margaret, wants to see her baby, but Dr. Kik refuses to release her to her husband, John, because her domestic situation does not conform to the ideal of the nuclear family:

> DR. KIK: He [John] can't take you home to that crowded house with all his folks around, you know that, Margaret. That's why you're almost well, because you know it. . . . John's trying to find a place just for you and him.
>
> MARGARET: And the baby?
>
> DR. KIK: Of course.

The geography of Juniper Hill organizes a parallel hierarchy of health whereby the patients closest to being well and to being released live on Ward 1. "Practically everybody goes home from 1," another patient tells Virginia. As the numbers of the wards increase, so does the illness of the residents and the number of locked doors. The mise-en-scène, bright and compositionally uncrowded on Wards 1 and 3, gives way to darker brick walls and strange shadows of bars and writhing bodies on Ward 33-33A. On Ward 12, the overcrowding is emphasized by the presence of a large area rug in the middle of the room that the patients are not allowed to tread on. Their staring, rocking, and moaning have been relegated to the narrow, teeming periphery of the room.

The spatial logic communicated by plot, editing, and cinematography carries out the hierarchical metaphor. Virginia is moved up the wards as she is deemed sicker and sicker, and this movement is continued by the camera, which finally rises on a crane to look back down at her caught on Ward 33 in the middle of the swarming "snake pit" of the insane. The highest-numbered wards seem to be the high towers of medieval exile. At her most desperate, Virginia is finally confined in a straitjacket, in solitary, in a narrow cell.

Besides its spatial articulation of the hierarchical nature of psychiatric power, the arrangement of the wards from top to bottom also reiterates Foucault's account of the historical development of confinement from chains to moral strictures. The upper wards evoke the eighteenth-century madhouse, the lower the early-twentieth-century asylum. When deluded, Virginia misrecognizes her place of confinement. She takes it for a prison. Brought back to reality, she knows it as a hospital. But the ideological thrusts of the two are equivalent.

Its strong patriarchal thrust notwithstanding, *The Snake Pit* does offer some countercurrents of resistance both on the level of ideological machinations that might have contributed to the film's reception as an advocacy tool for mental hospital reform and on the level of textual discontinuities that put into question the rationality of dominant psychiatric discourse.

The rules of Juniper Hill, as enforced by various individuals who work within the institution, are often portrayed as arbitrary or even sadistic and psychotogenic. Virginia is bound to obey Nurse Davis no matter what. At one point, however, Virginia has a sudden realization that Nurse Davis is in love with Dr. Kik and says so to her face. Nurse Davis becomes enraged and punishes Virginia by returning her to the upper wards where her illness deepens. Virginia's other removal to the upper wards is also caused by insensitive treatment at the hands of a member of the staff, this time a doctor, who is portrayed as rather eccentric himself. Because in each case Virginia is punished for acting out in response to what the plot presents as unjust treatment, the institution is implicated in the compounding of her madness.

In this context the voices Virginia imagines take on a fuller meaning than either that of internalized patriarchal instruments of control or mere symptoms of her madness. When Virginia's husband Robert comes to take her for a picnic on the grounds, a female voice supports her fears that the man she sees is not really Robert. The voice warns, "Watch yourself, honey. Everything counts against you." On one level, this is the voice of paranoia. But on another level, this warning is an appropriate response to conditions we have already seen Virginia experience as she was lied to and unjustly treated by the staff. Dr. Kik calls this distrust of Robert "the patient's main problem." But in Robert's account of Virginia's breakdown, Virginia shrieks an important line that goes unheard by the psychoanalytic work of the fictional doctor. In accordance with Kik's diagnosis, she does scream, "No, you can't make me love you." But she also screams, "No, you can't make me *belong* to you." This subversive brand of madness cannot be acknowledged by the overt psychoanalytic explanation provided, for neither can it be contained. Yet, though a fleeting line, this cry taps into a structured undercurrent of resistance to a film version of the institution of psychiatry and its narrative twin, the institution of marriage. We are encouraged to identify with Virginia's madness and through it with her resistance to psychiatric authority.

Virginia is joined in her rebellious actions by other more minor characters, and so an idiom of resistance is established that is a ubiquitous comment on overly rigid regimentation. For example, as the patients are being led back in from outside at the opening of the film, one patient breaks rank and sinks to the floor in a kind of sit-down strike. Later Virginia copies this act when she plops herself down on the out-of-bounds rug on Ward 12. When told to get up and off she does so, but another patient leaps forward onto the rug in a wild, erratic Charleston. Even though sanity is defined by the film as learning to accept authority, it is simultaneously defined as the natural, joyful desire to break the rules and to act jointly in doing so. Near the end of the film, Dr. Kik praises Virginia's loyalty to the mute Hester. Virginia replies to the effect that patients can understand each other better than doctors understand patients.

The film may also be read as providing a subtle commentary on social conditions that contribute to mental illness. The tidbits we learn about the lives of two characters who are sent home during the course of the film are illustrative. Margaret is held until a home can be arranged just for her, her husband, and the baby. But there is also Grace. Grace's view of going home is rather different: "Before long I'll be on my own, wondering where the next meal's coming from." As one of the film's few references to the outside world, this represents the acknowledgment of adverse social and economic conditions, an acknowledgment that is particularly pointed in a era touted as affluent. From this perspective, even Margaret's situation may be reread. Why, after all,

Figure 14. This evocative image of Virginia (Olivia de Havilland) in the "snake pit" interrupts the film's normally realist visual scheme. Production still.

was she living with a group of people who drove her crazy in the first place if not out of economic necessity?

But perhaps the film's most intriguing critique of adjustment psychiatry may be read not at the overt level of the plot, but at the level of cinematic signification. As spectators we are at various points in the film encouraged to identify with a certain textual madness most evident in the film's solicitation of our identification with Virginia's, the madwoman's, psychotic mental images, which are manifested in the film both visually and auditorally. Both the image of ocean waves sweeping over Virginia's inert body and the optically altered aerial shot of a miniature Virginia caught in a teeming "snake pit" of inmate serpents interrupt the film's realist visual scheme to function on the emotionally evocative level as refugee images from the avant-garde (Figure 14).

But here it seems useful to return to the perhaps less obvious recruitment of audience sympathy for mad texts in the form of the film's opening moments. As discussed above, one operation of psychiatric control exerted over the madwoman is that of the introjection of authoritative presence into her ego boundaries in the form of voices she hears. But further reflection reveals that this control tactic is actually quite problematic and opens to an alternative reading. Virginia is mad precisely *because* she hears and heeds that voice of authority. In other words, authority itself becomes a symptom of pathology. Furthermore, the audience is encouraged in this sequence to identify with what should be a pathological symptom setting Virginia apart from us, the healthy. When we hear Dr. Kik's query in the opening scene of the film, we are no more sure than Virginia whether the man is speaking from a proximate position just offscreen or whether his voice is, as we confirm a moment later, imagined by Virginia. It is only when the camera pulls back from the close-up of Virginia to an establishing shot of the bench on which she is seated that we can determine that the voice we heard was in fact imaginary. By that time Virginia has also figured it out. What is crucial, though, is not the moment of determination but that initial moment of indeterminacy when we share Virginia's auditory hallucination. In this moment the cinematic voice-over is to the audience what the delusional voice is to the character, and our identification with the film's main character is thus articulated through identification with her madness.

The particular dialog that passes between the representative voice of sanity and the certifiably mad woman is also significant. In fact, this opening mental conversation of the film bears comparison with Shoshana Felman's elegant and Lacanian interpretation of the "methodically mad" conversation between a salesman and a madman in a story by Balzac.[11] Felman argues that in this tale the madness of the madman's discourse, because it is taken for the discourse of a legitimate and successful banker by an illustrious and interested salesman, serves to demystify the mystification of the salesman's discourse, and by extrapolation, of the Balzac story, of realist literature, and of Western civilization itself. "What Balzac's text teaches us," writes Felman, "is that language has no master: this demystification is the function of the madman's discourse."[12]

Felman's analysis of the Balzac story concentrates on specific "linguistic techniques [that] transform delirious logic into a coherent counter-rhetoric."[13] As in a surrealist text, fragments of sentences spoken by the salesman are repeated by the madman and thus given a new inflection or a "different value." This, according to Felman, amounts to a "displacement of discourse" away from the conventional communicative function of speech and toward a "radical interrogation" of language. A similar discontinuous effect is created by the madman's taking the salesman's figurative statements literally and by the fact that the two interlocutors "only *understand* each other to the extent that they *do not listen* to each other."[14]

Similarly, the opening speeches of *The Snake Pit* involve a play with language across the two respective poles of sanity and insanity and also a play with specifically cinematic language, complicating both the authoritarian discourse of institutional psychiatry and the liberal reformist spirit of the film. Crucial in this "bouleversement" of the discourse of reason is the fact that the ostensible discourse of sanity is initially represented in the film as the psychotic imaginations of a madwoman. The film begins with a close-up of Olivia de Havilland (as Virginia Cunningham) and an offscreen question: "Do you know where you are, Mrs. Cunningham?" That opening question operates in the fiction as a standard gambit of psychiatric examination and simultaneously as a standard gambit of Hollywood storytelling rhetoric: setting the scene. But instead of a direct answer, and concomitantly, instead of an emphatic "Our story begins here, in . . . ," we get another question: "Where is he? It's as if he were crouching behind me. Why am I afraid to look at him?" Moreover, contrary to classical Hollywood editing and sound patterns, there is no cutaway from Virginia, no reverse shot signifying that a conversation is being held. Instead we get a strange hand-held camera move backing slightly away from Virginia, whose face appears puzzled and whose eyes shift about nervously. The sound of her speech is nonsynchronous so that her lips do not move and there is no guarantee that the voice we attribute to her is indeed hers. The film opens, then, with the displacement of discourse from "the effect of a *communication*" to the question of place, the enigma of a seemingly mad topography, and the troubling discontinuity of identities. Who is speaking and from where? Who is replying and how? If, as Lacan would have it, one constructs one's identity in the endless circulation of discourse between Self and Other, the film's sound and mise-en-scène interrupt that circuit before it has even begun. Later in the sequence we hear the same male voice, hailing Virginia once again: "Hello, Mrs. Cunningham." And once again, that voice is initially offscreen. This time, however, the doctor is actually present in the film's reality, as is made clear editorially a moment later. But, although on one level the film has neatly distinguished the voice of the doctor *as imagined by Virginia* from the voice of the doctor *as imagined by the conventions of Hollywood storytelling*, the film has also introduced an ironic dimension with regard to the attribution of presence, identity, and sanity. Felman calls the conversation in the Balzac story a "parody of Socratic dialogue, in which the madman plays the role of a clownish Socrates, an unwitting pedagogue who transmits an ironic teaching for which, of course, he is not responsible and of which he is not aware."[15] So, too, in *The Snake Pit* the standard diagnostic queries of the sane are made ironic by their situation as a product of a madwoman's imagination, the product of a split self whose symptomatic madness takes the form of a parody of sanity.

In keeping with Virginia's imagining of voices is her invention of a more fully blown, even novelistic, context for the characters she images. Like Balzac's madman, who imagines himself in various grand roles and who does so unconsciously so as "to achieve a desired image in the other's eyes,"[16] Virginia avoids admitting that she is in fact an inmate in a mental institution by stating that she's only there to study hospital conditions in order to write about them. Strikingly, Virginia's explanation is not simply novelistic, but rather involves very literally the casting of herself as the author of a novel. According to Felman's reading of the Balzac story, the device of a character in a novel who makes himself into a character in a novel puts into question psychological realism itself: "His [the madman's] delirious confabulation does not point to a referent of a psychological order, but rather to the dynamics of a language game. He is not defined by his motivation, but by his role in the narration and by his place in discourse."[17]

In the case of *The Snake Pit*, Virginia's verbal misrecognition of the mental hospital as a prison and the supporting subjective shots of crowded-together inmates behind restraining bars call into question the fictive pretense that Virginia is wrong to read her surroundings as a prison. Moreover, the language of the dialog may be seen to link "the dynamics of the language game," that is, the realist illusion, with the discourse against authoritarian psychiatry. As she files in from the yard along with the other inmates, Virginia has the following conversation with her sympathetic companion, who nevertheless hears Virginia's words but fails to understand them:

VIRGINIA: I don't like regimentation.

GRACE: Please, Virginia. [Talking in line is not allowed.]

VIRGINIA: I may have to make a speech against it.

GRACE: Against what?

VIRGINIA: Regimentation, of course. But I can't make a speech without writing it.

In this conversation the two women talk at cross-purposes, all the more crossed for the fact that the object of Grace's dialog is to stop Virginia from speaking. And Virginia herself acknowledges the effective failure of speech in the absense of writing. Only the power conferred on the author of a novel will free Virginia, at least in her imagination, from the confines of the mental institution. But at the same time, the character Virginia herself recognizes her disenfranchisement from the power to write.

Going beyond the comparison with the Balzac story, but offering a felicitous comparison with Felman's other work,[18] the relationship of language and madness in *The Snake Pit* is focused very specifically as a problem of language, madness, *and femininity*. When the camera finally pulls back to an establishing shot of the bench on which Virginia is seated at the opening of the film, another woman, Grace, is revealed seated next to Virginia. This woman is visible to Virginia even when she is under the power of her delusions and imagining the voice of Dr. Kik, and Virginia mentally asks herself, "But who is that and what's happened to him?" Virginia suspects at first a physical continuity whereby Dr. Kik has transformed himself into Grace:

> He's clever, but he can't fool me with his magic. It's an old trick, changing into a girl.

But she immediately makes the appropriate distinction between the two:

> Oh, she can't be he, she doesn't ask questions.

The basis on which Virginia makes her distinction between male and female conversationalists is revealing in relation both to the parodic Socratic discourse attributed above to the questioning of the discourse of reason and to the construction of identity in this fiction. To acknowledge that "she can't be he" *because of a mode of speech* is precisely to acknowledge the binary law described by Lacan, under which a biologically gendered subject is obliged for the entry into symbolic language, and hence for the psychological construction of identity, to take up one or the other of two possible psychosexual positions. Even under her delusions, the supposedly mad Virginia is capable of taking account of sexual difference, an acknowledgment otherwise avoided by the film's sexual politics (as when Dr. Kik ignores Virginia's statement to her husband, "You can't make me belong to you") and by the operation of classical Hollywood cinema, which hinges typically on the denial of sexual difference. The inherent contradictions in the feminine position are also made clear in the upshot of the scene in which Virginia is confronted for the first time in the film by the real Dr. Kik and by her husband. Already, in the first few minutes of the film, the dialog has very pointedly provided several opportunities for Virginia to be addressed by her married name, "Mrs. Cunningham." Then, when Dr. Kik asks Virginia to state her full name as proof of her lucidity, the film is able to capitalize on Virginia's error in giving her maiden name rather than her married name, and here too, as in a subsequent scene already described above, the plot makes much of Virginia's contradictory claim that she is married but has no husband. This may be read, on one hand, as clear evidence of Virginia's removal from reality. But, on the other hand, and in contrary relation to the film's authoritative insistence on conformity to patriarchal patterns, it may be read as a covert strategy of dissidence, a linguistic dissension from the unquestioned normalcy of the patriarchal nomination of married women.

In general, the character of Virginia functions not only to lead the way down the road to proper femininity, but in its split subjectivity, in the interstices between the world as it is and the world as it is imagined or hallucinated, the character of Virginia functions also to suspend the domination of the pedantic discourse of reason.

The Cobweb

The case of melodrama has been proffered by such writers as Thomas Elsaesser, Geoffrey Nowell-Smith, and D. N. Rodowick as one that illuminates with unique nuances the textual operations of patriarchal dominance and disturbance, which much of the seventies' and eighties' theoretical work on film has argued are typical of Hollywood classical cinema overall.[19] I turn now to *The Cobweb* (1955) as a way of illustrating how the symbioses and dissonances *within* historical psychoanalytic psychiatry and its narrative figurations are particularly inflected in the context of a psychiatric institutional film that is also a melodrama. In *The Cobweb* the authority of psychiatry aligns with marriage, but both are systematically undermined to a greater degree than in *The Snake Pit*. A main contributing factor to the subversion of patriarchal authority is the division of the narrative into two interconnected plots. One plot primarily concerns Dr. Stuart McIver's (Richard Widmark) work at the luxuriously endowed psychiatric clinic, the other his relationship with his wife Karen (Gloria Grahame) and their children.[20] Having established these parallel plots, the narrative proceeds by intercutting between them so that elements of one plot are continually translated into the terms of the other plot. Ultimately however, the two plots of *The Cobweb* work against each other.

The clinic plot by itself resembles the narratives of *The Snake Pit* and *Whirlpool* in that the basic elements of patriarchal family structure are superimposed on the regular relationships between doctors, nurses, orderlies, and patients, and are used to naturalize the curative process. In *The Snake Pit* a rudimentary "therapeutic family" is established in which Dr. Kik takes the structural role of father, and Virginia the role of daughter. The "father" ultimately passes his newly matured daughter into her husband's care. There is even a mother, albeit a "bad" mother, in the person of Nurse Davis, who has a crush on Dr. Kik and who competes with Virginia for his love. This "therapeutic family" is even more explicit in *The Cobweb*, as Geoffrey Nowell-Smith argues. Dr. McIver is the virile, dedicated, modern father. He attends meetings with patients and encourages them to take responsibility for their own governance. The child and primary patient in the clinic family is young Stevie (John Kerr). His position as child is made clear structurally, but it is further evidenced in the infantilizing diminution of the name of this boy in his midteens. As doctor and patient, McIver and Stevie are involved in a modified Oedipal conflict, exacerbated by Stevie's attraction to McIver's wife, whom he has met accidentally. McIver's protestation, "I'm not your father, Stevie," only serves to underscore the extent to which the narrative does structure him as such. Meg Rinehart (Lauren Bacall) is the nurturing mother to whom Stevie opens up. In this plot, not only do Meg Rinehart and Dr. McIver work to make Stevie well, they actually have an affair that "consummates" the clinic family marriage (Figure 15). "We're different, we're good parents," says Meg to Stuart. The harmonious personal and therapeutic goals of the clinic family are encapsulated in one image in particular: that of the rustic, homey, Italian supper Stuart and Meg share with an artist friend and his pregnant, contented wife.

However, the harmony of the clinic family is disturbed by the presence of Dr. McIver's actual family—a narrative complication obviated in *The Snake Pit* by the fact that Dr. Kik makes it clear that he has no real family. The presence of the family members in this second plot discompose the first plot's interdependency on patriarchy and cure by suggesting (1) that mental problems may exist outside of treatment centers—it is not only "patients" but people in general who are disturbed, (2) that these problems may be the result of the heightened sensibility of disturbed individuals—the appropriate response to a disturbed world, and (3) even psychiatrists are subject to problems of interpersonal relations. The family, then, becomes an outside, unregulated site of perturbation.

McIver's wife, Karen, represents a central source of the disturbance, in keeping with Rodowick's claims about the excess of feminine sexuality in 1950s melodrama.[21] Near the beginning of the film, a title that reads, "The Trouble Began" is written out across the screen as Karen drives up to the clinic. The immediate "trouble" is that Karen has stopped to give Stevie a lift and that she takes the initiative to order draperies for the common room of the clinic without going through channels. Plotwise, "the trouble" is Karen's performance of wifely duties. According to Stuart, "I'd be home more if there were something to come home to . . . a real woman."

Figure 15. The "therapeutic family" in *The Cobweb* is illustrated in this production still of Dr. McIver (Richard Widmark), occupational therapist Meg Rinehart (Lauren Bacall), and their patient, Stevie (John Kerr).

At a deeper level, however, "the trouble" is Karen's sexual desire, which her husband cannot or refuses to fulfill. In this way female sexual desire comes to embody textual trouble. One scene in particular links the heat of Karen's desire to her lack of sexual relations with Stuart. In the right foreground we see Karen, perspiring, lying restive in her bed. At the left of the frame in deep space, we see Stuart open an adjoining door and look at her. But he doesn't enter, and the sense of incompletion is enormous.[22]

On a more abstract enunciative level, Karen's physical, feminine presence overwhelms the codes of dress and gets expressed as art direction, according to the melodramatic principle whereby highly charged psychological states are symbolized as opulent decor.[23] When she picks up Stevie, the entire back of the station wagon is filled with brightly colored flowers, and Stevie remarks upon them. Karen relates them to sensual desire, asking, "Isn't it enough that they have color and form, and that they make you feel good?" In this way the character Karen comes to be associated with the color image of the film itself. The association is extended in Stevie's response. He speaks of a French painter who died in a hospital room "in a white bed in a white room with doctors in white standing around. The last thing he said was, 'Some red, show me some red. Before dying I want to see some red and some green.'" Here color—the iconography of Karen's visual representation—is given a higher valuation than the white of the hospital setting, for here that setting is linked with death. But perhaps the clearest decorative allusion to Karen's unfulfilled desire is the drapery.[24] When Karen shuts herself in a phone booth to arrange for the drapes, her perspiring and radiant image appears explosive. But both staff and patients reject the rich brocade with which she has attempted to furnish the clinic and make her presence felt.

The final sequence of the film attempts the joint resolution of the two plots through the therapeutic pacification of the two sources of trouble, Stevie and Karen. On a stormy night, Stevie has fled the clinic, and search crews drag the river for his body. Meg breaks off her relations with Stuart, and he and Karen reconcile. Apparently Karen has taken the advice of an older counselor: "Don't nurse your wounds, nurse his." As they pull up to the house, their headlights flash on a bedraggled Stevie, alive and waiting for his doctor. The last shot of the film is of Stevie, lying on the McIvers' couch covered with the rejected draperies. Stuart supervises from the rear, and Karen prepares to spoon hot milk into Stevie's mouth—the maternal role embodied (Figure 16). The superimposed title reads, "The Trouble Was Over." A maternal Karen is no longer a threat to Stevie, nor an unbridled sexual disturbance. Karen's draperies have become a comforter.

Neat as this ending seems at first, another look reveals that its success rests on mutually unsatisfactory narrative displacements. The problems of the clinic plot are seemingly resolved within the family plot and vice versa, but in fact this transposition encourages the elision rather than the resolution of the problems raised in each individual

Figure 16. In this production still from *The Cobweb,* Dr. McIver's wife, Karen (Gloria Grahame), comes back into the fold as comforting helpmeet.

plot. The interchange between the two plots does not represent the symbiosis of psychiatry and family as in plot one, but rather the endless multiplication of problems and the impossibility of real resolution. Stevie's disturbance can only be resolved by the constitution of a family that desexualizes the woman, for her sexuality poses the threat of an Oedipal feud between father and son.

But the resolution of Karen's personal disturbance would require the opposite. It would require the *expression* of sexual desire in the relationship with her husband.[25] But the scene of the reconciliation between Karen and Stuart is repressed in the film both temporally and cinematographically. Only the tail end of this scene is shown, and what is shown is photographed in extreme long shot. Because it is therefore difficult to determine whether it is Karen or Meg with whom Stuart speaks, and because we never learn what issues were raised and discussed, the peace afforded by the ostensible reconcilliation is unexpected and uneasy, and the memory of Meg remains current.[26]

In short, the real problem of the narrative is that there are two women, but only one man. The interchangeability of the women cannot erase their number, and that number is double what the familial scheme of the narrative can abide. *The Cobweb* ends with an extra woman, or an excess of feminine sexuality.

Another way of looking at it would be to see it as a problem of McIver's insufficiency. He has a bigamous relationship to the narrative structure. If he devotes himself to Meg, to the world of the clinic, he shortchanges his own wife. His energies are also insufficient to the needs of the children. Just as Karen and Meg are doubled, Stevie and his young friend Susie (Susan Strasberg) are doubled in McIver's son and daughter. But, as both the film's dialog and its mise-en-scène make clear, conscientious attention paid to the clinic offspring necessitates the neglect of the biological offspring. Karen reports that when their daughter was asked what she wanted to be when she grew up, she answered, "A patient." The editing and the composition of the film's final sequence describe the actual son's abandonment by his father. When McIver pushes open the swinging door of what he takes to be an empty kitchen to warm some milk for Stevie, the door initially blocks his view and ours of McIver's own son, Mark, who is seated at the kitchen table. Mark is occluded by his father's errand of mercy for the other boy. We only see him after the door swings shut again. Once McIver notices Mark, he attempts a mumbled apology, "Sometimes it's easier for a doctor to take care of his patients than someone of his own." His son interrupts him, saying, "I know, Dad, that's your *job*," and McIver exits, his guilt assuaged. But the gloom of the boy, dressed inexplicably in a dark, even funereal suit and sitting alone late at night, belies the supposed satisfaction of this solution. Instead of reenforcing a social ideal in which the man's breadwinner role suffices as his duty to his family, this film suggests that an overemphasis on career deprives a man's family of the quality of his attention.

Finally, in *The Cobweb*, as in *Tender Is the Night*, the emotional stability of the psychiatrist himself is impugned. In the car with Karen at the beginning of the film, Stevie implies that doctors are as ill as patients: "Everybody's tilted here. You can't tell the patients from the doctors." Karen's reply goes even further, questioning not only the mental health of doctors but their prognosis as well: "Oh, but I can. . . . The patients get better." Even Dr. McIver's monologue at the opening of the film contributes to this doubt about the mental health of doctors. Dictating a letter to his secretary, he speaks the following words, which are interrupted by the arrival of a patient: "In dealing with the . . . ah . . . borderline patient, that is to say the people who find it difficult to cope with the normal strains of living, in whom the danger of a psychotic break is always present . . . " Although motivated by the narrative and ostensibly a discussion of borderline psychotics, this speech, delivered directly to the camera, could be read alternatively as an account of the psychiatrist's own role in the narrative, for *The Cobweb* is about McIver's own difficulty coping with the "normal strain of living." He is the "borderline patient." In fact, as a doctor whose mental health is questioned, he is the perfect borderline patient—on the border between authority and its critique.

If, as suggested previously, the fictional character of the psychiatrist can stand as the narrative representation of psychiatry itself, so that his mental illness couches the film's indictment of that institution, *The Snake Pit* would seem to imply that institutional psychiatry can malfunction. But where *The Snake Pit* answers with a good, omniscient, and sane psychiatrist in a main role who represents the institution at its ideal best, *The Cobweb* deepens *The Snake Pit*'s complaints against psychiatry by locating mental disturbance in the central authority figure himself, the best psychiatrist at the clinic, whose own words constitute a revealing self-analysis.

Snakes, Spiders, and Mythical Creatures

Lilith (1964) is a story of love, psychosis, and destruction centering around a female mental patient and the man assigned to take care of her. The film is similar to other films discussed to this point in that it begins with the premise of a woman's illness. It is especially similar to that other 1960s film, *Tender Is the Night*, in that both films also develop the question of the mental health of the ostensibly sane male caregiver and the mental health establishment he represents. What will be explored in this section is the film's contrary take on mental illness as manifested distinctively in women and men. Paradoxically, in light of the reverse impulse in American psychiatric literature, female mental illness is linked to basically female and enlightened, though socially derogated, thought processes, whereas male mental illness is linked to a *psychological* drive, perceived as masculine, toward death and destruction, and is seen as responsible for the creation in the first place of brutish social practices.

Lilith embodies both the familiar literary equation of irrationality with femininity[27] and the philosophical equation of women with a threatening prehistorical, prelinguistic matriarchy,[28] in keeping with Elaine Showalter's suggestion that female madness is often perceived as "the essential feminine nature unveiling itself before scientific male rationality."[29] At one point the camera loses and then finds Lilith emerging from a heavy mist over a marshy body of water. It finds an emblazoned shibboleth over her bed, "HIARA PIRLU RESH KAVAWN," that she

Figure 17. Lilith (Jean Seberg) is associated with refracted and reflected light, as in this production still from *Lilith,* in which she is shown turning a prism to catch the light.

protests is not her language, not the language of schizophrenia, but the language of "her people." In the spirit of her namesake, the mythological Lilith who was either an evil spirit, Adam's first wife supplanted by Eve, or a famous witch in medieval demonology, this Lilith demands that men risk their lives for her.[30]

If the description does not recommend Lilith as a feminist role model, it does suggest her interest from a feminist perspective. *Lilith* (1964), much more so than either *The Snake Pit* (1948) or *The Cobweb* (1955), gives free rein to the feminine psychosexuality so carefully regulated in the earlier films, partly denouncing that sexuality while taking care to articulate it. Thus, in the context of the wider social formations being studied, *Lilith* may be read as a narrative refiguration of the ambivalence around femininity and masculinity, and around feminism and the feminist challenge to psychiatry.

Lilith's self-proclaimed joy and unquenchable love are expressed in a dazzling mise-en-scène of bright light, refracted and reflected (Figure 17). Her madness is seductive and threatening, but simultaneously visionary, taking up, as one character notes, the Shakespearean association of madness with rapture, innocence, and ecstasy. Lilith more often is shown outside the clinic than within its walls. On her first outing with the staff and patients, her point of view elicits a number of rather abstract shots of the sun glinting and sparkling off the water, filling the frame and momentarily halting the narrative. The association of Lilith with light is continued later, when Lilith is taken on outings, or actually dates, by Vincent Bruce (Warren Beatty), an occupational therapist trainee. In town for a local fair, Lilith and Vincent pass a boy selling watermelons. In an oddly seductive moment, Lilith asks for a shard of ice from his tub and describes it as a diamond. Later, she stands at her window turning a crystal to catch the light streaming in.

A psychiatrist at the clinic where Lilith resides, Dr. Lavrier (James Patterson), links these otherworldly images of light and diamonds to schizophrenia. But he also characterizes schizophrenia itself as heroic:

> Some of these people have such extraordinary minds, such extraordinary sensibilities. Too extraordinary, I think, sometimes. . . . Maybe it's romantic, but I often compare them to fine crystal which has been shattered by the shock of some intolerable revelation. I often have a feeling when I talk with them that they have seen too much with too fine an instrument, that they've been close to some extreme, some absolute, and have been blasted by it. . . . They are the heroes of the universe; its finest product and its noblest casualty.

Thus, inasmuch as we are attracted by the beauty of these luminous images, we are attracted to a nobly schizophrenic vision, called forth by Lilith, the embodiment of female sexuality.[31]

But if Lilith is the film's most effective spokesperson of the altered mental state, the central enigma of the film is actually Vincent's, and not Lilith's, madness. Vincent Bruce is Lilith's caretaker and lover, thus standing as the counterpart of the psychiatrist-husbands in the other films, even though Vincent is not literally a physician. The very fact that he is not a physician, but rather a staff member whose work is supervised by physicians, may be read precisely as part of the film's erosion of psychiatric authority, rather than merely as a plot device designed to salvage psychiatric authority by shifting the ill-advised psychiatric treatment of Lilith to a layman. And if questioning the sanity of the doctor is generally a way of questioning the normalizing authority of psychiatry as I have shown, *Lilith*, through Vincent, takes this query even further. As Dr. Lavrier, Bea Brice (Kim Hunter), who runs the clinic, and even Lilith herself all intimate, the boundary between caretaker and patient is a semipermeable one, and the very qualities that make Vincent a good caretaker may also make him especially vulnerable to mental breakdown.

Effected in large part by Beatty's muted and disjointed dialog and performance, a sense of Vincent's real estrangement from reality is communicated.[32] Vincent's relationships with people are inexplicable and fumbling. When he reencounters a woman, Laura (Jessica Walters), who had been his girlfriend before the war, it is revealed that he had never made his intentions clear to her. And the scene in which Vincent is introduced to Laura's husband, Norman (Gene Hackman), is one of the most uncomfortable in the film because of Vincent's failure to engage in appropriate, typically masculine repartee. Here, as in the scenes in *The Snake Pit* underlining Virginia's failure at conventional and effective communication, are overly long pauses as we wait for Vincent's reply, and the unconsummated humor of bawdy jokes told by Norman (about his brother the traveling salesman with an "unusual line," Norman jokes, "Every time I see him now I say, 'Nick, I never thought I'd see you in ladies' underwear' "). But this attempt at humor is left totally unremarked upon by Vincent. These instances of missed communication add up to the displacement of discourse identified by Shoshana Felman as characteristic of a character's embodiment of the madness of a text.

Vincent is mad in part because he succumbs to Lilith's advances, and accordingly, to her mad worldview. But the film also suggests that Vincent was *already* mad before he met Lilith. It does so by providing ample hints about the etiology of his madness in fragmentary references to his dead mother's mental state and to his wartime service experience. In fact, the film's suggestion that Vincent's madness is attributable to his relationships with the two simultaneously seductive and psychotogenic women in his life, Lilith and his mother, is complicated by the narrative association of the two women. On his bedside table Vincent keeps a photograph of his mother as a young, attractive woman that is signed, "To little Vincent with love, Mother." Later a photograph of Lilith appears next to the photograph of Vincent's mother, and the physical similarity between the two women is unmistakable.

The film offers two possible interpretations of the association of Vincent's madness with women. On one hand, it pejoratively depicts the mad-making matriarchy implied by the proliferation of women in Vincent's life: grandmother, mother, old girlfriend, Bea Brice, Laura, and the girl in the bar near the end of the film who looks like Lilith and whom Vincent calls "bitch." On the other hand, from a feminist perspective, the danger of this matriarchal world may be read *as a product* of Vincent's crazed psyche—the violence arising precisely from his *fear* of feminine sexuality.

The latter reading is particularly compatible with the association of Vincent with darkness, war, and death. Vincent's instability unfolds as he prowls the city streets by night under the gloom of cloudy, rainy skies, a contrast highlighted by the film's use of black-and-white film stock. Even the interior of the home Vincent shares with his grandmother is full of strange and ominous angles. The shots of the stairway up to his bedroom are expressionistic, by virtue of distorted perspective communicating a feeling of claustrophobia. One night Vincent is awakened by a storm, the banging of a shutter, and the strange dreams represented on the sound track as crazed laughter and Lilith's voice. From one perspective, this is further evidence that his madness is her fault, but from another perspective, the dreamy voices he hears along with the banging of the shutter and the storm itself are an expression of his internal mental state, and they suggest that he is the madder of the two.

If the imagery of Lilith's world is based on the cultural connotations of femininity, the images of war that define Vincent's mental landscape are linked to stereotypical views of masculinity. And stereotypical, violent masculinity is presented as masculinity gone mad. One scene in particular underlines this condensation of Vincent's madness with Vincent's maleness. The scene begins with a dissolve to the photograph of Vincent's mother on his bedside table, and cuts to reveal Vincent himself stretched on the bed at night watching television. A second shot of the photo of his mother is interposed before a cut to the television, where a battle scene from a graphic war movie is underway. Crushing the beer can, Vincent mutters, "Yeah, he'll die. She dies. Everybody dies." At the level of plot the meaning of the scene remains uncertain, but, like a series of images from a dream, the sequence links the psyche of the dreamer with the male world of mayhem and death and with the portrait of a beautiful dead woman. The issue of Lilith's possible treachery in drawing Vincent into the source of her feminine dazzlement is rendered benign by comparison with the dark alternatives of the male world of loveless marriages and death.

Lilith resists the dark destruction represented by Vincent, the mad, masculine psychiatrist proxy, and celebrates the codes of light linked with feminine and polymorphous sexuality. But to complicate matters further, the connotations of light in *Lilith* have been redefined. In *The Snake Pit*, as in wider cultural discourses discussed in chapter 2, light is associated with science, rationality, and sanity.[33] For example, Dr. Kik uses the metaphor of a light switch to describe the maintenance of sanity:

Look, it's as though you were in a dark room like this one [switches off the light], and you wanted to turn on the light, but you couldn't because you didn't know where the switch was [switches on the light]. Now you do. You may never know why turning that switch makes the light go on, but you don't have to as long as you know where it is. You don't ever have to be afraid of being in the dark again.

Alternatively, in *Lilith* light is associated with pleasurable, aberrant behavior. To illustrate his talk on schizophrenia, Dr. Lavrier shows some transparencies of spider webs. As the show starts, we see him in medium close-up framed between the legs of the projector. A giant circular beam of light projects toward the camera from above his forehead— the light of scientific knowledge. The sequence cuts to images of the webs of spiders in which schizophrenia has been induced, and Dr. Lavrier explains: "The mad ones spin out fantastic asymmetrical and rather nightmarish designs . . . a most unsettling fact." When the scene cuts back to Lavrier, he is seated to the side of the projector on which the beam is no longer visible, and he is now lit by the reflected light of the projected slides themselves. The light of scientific rationality has been replaced by the light of the "fantastic designs" of madness. Moreover, the lines of the spider webs echo the lines and butterflies of the film's title sequence, so that exotic aberrance is appropriated as an acceptable feature of filmic design.

The conflict in *Lilith* between male and female madness is also a question of sexual politics. Lilith's is a bisexual, nonmonogamous world where desire is free-floating. We gather that she was involved in an incestuous relationship with her brother, who committed suicide "because he didn't dare love me." Her relationship with Mrs. Meaghan is also a sexual one, as evidenced by exchanged glances and our brief glimpse of the two women about to make love on the straw bed of a barn. Even little boys share her sensuality. She kisses the little boy who gave her the ice shard and whispers suggestively in his ear. Later, seated spread-legged on her bed and reaching down to her genitals, Lilith describes her passion: "She wants to leave the mark of her desire on everything in the world. If she were Caesar, she'd do it with a sword. If she were a poet, she'd do it with words. But she's Lilith. She has to do it with her body."

Vincent does have a sword, that icon of male strength and desire. In its literal form, his sword is the lance with which he wins the jousting contest at the fair, a contest realized imagistically as a series of close-ups of tiny rings, penetrated and wrested from their hooks one after the other. Even more abstractly, his sword is the law of the patriarchy, with its rigid demands of sometimes lethal heterosexual monogamy. For example, Vincent interrupts the scene of Lilith and Mrs. Meaghan's

Figure 18. Lilith gazes out through the confining wire mesh of her window. Production still.

lovemaking by flinging Mrs. Meaghan from the barn and shaking Lilith while calling her a "dirty bitch." Near the end of the film, Vincent causes the suicide of a male patient whom he perceives to be a competitor for Lilith's love. The patient, Steven, commits suicide by falling onto the blade of a kitchen knife, and so it could be said that the force of Vincent's proprietary rule has pierced the heart of his rival.

Rivalrous masculine and feminine sexuality is also articulated through dueling point-of-view shots. Through the wire mesh of her window we see Lilith gazing down (Figure 18), and in the shot that follows we see her point of view of Vincent crossing the grounds of Poplar Lodge. Conversely, there are shots of Lilith from Vincent's point of view. When Lilith and Mrs. Meaghan walk across the fields, Vincent chases behind, fixing them with his gaze. A challenge to this controlling male gaze comes in the form of Lilith's fascination with her own reflection in a pool of water, her gaze at herself. Vincent is displeased when she speaks to this image. Later, the water reflects the subversive sexual images of Lilith and Mrs. Meaghan. In one shot their hands are joined, and in another, a close-up, the two lie back, heads together, eyes closed.

But in spite of this editorial challenge to the male gaze, the last shot of the character Lilith reinstates it. During Vincent's initial tour of the clinic, Mrs. Brice takes him to a corridor where the catatonic patients are housed. Vincent approaches the small square window in the door of one of the cell-like rooms, and there follows a shot from his point of view. Through the wire mesh of the window we see a young woman seated on the floor beside her cot. She sits immobile and staring in an open cross-legged position. Near the end of the film the two shots are repeated, but this time the young woman is Lilith. It would seem that male control is ultimately reestablished in *Lilith*, the challenge to it deflected as in *Whirlpool*.

Yet what has come before affects our reading of this last shot of Lilith, overlaying it with a malevolence that rewrites its power as undesirable. The film suggests that it was Vincent himself who brought Lilith to her catatonic, sightless state, and not the turnings of her own psychosexuality. Earlier in the film we see Vincent steal a small princess doll from Lilith and "drown" it in his aquarium. If Lilith is "queen of love and beauty," as she was crowned at the fair, this doll must be her effigy, and so the act is one of violence against her. The mise-enscène of Vincent's theft is shadowed and sinister. In the first shot a hand reaches for the doll, as in countless detective films and television shows where the identity of the killer is hidden and his evil nature enhanced by the power of the imagination. Successive shots and dialog reveal Vincent's identity, and we are forced, retrospectively, to assign him a malevolence of which we were previously unaware. Finally, just before Vincent peers through the window at Lilith, the camera pans Lilith's room, now a scene of destruction, her loom tipped over and her slogan blacked out.

The victory of Vincent's final glance is a pyrrhic one. Far from enacting a happy regulation of previously deviant feminine sexuality, this gaze has destroyed feminine sexuality, and sanity and light along with it. Earlier in the film Lilith had asked the following question about the process of the cure: "Do you think they can cure Lilith? Do you know what she wants? You think they can cure this fire? Do you know what they have to cure?" By the end of the film, the fire has been "cured," but the "cure" is the destruction of Lilith.

In the last sequence of the film, Vincent begins to walk off across the grounds away from the clinic, while Dr. Lavrier and Mrs. Brice watch from the doorway. Several shots of Vincent's hurried flight resurrect Lilith's point of view, for they are taken from a perspective similar to the one she took when she looked down at Vincent from her room. In the end, however, Vincent turns back and approaches the clinic. The last shot of the film is a close-up of Vincent pleading, "Help me." Since, formally speaking as well as literally in the plot, the therapist has become a patient, this sequence may be read as repeating the work of the film, which is to emphasize the ongoing possibilities of feminine sexuality expressed through Lilith, and the flaws of patriarchal models of psychiatric authority.

No evocation of metaphoric madness, neither "snake pit" nor "cobweb," can exhaust the description of the dichotomous relation between the sane and the mad; for neither stresses properly the *creative* operations of its fictive author, be she Virginia, author of a hallucinated pit of vipers in *The Snake Pit*, or Lilith as schizoid spider in the eponymous film; and neither emphasizes properly the exterior and pervasive venom of patriarchy gone mad. Lilith is mad enough to want to weave a golden cloth of her own hair, but Vincent in his madness destroys the loom itself.

Like the films of chapter 3, *The Snake Pit*, *The Cobweb*, and *Lilith* are organized according to a double narrative structure that supports the psychiatric adjustment of women to traditional sexual roles, as well as supporting a challenge to the social order implied by that adjustment. But here the double impulses of adjustment and resistance are played out in an institutional setting that both expands the apparatuses of control and deepens the subversive connotations of madness.

Also like the films of chapter 3, the three films of this chapter illustrate the changing roles and relationships between doctor and patient from the 1940s to the 1960s. The omniscient, sane, authoritative psychiatrist of *The Snake Pit* gives way to the self-doubting, unstable trainee of *Lilith*, while the irregular wife and mother gives way to the highly sexual Lilith, so that *Lilith* most profoundly represents a feminine challenge to masculine psychiatric authority. Thus, these films, and *Lilith* especially, may be read as narrative refigurations of the growing social ambivalence about psychiatric power and women's subjugation to it.

5

Psychiatry and the Working Woman

Women make the best psychoanalysts . . . until they fall in love. Then they make the best patients.

—Dr. Bruloff in *Spellbound*

The story of *Lady in the Dark* (1943) concerns a single career woman who is editor-in-chief of a women's magazine. Like its real-life counterparts, the fictional *Allure* magazine holds up to its female readership a frilly, feminine manner of dress and behavior, but its editor, Liza Elliott (Ginger Rogers), rejects this model as a personal style, opting for dark-skirted suits and a lover to whom she is not romantically attracted. As Mary Ann Doane has observed, clothing in this film is the most "explicit indication of sexual difference."[1] But Liza is ill. She has "lost the power of making decisions" and is forced to consult a psychoanalyst. From the minor-keyed tune that she hums and the sound track embellishes to the dreams she recounts in the form of opulently costumed and staged musical numbers, Liza's symptomology embodies the most spectacular aspects of the film. In her dreams (dreams that showcase Ginger Rogers's actual talents and her familiar musical comedy persona) she is talented and supremely feminine, dancing and singing her way through stylized scenarios of desire, courtship, and marriage. Since the work of Liza's analysis is to release her from a "repressive" career to the freedom to be Ginger Rogers, one could say that a woman's desire for a career is handled in this story as a neurotic symptom.

If *Lady in the Dark* (1943) presents a textbook case of how Hollywood narrative manipulates two thematic variables, psychiatry and the working woman, in a manner consistent with conventional gender-allocated social arrangements of the period, the film is not alone in that regard. *Marnie*, for example, stars Sean Connery as an amateur head-shrinker who forces a working girl (Tippi Hedren) with the bad habit of stealing from her employers to leave this line of work and marry him. *The Three Faces of Eve* takes an attitude of pity for the series of unsatisfying service jobs in which Eve is forced to work until she is healthy enough to remarry.

From the point of view of contemporary advocates of better roles for women, the response to this prevalent and even banal equation of the working woman with the neurotic analysand might be to conclude that the character of the *female psychiatrist*, by herself embodying psychiatry at the same time that she holds a place in the work force, might represent a solution to the ideological intransigence of stories along the lines of *Lady in the Dark*. As has been noted both by analysts of filmic representation and by psychoanalysts interested in the representation of their profession, female psychiatrists were far from rare, taking the lead in *Spellbound* (1945), *She Wouldn't Say Yes* (1945), *Shadow on the Wall* (1950), *Private Worlds* (1935), *Nightmare Alley* (1947), *Knock on Wood* (1954), and *Three on a Couch* (1966), among other films.[2] Furthermore, it may also be observed that when the psychiatrist is a woman, the man must take the complementary role of patient, due to the consequences for the therapeutic couple of Hollywood's convention of romance.

In part, the feminist promise of this role reversal is realized. *Spellbound*, for example, has been seen to represent the utopian possibilities of the symbiosis between love and professionalism (read professionalism feminized) in the character of Dr. Constance Peterson (Ingrid Bergman), for it is precisely Dr. Peterson's love for her patient (Gregory Peck) that leads her to pursue his analysis to its satisfactory termination against the professional counsel of her male training analyst, Dr. Bruloff (Michael Chekhov).[3] Bruloff scolds Constance for taking her amnesiac patient as a lover and for believing in his goodness: "We are speaking of a schizophrenic and not a valentine." But though her patient may not quite be a valentine, in a Freudian slip of the plot, he does turn out to be a Ballantyne, John Ballantyne. In fact, the very work of *Spellbound* is to infuse the didactic psychoanalytic charter with which the film begins with the emotionally restorative properties of romance. The opening explanatory title reads as follows:

Our story deals with psychoanalysis, the method by which modern science treats the emotional problems of the sane.

The analyst seeks only to induce the patient to talk about his hidden problems, to open the locked doors of his mind.

But, crucially, it is not "modern science" as much as old-fashioned passion that can blast open the locks on the doors of the mind. When the lovers embrace for the first time, the music wells up on the sound track, and the image track dissolves to a door that opens to reveal another door that opens in its turn to reveal yet another door, and so on until a whole series of open doors is revealed extending into deep space.

Perhaps paradoxically, but at least consistently with the ideology of sex-role feminism, at the same time that these films propose love as an enabling force when combined with psychoanalysis, they also present a critique of the institution of marriage. For example, the female psychiatrist in *She Wouldn't Say Yes* (1945), played by Rosalind Russell, gives the following explanation of why she doesn't want love in her life: "If you could see the miserable women who troop in and out of my office every day you'd know why; women who are ill, women who have lost their pride, women who cry in vain, *women who've lost themselves completely as individuals always because of a man*, the 'right' man, or the 'right' men." Indeed, representational models of professional women and this voiced critique of marriage can recirculate and encourage progressive social currents.

But here the limitations of sex-role analysis show themselves. What I find compelling is not so much the role of the female psychiatrist per se, nor the assignation of a film on that basis to a position on the progressivity scale, but rather the formal textual conflicts introduced by the representation of the female psychiatrist and by the narrative impulse to refeminize or repatriate her—to make her the object of psychiatric investigation. Chapter 1 of this book mentioned some of the conflicts between various discourses on women's roles, particularly the conflict between discourses that celebrated the woman as exclusively wife and mother and discourses that recognized and approved of more and more women, including women with children, in the post–World War II work force.[4] Examining a series of recruitment posters circulated by the War Manpower Commission, Leila J. Rupp points out another rhetorical contradiction in the issue of women and work, one that is particularly relevant as it concerns an imagistic text.[5] Rupp argues that while the posters encouraged women to take industrial jobs normally held by men, the depiction of the working women on the posters maintained the traditional conception of femininity, addressing women primarily as wives and mothers and not as independent wage earners. Films about a female psychiatrist similarly have it both ways, and so take up the complications of the wider social discursive formation. They depict career women, but at the same time the narratives work to question the fitness of these women for their careers on the basis of theories about the limitations or idiosyncracies of feminine nature—they subject the woman psychiatrist to a certain textual curiosity. As Gabbard and Gabbard state in *Psychiatry and the Cinema*, "When women are cast as psychiatrists, they are almost always portrayed as effective professionals whose inadequacy as women emerges as a central theme in the films."[6] Furthermore, Gabbard and Gabbard find only two films containing a female psychiatrist who does *not* succumb to the advances of her male patient, and both films are outside the time frame of this study.[7] The working woman role model is thus consistently undercut by the textual proclivity to designate the woman psychiatrist as more woman than psychiatrist, as if the two were mutually exclusive, and by the concomitant textual proclivity to designate the woman psychiatrist as more of a *patient* than a psychiatrist.[8]

A shift in the representation of femininity naturally affects the representation of masculinity, and indeed, these films raise masculinity and its social preserves as no less of a complicated problem than femininity. Prior chapters explored the dual function of the male psychiatrist character simultaneously to uphold masculine authority and to provide an entry point for its critique. Here we turn to the similarly double functions of the male patient. In these films the male patient is paternal caretaker of the errant female professional and amateur analyst, as well as being a hopelessly dependent neurotic.[9] If authority generally resides with patriarchal psychiatry, represented in the narrative by a male psychiatrist, these films find a unique way to mount the inevitable challenge to that order: a woman now acts for psychiatry, and a male neurotic for patriarchy, so that the woman now represents the interests of psychiatry in the fiction, and neuroses and psychoses normally associated with femininity are now attributed to the female *psychiatrist*. Because a male now plays the patient, the neuroses and psychoses usually associated with femininity may also be explored in relation to masculinity.

The Representation of Femininity as a Problem

Near the opening of *Spellbound*, a male colleague suggests to Dr. Constance Peterson that her professional demeanor is inappropriate: "I'm trying to convince you that your lack of human and emotional experience is bad for you as a doctor . . . and fatal for you as a woman." She replies with astute insight into his motivation, "I've heard that argument from a number of amorous psychiatrists who all wanted to make a better doctor out of me." Her answer shows that she is well aware that his motivation is personal and that his commitment to making her a better doctor is a ruse. Nevertheless, the ruse is that of the film itself—the story of a woman's romantic awakening. And yet, the woman-as-psychiatrist component of the plot in *Spellbound* complicates the film's more conventional romantic tendencies by engaging a formal and visual rhetoric of vision and identity that proceeds as an endless series of shifts and reversals.

When John Ballantyne, alias Dr. Anthony Edwardes, J. B., and John Brown, dreams of Dr. Constance Peterson, he dreams of a scantily clad sprite, flitting about the 21 Club entertaining the customers. This dream borrows from the constitutive scene of Hollywood classical narrative cinema—the specularization of the woman through costume and performance. But while the character Gilda in the film of that title is indeed a singer-dancer who rivets the attention of her fictional and real audiences with her undulating striptease, the flirtatious Constance is only a mirage—an oneiric wish-fulfillment. In story "reality," the seductive sprite is a determined psychiatrist who nags and pushes J. B. to research, reorganize, and reconstruct his psyche.

The specularization of femininity in *Spellbound* thus poses a problem for J. B. and for the text. The very moments when Constance appears most feminine are the moments that set off J. B.'s uncontrollable rages. Early in the film, Constance rises from bed in the night, slips on her robe, brushes her hair, and steals up the stairs ostensibly to consult a book, but actually to see "Dr. Edwardes." Her romantic motivation is obvious and the two embrace. But as they do so, Edwardes's gaze fixes on the white wale of Constance's chenille robe, and he pushes her away confused. The robe may be compared with the "particular hair-coloring or clothing" that Freud describes as the sexual object required to fulfill the condition of the fetish in the primal scene. When faced with the overwhelming sight of his parents' intercourse, the child substitutes another object.[10] Like the fetish object, the robe hides the sex, yet also marks it; provides pleasure and offends.[11]

This ambivalence toward the figure of the woman analyst may again be observed later in the film in another setting where personal domestic space is pressed into service as an impromptu analytic scene. When Constance Peterson flees with the Gregory Peck character (now calling himself John Brown), she flees to the home of her former training analyst, the wise old Dr. Bruloff, whose character and status as a European analyst epitomize benevolent psychiatric authority. Finding herself once again in her old room, faced with the mirrored image of her younger self, Constance takes up old habits such as making coffee for Dr. Bruloff, and she appears relieved to trust herself to his keeping and to his aid in the analysis of John Brown. Masquerading as a honeymoon couple, the two debate who shall sleep in the bed: the doctor or the patient, the man or the woman. The decision that Constance shall take the bed implies an acceptance of the binary and exclusionary principle around the terms doctor/patient and man/woman, under which principle accepting the privilege of the bed implies a further abnegation of the role of doctor and an acceptance of the role of woman as being similarly unempowered to that of patient.

Significantly, John Brown's vision of the sleeping Constance extends the ideological possibilities of the sequence and makes more complex the role of the woman in it. Restless in the night, John Brown becomes deranged at the sight of blindingly white bathroom fixtures, and his glance follows a trail of white up the bedspread tucked in at Constance's chin. Disturbed by the sight of Constance's face, he goes downstairs carrying an open razor. The paternal Dr. Bruloff is sitting vigil below in fear for Constance's life, and he intercepts John Brown's violence (in a symbolic castration) by feeding him bromides in his milk, "enough to knock out a horse." John Brown must retrieve his identity by researching his past, but his way is initially barred by Dr. Bruloff, who, in prohibiting John Brown's murderous desire for Constance, prevents both his incestuous desire for a mother figure (Constance as doctor, Bruloff's partner) and for a sister figure (Constance as Bruloff's daughter). Any appropriate romance between Constance and John Brown is deferred at this point by Brown's infantilization. According to Freud's account of the primal scene, the child who sees or hears parental intercourse desires his mother but fears his father's retribution.[12] This scene in *Spellbound* presents a covert primal scene in which the bed where Constance sleeps, though literally empty of a male partner, holds in its fantasy construction either its owner, Dr. Bruloff, or its potential guest whose rights to the bed had only just been debated. In the logic of *Spellbound*'s fiction, John Brown's gaze at Constance invites him into a dangerous rivalry with the father. And yet this desiring gaze at the supine woman simultaneously, like the primal gaze, outlines a fantasy position that for a heterosexual male will be attained at a future time. For *Spellbound* is a fiction, and in a fiction, as in a fantasy, desire may be impossible and possible both. John Brown can and does supplant his father and possess his mother.

Except for one thing. Constance's professional role aligns her with patriarchal authority, and so casts *her* as father as well as mother. Her quick mind and analytical powers enable her to figure out the final meaning of John Brown's dream, and this psychic sleuthing leads to the suicide of the head of Green Manors, Dr. Murchison, the very man whom John Brown had attempted to replace while impersonating Dr. Edwardes. In this sense, Constance Peterson's role in the Oedipal scenario is that of the son who matures into the victorious rival of the father.

Like *Spellbound*, *Knock on Wood* oscillates between embracing stereotypical, specularized femininity on one hand, and on the other hand bracketing it off as a male fantasy. The problem Jerry Morgan (Danny Kaye) explains to the first psychiatrist he sees (a man) is a compulsion that depends on the interchangeability of identical women, and indeed on their endless supply: "It's happened the same way five times. I meet a girl, fall in love with her, and when I begin to think of marriage, Clarence [Jerry's ventriloquist's dummy] suddenly comes to life and breaks it up."

Even the root of the problem raises this interchangeability. A flashback to Jerry's childhood reveals that his mother's appearance is extremely similar to that of his latest girlfriend and to his second psychiatrist, the female Dr. Nordstrom (Mai Zetterling). Of course this interchangeability of partners is regarded as unnatural, as a *problem* of Jerry's. To be cured, he must break the chain and settle on one partner. Still, it is not the individuality of the final partner that is important, but the social obligation to settle on any one of many. The interchangeability of women still stands socially.

According to the film-as-analyst, the notion of stereotypical femininity originated in Jerry's past. As we learn from a flashback motivated by Jerry's narcoanalysis, his parents were vaudeville entertainers, one of whose acts was a musical dance number describing a successful courtship ritual displaying traditional male and female roles. Offstage, however, his parents behaved differently, "fighting and yelling and screaming at each other and throwing things and everything." Jerry's ideal of his parents, then, is not the whole flashback, but the performance within the flashback, a performance shot from the five-year-old Jerry's point of view from the wings of the stage. As such it is another primal scene, or perhaps a family romance in which real parents are replaced by more desirable surrogates.[13] That Danny Kaye himself plays his own dancing and singing father makes the Oedipal connotations even clearer. But in spite of the character Jerry's desire to live this musical idyll, the film presents the courtship ritual as an impossible scenario, one that may be realized only through theatrical artifice. The spectacle of the docile, romantic, specularized woman cannot be sustained, for offstage the fights begin. Nor can the image of the virulent man, of which more later.

Another example of the impossibility of woman-as-spectacle comes in Jerry's interaction with Dr. Nordstrom (Figure 19). His inclination is to make challenging love to her: "When was the last time a man held you in his arms? When was the last time a man told you you were young and beautiful? And you are young and beautiful. . . . What are

Figure 19. The patient (Danny Kaye) with his female psychiatrist (Mai Zetterling) in this production still from *Knock on Wood*.

you fighting? What are you so dreadfully afraid of?" But Jerry is interrupted in the process of praising her physical appeal, "blue eyes, lovely hair," by an injection she administers to make him sleep and remember. As a result of the drug, his adult masculinity is replaced by the infantile sexual researches described. After the flashback, he emerges from narcosynthesis insisting on her feminine attributes, repeating "blue eyes, lovely hair," but Dr. Nordstrom will not easily submit to a passive role as proper object of the gaze. In a later scene, Jerry peers around the corner of a building to spy Dr. Nordstrom striding forward, having betrayed Jerry's whereabouts to the police. In this case the gaze of the male character fails to articulate a rhetoric of control and in fact stands precisely as a mark of his failure to dominate. The female character is here made to repulse or betray the domination of vision at the same time that she is made the object of the gaze.

Perhaps the humorous words of an obstetrician in *Three on a Couch*, spoken to psychiatrist Dr. Elizabeth Acord (Janet Leigh), express most succinctly the problem of femininity and the working psychiatrist. "Any girl that won't get married and have babies," he claims, "is antibusiness." Of course the obstetrician speaks literally: his "business" is delivering babies. But he also speaks for the business of the social system at large, in that postwar monopoly capitalism depended on the wives who freely gave their labor to run the homes and organize the leisure time of male workers. But the compelling difficulty of the working woman is not so easily resolved. The patriarchal proposition is put clearly by this colleague when he tells Dr. Acord that she must decide whether she is "a woman or a doctor or both." Of course he offers his own opinion: "From here you look like a woman, doctor." But his opinion, though in one sense clear in its essentialist rhetoric, is, at the same time, grammatically and inherently contradictory.

The Representation of Masculinity as a Problem

If the specularization of the woman is undermined in these female psychiatrist films, the specularization of the man is encouraged. Here the male is often the one who is shot with his head against the white of a pillow as he sleeps or lies ill, and the female is the one who looks down at him sympathetically, unlike the common and opposite case exemplified by *Notorious*, where Ingrid Bergman's descent into illness prepares the ground for her rescue and romance with the Cary Grant character. This alternative dispensation of the look, like the problematization of its conventional female object, loosens the theorized male monopoly on vision.

The filtered close-up of Ingrid Bergman in *Spellbound* as she sets eyes on the Gregory Peck character for the first time is matched by another close-up—this time of Gregory Peck. Because no stylistic differentiation is made in who is gazing at whom, this early exchange creates a precedent for an alternating system of looks, of which the male is at least as often if not more often the object. On their walk later that afternoon, the imposter Dr. Edwardes admires "the view," meaning his view of Dr. Peterson and not of the hills and meadows over which she gazes. But this incident occurs relatively early in the plot. Later, the film provides Dr. Constance Peterson with many opportunities to answer his look. These opportunities naturally follow from *Spellbound*'s narrative enigma concerning the mystery surrounding the true identity of the imposter. The reverse of previously discussed narratives wherein a woman's autobiography is rewritten by representatives of social authority, *Spellbound*'s narrative unfolds according to Dr. Peterson's need to fathom Dr. Edwardes's appearance and psyche.[14]

Like Ann Sutton in *Whirlpool* or Virginia Cunningham in *The Snake Pit*, Dr. Anthony Edwardes is ill, and his illness motivates an investigatory response. When Constance rises in the night to seek Edwardes, she finds him asleep in a chair, where she is able to watch him unobserved for a few moments before he awakens. Similarly, after Edwardes has collapsed in surgery, Constance watches "the patient" from his bedside, her glance alternating between his sleeping form and the book he has supposedly written, as she tries in vain to make sense of Edwardes as author rather than patient. In another reversal of visually attributed dominance at Dr. Bruloff's home, John Brown's look at the sleeping Constance is shortly answered by her anxious rush to find him, and by her subsequent discovery of the film's male lead disarmed and stuporous on the couch downstairs.

The Peck character's numerous collapses or "spells" further express his powerlessness through the device of physical deflation and its concomitant vulnerability to being looked at without one's knowledge. The collapse in surgery is followed by a collapse at the train station as Constance tries to propel him forward to purchase a train ticket to the same place he went before his amnesia. Throughout the film, the Peck character is made to suffer illness and attacks, to be hunted, to be arrested and jailed, and in short, visually and narratively to be spellbound.

The final mark of his visual and narrative bondage is the transformation of his body into a source of clues: "Your hand has been burned, you've been in an accident," Dr. Peterson exclaims. The "medical gaze" that Mary Ann Doane observes in a subcategory of the women's film, a gaze that requires the despecularization of the woman and her respecularization as the object of scientific inquiry, is here directed at the man.[15]

But perhaps the most extreme manifestation of the specularization of the Peck character occurs within the very dream sequence in which Edwardes/J. B. had imagined Dr. Peterson as a sexy serving girl. As J. B. sits playing cards in the 21 Club, he is surrounded by the famous and numerous oversized painted eyes of Salvador Dali, which stare out at him from the drapery. Dr. Peterson interprets these eyes as belonging to the inmates of Green Manors, but they seem also to articulate a local instance of a whole relay of authoritative looks. In the dream, the flirtatious Constance surrogate cuts the eyes with a giant pair of scissors. Especially if seen in concert with a previous act of slicing, the famous incision of Dali's other joint film project, *Un Chien Andalou*, Constance's act here may be seen to underline, metaphorically, her command over vision, her power to blind or to give sight. As a psychoanalyst, she has the power to interpret correctly the images of the dream—reaching into J. B.'s psyche with a sureness even he does not possess. She even animates his memory, entering the scene of the dream by helping J. B. reenact the murder on skis of which the dream is a symbolic representation. In this sense, Constance Peterson is the narrator of the film's authorial regime, which includes Bruloff, a supervising analyst; Salvador Dali, the designer of the dream images; and Hitchcock, the film's director.

Where the male point of view is insisted upon in *Spellbound*, where J. B. is "author" rather than "patient," this point of view is characterized as mad or dangerous. J. B. did not after all kill the real Dr. Edwardes as he believes until the very end of the film, but he did accidentally kill his little brother when they were boys. In this connection, one wonders whether the psychoanalysts on the staff of Green Manors aren't wrong in their diagnosis of another patient, Garmes, whose claims to have killed his father are dismissed as paranoid.

The specularization of the male, motivated primarily through his status as a patient in *Spellbound*, is furthered in *Knock on Wood* by the film's musical comedy format. Not only is Jerry Morgan the patient object of the "medical gaze," but the presence of a variety of staged musical numbers make him a spectacle as well. In fact the film is highly overdetermined, generically being both a musical comedy and a comedy with an additional spy plot: Jerry performs on stage not just because the film is a musical and Jerry is played by the dancing, singing Danny Kaye, but because he is forced into a series of charades in his efforts to elude the police and the bad guys (in the tradition of Richard Hannay's [Robert Donat] impromptu and unintentionally sarcastic political speech in Hitchcock's *The Thirty-nine Steps*).

His character circumscribed by multiple authorial layers, Jerry takes the position that contemporary film theory has usually reserved for the woman, as in Mary Ann Doane's use of *Gilda* to illustrate the objectification of the body of the (female) performer in Hollywood representation.[16] That Jerry is *obliged* to perform instead of performing of his own free will further suggests the performer's subjugation. But *Gilda* has also been used to illustrate the opposite: the possibility that discursive *resistance* attaches to the performance component of the film.[17] It is perhaps the very contradiction that these divergent readings suggest that forms the most apt comparison with *Knock on Wood*.

The specific content of Jerry's performances is significant in this regard. When forced to appear on stage in the middle of a ballet, the role Jerry performs is that of the romantic lead who wins the royal princess with his physical prowess. The contrast between his awkward, confused movements (he cannot dance ballet) and the technical ability of the other dancers (who attempt to go on as if nothing were amiss) is amusing. But more than that, the comic pas de deux specifically acts to parody the formulaic nature of the roles being romanticized in the ballet and the roles his father and mother danced in the fantasy.

There is one performance of Jerry's that is not a forced performance, but it too is articulated through a series of authorial devices, and in fact it seems to initiate his placement as object of the gaze. His character is introduced in the opening of the film by the voice of a male narrator used for expository purposes at the start of the film. The typically deep narrator's voice explains that Jerry is about to be involved, *unknowingly* and *against his will*, in one of the most infamous crimes in the history of international espionage. The visuals echo this authorial bracketing in that Jerry's photo on the night club marquee is introduced before Jerry himself. Later, another photo of Jerry, this time published in the newspaper, will identify him as the object of a manhunt, as a similar photo identified Constance in *Spellbound*. After the photo on the marquee comes yet another mediation between our gaze and Jerry's presence: a shot of the nightclub audience. When the film finally cuts to Jerry, he is nonverbal, scatting the finale of his song. At the song's end, he tries to speak, to bid the audience good-bye, but his ventriloquist's dummy comes to life and undercuts his good intentions. Far from enjoying the powerful prerogative of a ventriloquist, Jerry himself has become the "dummy" in a complex web of authoritative narrational devices.

The discursive authority of the character Jerry Morgan is undermined also by constant demasculinization or even feminization. At one point in the ballet, Jerry finds himself whirling with a new and, from a heterosexual point of view, comically inappropriate, partner, a male archer. Jerry is repeatedly referred to as the "red-headed ventriloquist," an eponym evocative of the way women more than men are referred to, metonymically, by their hair color, as "blondes," "brunettes," or "red-heads." At one point when the head spy finds out Jerry was unknowingly carrying top secret documents, the spy calls Jerry "a red-headed fool [who] is nothing but a mailbox." Whether intended by the screenwriters or not, this appellation aptly describes how Jerry functions in the text: as a "male box," with all the reference to female anatomy as inclusive receptacle that the slang "box" might imply.

As a male in a female position, Jerry's body becomes an issue, as did the body of the Gregory Peck character in *Spellbound*. In a comic echo of the striptease in *Gilda*, a shower-room scene draws attention to the prospect of Jerry's nakedness under his clothes. Jerry walks sleepily into a shower room, failing to note either the word "Damen" on the door or the fact that a woman occupies one of the two stalls. A cut hides his initial disrobing, but we soon see the two occupants in adjacent cubicles. The bathroom architecture divides the two from one another, but reveals them framed from the shoulders up to the privileged straight-on view, that is, to the view of the cinema spectator (Figure 20). This arrangement occulting the mutual view of the shower-room occupants soon gives way to the possibility of nudity revealed in the common downstage space. The two notice each other, and it is revealed that the woman is none other than Jerry's psychiatrist, Dr. Nordstrom. Immediately, while still unaware of the implications of her act, she commands Jerry to leave the shower room. He opens his shower door and starts to emerge when he leaps back with the realization that his unclothed body had been about to be revealed. The scene turns on the titillating trope of the promise of nudity made simultaneously to fictional and real spectators. But this time the promised but withheld body is that of the male.

The problem of the narrative is that Jerry cannot fill his father's shoes. The only shoes he does seem to fill are Dr. Nordstrom's pom-pommed slippers, which he accidentally dons . . . twice, in the comic tradition of male cross-dressing exemplified by Billy Wilder's *Some Like It Hot* (1959). He cannot become that idealized image of himself from the fantasy, for he can neither perform successfully nor marry. At the end of the film, after unmasking the chief spy, Jerry is given a drink. As he crumples to the ground a detective tries to help him. "I'll do it," says Dr. Nordstrom, "I have a feeling I'm going to get used to it." The next and final scene is Dr. Nordstrom's and Jerry's exit from the church as newlyweds. What Dr. Nordstrom will have to "get used to" is Jerry in the impossibly contradictory roles of husband and patient.

In this film, then, the psychiatric context joins with that of the comedy genre to provide a pretext for Jerry's bizarre symptomology: personality dissociation is expressed simultaneously as a diagnostic category (Jerry seeks help from a psychiatrist) and as a vaudeville act gone awry (Jerry atones by doing time on the classic stage). And cross-dressing undressed and the other attendant flirtations with feminine

Figure 20. Male patient and female doctor find their positions compromised in this production still from *Knock on Wood.*

sexuality reveal Jerry's troubled attitude toward women as well as fitting in with the gender confusion common to fifties comedies.

The character of Dr. Elizabeth Acord's fiancé in *Three on a Couch* introduces even more complications than were introduced by Dr. Anthony Edwardes and Jerry Morgan in *Spellbound* and *Knock on Wood*, respectively. Although Christopher Pride (Jerry Lewis) is not actually a patient of Dr. Elizabeth Acord (Janet Leigh), but merely her artist lover, the chaotic use of language and physical expression that is typical of Jerry Lewis's comic style suggests that Pride is at least as wacky as his patient precursors. Moreover, Lewis's brand of physical and verbal comedy is known particularly for transgressing the boundaries of the male position and flirting with feminization.[18] *Three on a Couch* may be regarded as the felicitous intersection between characteristic aspects of the Lewis oeuvre, such as Lewis's play with the social boundaries of masculine and feminine, and the cinematic refiguration of sociocultural issues surrounding psychiatry and the working woman. In part the Jerry Lewis character is an active narrational agent who achieves his goal of getting Dr. Acord to marry him and go with him to Paris. At the same time, however, he takes over from Janet Leigh rather decisively as the feminized object of our fascinated gaze.

Three on a Couch parodies masculinity by taking it to an extreme.[19] Supermale Pride woos not only Dr. Acord, but her three female patients as well (under the impression that the only therapy they require is a good man), and woos them by adopting three stereotypically male disguises: cowboy, zoologist (i.e., scientist), and sportsman. Ironically, one source of comedy is the *failure* of each of these ultramasculine caricatures to live up to his promise. The cowboy ends by roping himself instead of the calf, the zoologist prances effeminately after butterflies, and the sportsman is continually defeated in physical contests by the woman he dates. Failure turns to perverse success, however, as these ignominious experiences serve only to endear the man to his girl.

As in other female psychiatrist films, and other Lewis vehicles, feminization of the male is accompanied in *Three on a Couch* by the tendency to make a spectacle of him. Christopher Pride does not literally go on the stage, as does Danny Kaye, but the multiple characters Pride plays constitute the film as a series of performances within a film performance. These performances are further bracketed as such by editing and composition. For example, when Pride sets out as cowboy Ringo Raintree to woo Anna, his friend the obstetrician coaches and watches his "performance" from behind a corner.

But perhaps the most notable play with problematic masculinity occurs when Pride cross-dresses to become Heather, the sister of the zoologist. If the zoologist is no paragon of masculinity, neither is his sister a paragon of femininity. Unlike the character Dustin Hoffman plays in *Tootsie* (1982), Heather is a character in crudest drag. If the crudity of the artifice were not already clear, it is pointed up in the scene in which Pride has to pretend to be both Heather and her brother, Rutherford, at virtually the same time. Heather has retired to the bedroom supposedly to convince Rutherford to greet Dr. Acord's patient, Mary Lou, in the living room, but of course the conversation between Heather and Rutherford is created in order to be overheard by Mary

Lou. While carrying on a rapid conversation between the two invented characters, one male and the other female (à la *Psycho*), we see Lewis frantically stripping off the clothing of Heather to become Rutherford. Perhaps the most complex moment in the transformation is when Lewis sits on the bed wearing a heavy corset and pops two oranges out of the top of his bra. Simultaneously on view is the artifice of femininity (Heather), the emergent male (Rutherford), the fiction behind the artifice (Christopher Pride), and the hairy chest of Lewis himself. This moment of transformation from female to male (underlaid by the audience's additional knowledge that Heather is no female to begin with) draws attention to the "masquerade of femininity," the notion that femininity is always an assumed disguise, an unstable construction, rather than an innate quality.[20] In fact *Three on a Couch* and this quick-change scene in particular draw attention to the unsuitability of both masculine and feminine suits.

Spellbound, *Knock on Wood*, *Three on a Couch*, and the other female psychiatrist films articulate the problem of psychiatry and the working woman without resolving it. They suggest that women may be authorities in the field of mental health and simultaneously that this role would present a problem for the social construction of femininity. They also suggest that to position a man as a psychiatric patient is to undermine the social construction of masculinity.

In these films, even more clearly than in the films of the preceding chapters, the man's possessive look at the woman, generally the crucial site of spectator identification, is made to seem a romantic mythology and a neurotic fantasy. The presentation of an alternative in the form of the woman's possessive gaze at the man is no more viable, for it too may be read for what it is, an inappropriate exercise of power rather than a step toward sexual parity. In general, the films of this chapter lend focus to Hollywood cinema's characteristic concern with identity and psychosexuality by articulating these issues in terms of the specific sociocultural debate around psychiatric authority and ideas about masculinity and femininity.

In "Womanliness as a Masquerade," Joan Riviere has described a type of successful, intellectual, and usually professional woman who, to mitigate the anxieties stemming from her success in the masculine mode, has had to assume a mask of excessive femininity. More specifically, what Riviere speaks of in the main case history used as an illustration in the article (a case history that may have been a compilation of any number of real patient histories) is the "incongruity of attitude" apparent in a woman patient who required reassurance from men in the form of sexual advances after every "public performance" she made. Here, again, as in the films, we find the problematic coupling of performance and sexuality. But, vis-à-vis the films under study here, what Riviere could be describing is the passage from performance to romance enjoyed by the *male*: a dream recounted, a ventriloquist's dummy as performative medium, a donning of fluffy robes and pompoms, a bra stuffed with oranges, all performances attended attentively by unflinching and attractive female psychiatrists who take their patients to heart very literally in the marriages with which these films end. As for the women characters themselves, the scenario is Riviere's on its head. In the place of excessive femininity as a cover for threatening professional success, these films sport excessive masculinity (the overly serious professional who needs only to let her hair down) as a cover for an essentially feminine nature.

And yet, although apparently paradoxical, the two differently derived and figured accounts (Riviere's and that of the films) of the problems of masculinity and femininity in professional women contain a similar interest: the anxiety produced in women (Riviere) or in men (the films) by a woman's public professionalism. For the films, the woman character is only apparently at stake. The true stake here is the masculine fear of the professional woman reflected in the text's work to construct neurosis as a masquerade for female professionalism. As Riviere states clearly and as one might derive from films that insist on placing a comma in the term "woman doctor," there is no salient distinction but only contradiction and instability between real womanliness and its "masquerade," or between femininity and the professionalism of the female psychiatrist. Similarly, as evidenced in these films, there is no salient distinction but only confusion and instability between masculinity and its masquerade, between masculinity and the male patient.

6

Psychiatrists and Cinema
A Correspondence

? is: good done by "experts" wr. intentional
& unintentional evil (s. 141)
142
but discussions here are slight
& obvious

American psychiatry was well aware of its own image in relation to women, and, following World War II, organized psychiatry intervened in Hollywood film production on behalf of that image and its recipients. This chapter, as a way of consolidating and opening out questions of psychiatry, women, and cinema, presents a case study of the influence of American psychiatry on textual patterns of gendered power by investigating the epistolary and ideological correspondence between psychiatrists and the creators of three films about female mental disturbance: *Shock*, *The Snake Pit*, and *Freud*.

Shock

On March 8, 1946, the American Psychiatric Association voted to have its president, Dr. Karl Bowman, write an official letter to the Motion Picture Association of America (MPAA) stating the opinion of the membership that the film *Shock* (1946), produced by 20th Century–Fox, is "an unsuitable and undesirable picture to be shown to the general public and that it will do a great deal of harm."[1] In the same month the New York Society for Clinical Psychiatry voted unanimously to go on record strongly protesting the circulation of *Shock* for the "lurid and distorted manner" in which it portrayed insulin shock treatment, a treatment deemed by the society's membership as invaluable for patients formerly considered "hopeless and incurable." "All in all," read the letter, "this problem of shock treatment has broad implications as far as public health is concerned, and an important avenue of information such as the motion picture, should further public enlightenment and not distort it."[2] This collective action by the respective and respectable professional societies represented the result of a flurry of correspondence among members of the psychiatric profession and motion picture industry personnel regarding the propriety and in fact the raison d'être of the film in question. It also represented the beginning of a process of negotiation between and within the two preeminent institutions, each at the height of its power.

The film *Shock* tells the story of a weak and morally diffident psychiatrist, played by Vincent Price, who confines in his psychiatric clinic, and attempts to control the mind of, a woman who inadvertently witnessed the psychiatrist's unpremeditated murder of his own wife. Twentieth Century–Fox must have been apprehensive about this story's possible reception, for they engaged the counsel of the Medical Information Bureau, whose executive secretary, Dr. Iago Galdston, hosted a screening of the film at Fox Studios to which he invited such psychiatric dignitaries as A. A. Brill, first translator of Freud into English, first American to proclaim himself an analyst, and founder in 1911 of the New York Psychoanalytic Society; Dr. Clarence Oberndorf, eminent psychoanalyst and historian of American psychoanalysis; and Dr. S. Bernard Wortis, director of Bellevue Psychiatric Hospital. Fox's motive in contacting the Medical Information Bureau and arranging a preview screening would have been to recruit the support of the medical community in advance, thereby advertising the seriousness and palpability of the film for knowledgeable parties and paving the way for a Production Code Administration certificate and a positive response from the reviewers.

Instead, the preview screening inspired formal protests by the psychiatric community and catalyzed the specification of how this community would wish its theories and practices represented. The psychiatrists took great pains to assure film industry personnel that their objections did not lie primarily in the negative portrayal of the psychiatrist. It was understood, they claimed, that there would be villains in a fiction. Their objections, rather, were self-defined as being based in altruism. Each of the doctors responding to Galdston after the screening stressed the detrimental and even "pernicious" effect on the public should it be suggested that a psychiatrist "had unlimited opportunities and abilities to do whatever he pleased with his patients," that hospitals were places where "a sane person could be maliciously detained,"[3] or that insulin shock therapy could have other than a positive therapeutic effect.[4] Furthermore, this detrimental effect was described as being more severe in the uneducated, in adolescents, and in psychiat-

ric patients and their families. And the appeal to protect this latter
constituency carried great weight because an inordinate number of
psychiatric patients were veterans of the war, and therefore popularly
perceived as being among the most patriotic Americans, worthy of re-
spectful treatment. Bosley Crowther in a *New York Times* review challenged *Shock* as a "social disservice" in light of the psychiatric treatments currently being practiced on "thousands of men who suffered
shock of one sort or another in the war. A film," he continued, "which
provokes fear of treatment, as this film plainly aims to do, is a cruel
thing to put in the way of those patients or of their anxious relatives."[5]
That this argument reflected the common view is further illustrated by
the fact that Joseph Breen himself, head of the Production Code Administration (PCA), responded empathetically to one objecting psychiatrist with the information that his own son had been badly wounded
on Guam and "came near to being what might be called a serious mental case."[6]

The motion picture industry was thus put into a position to defend
the film, and it did so through the Motion Picture Association of America (the industry organization responsible for censorship) by pointing
to the balance afforded by the existence of sympathetic portrayals of
professional men in other films (the relative sympathy of various characters is clearly referenced in documentation kept as a matter of
course by the PCA), and by informing the psychiatrists that the voluntary Production Code didn't provide for judgments on the grounds
raised in their letters—it didn't provide for judgments on policy matters but only on morality and decency.[7] But, in spite of these obligatory
defenses registered by the MPAA, that office did take heed of the psychiatric point of view, a point of view Breen termed "interesting and
illuminating,"[8] and it circulated the psychiatrists' letters among its
personnel and distributed them to the studios.

But perhaps even more significant than the details of this immediate
correspondence are its implications for ongoing discourses internal to
American psychiatry. Although the psychiatrists who advocated intervention in film production did not speak overtly about the filmic depiction of women per se in relation to institutional psychiatry, documents reporting psychiatric opinion do display a fundamental subtext
concerning questions of female subjectivity. In *Shock* a woman's reci-
tation of the truth (she did see the Vincent Price character, "Dr.
Cross," clobber his wife to death with a candlestick) is defined by Dr.
Cross and initially accepted by his colleagues as a delusion or hallucination that calls for insulin shock treatment. It is Dr. Cross's plan to
administer a fatal overdose in the fourth treatment. The film does
seem to imply, as Galdston and his colleagues complain, that psychia-

try can rewrite truth to suit itself and, moreover, that psychiatric treatments may be invasive and inappropriate. And these, of course, are precisely the implications that psychiatrists advocating the use of shock treatment wanted to avoid. But to complicate matters, they are also the very characteristics of shock treatment that opened to criticism the use of shock treatment (see chapter 1). From this perspective the handling of the woman's "treatment" in *Shock* does echo in a disturbing fashion real cases where patients' objections to insulin shock treatment were attributed as symptoms and on that basis dismissed.

This is not to imply that there were actually patients in the situation of the patient pictured in *Shock* who was subject to criminal acts, but rather to say that psychiatry's diagnostic uncertainty, as well as its inherent altruism, contributed to the zeal and prolificness of debates about the public, cinematic portrayal of shock treatment.

The Snake Pit

If the film *Shock* had caught psychiatrists by surprise, its release did prepare them for an early and focused campaign responding to the development of *The Snake Pit* (1948). Correspondence with motion picture personnel on the subject of the former (finished) film had brought to the attention of psychiatrists the fact that *Shock* had after all been prepared with the aid of an on-set technical adviser, a Dr. William Brophy of the Good Samaritan Hospital in Los Angeles.[9] Thus, the general objections to the finished film *Shock* and to Brophy's judgment and/or influence (or lack thereof) made it clear to organized psychiatry that ad hoc consultation was not sufficient to its needs. In good part as a result of the unhappy experience of *Shock*, the American Psychiatric Association moved to *formalize* the process of technical consultancy in relation to the film industry, beginning with *The Snake Pit*.

By the time the American Psychiatric Association (APA) became aware of the film script being prepared from the novel, *The Snake Pit*, its producers had in fact already engaged the aid of a reassuring number of advisers: "three eminent psychiatrists" at the script stage, and two psychiatrists from the staffs of institutions such as the one pictured in the film who were present on the lot during the shooting of the film.[10] However, this knowledge did not satisfy Dr. C. C. Burlingame, chairman of the Committee on Public Education of the American Psychiatric Association. For one thing, the names of the advisers were being kept confidential (at their own request, it turned out), but more important, they had not been engaged through what the APA regarded as proper channels. As "Burley" put it in a letter to Joseph Breen:

I am beginning to think that you and I are much in the same
boat—we are both running a flock of opera singers. As far as the
psychiatrists are concerned, they must either agree openly and
officially to perform any function that you gentlemen need, or else
they must stop talking and criticising. . . .

I am anxious to break through this barrier of nonsense and will do
whatever you say. If you like, and want to notify your companies, we
will undertake officially to name competent men, and officially notify
them that the American Psychiatric Association has proposed them.
On the other hand, if you want any particular psychiatrist who has
the special talent or qualification you are seeking, I will see that his
name is officially proposed, unless there is some valid objection.[11]

Joseph Breen moved with alacrity to respond positively to Burlingame,
notifying the studios of his offer to "name competent men." One gath-
ers from the correspondence involved that the APA's desire to formalize the process of technical consultancy was shared by the motion picture industry, though the industry had its own set of reasons for
welcoming organized consultancy.

For one thing, the MPAA and film studios had received notice of the
public perception that the representation of mental illness could be injurious to audience members and of the concomitant perception that
motion pictures tackle such themes for the sole motive of profit. In the
words of a self-described "Motion Picture Patron,"

Pictures treating of psychiatry and of mental disorders undoubtedly
satisfy the curiosity of the mob; but they also reopen bitter memories
in the minds of many. . . . there are literally millions of us in this
country, including parents, husbands, wives and children of the
victims of psychiatric diseases, whose lives have been deeply touched
by these strange and terrifying illnesses so convincingly portrayed in
books and on the screen. This great industry should pay attention not
only to the *profits* that might be made, but also to the propriety of
avoiding the infliction of pain and anguish upon a very large number
of patrons.[12]

In England the perception that psychiatric themes could be injurious
was confirmed in a flurry of national publicity when the press reported
that a woman was driven mad as a result of seeing *The Snake Pit*. According to a report by the *Daily Mail*:

A 52-year-old Luton woman left a West End cinema after seeing "The
Snake Pit"—the film about mental hospitals in America—and at once
began to act strangely. Now she is a voluntary patient in Arlesey
Mental Hospital.

Her story was told yesterday by her bus-driver husband. When
they left the cinema, he said, her first remark was: "It's terrible what

those poor souls go through". She refused a cup of tea, then left an ice cream because, she said, she thought it was poisoned. . . .

Twice in the next two days she went to a doctor. She wanted everything in the house analysed. She advised her husband to take a course of shock treatment.[13]

Apparently Breen and company felt that professional advice could diffuse public protests against psychiatric themes—freeing the film industry to broach with impunity such popular and timely subject matter.

And in addition to allaying public outcry against the film industry, the acceptance of the APA's consultancy plan would have had the even more direct result of recruiting the blanket and prior psychiatric professional support hoped for and not received in the earlier case of *Shock*.

Freud

When, a decade after the release of *The Snake Pit*, John Huston began to prepare his biographical film *Freud* (1962), he did so with a wise eye cast at professional psychiatry. He, like prior producers, would attempt to garner psychiatric support for reasons of public relations and in order to facilitate acceptance by the Legion of Decency and a certificate of approval from the MPAA. In fact his efforts to seek technical advice were remarkably intensive given that by the 1960s the Production Code was weakening and beginning its change from a rigid censorship apparatus to a classification system. These changes, even in the absence of psychoanalytic approval, would most likely have allowed Huston to explore in some manner the controversial and previously taboo issues of infantile sexuality, repression, transference, and child molestation.

But Huston's pursuit of professional counsel displays a more genuine and scholarly concern for the substance of the psychoanalytic intellectual history pictured than was displayed in the cases of *Shock* and *The Snake Pit*. Whereas Darryl Zanuck actually advised against going overboard in *The Snake Pit* with "the intimate details of life in an insane asylum," saying that to portray them was "neither courageous nor clever" and probably "most uninteresting and dull,"[14] Huston attempted to render meticulously the substance and detail of Freud's ideas. In a meeting in Ireland with psychiatrist Earl Loomis, who would become the film's credited technical adviser, Huston apparently "probed very deeply into the technical facets of the script as it relate[d] to the life of Freud."[15]

On September 21, 1960, Geoffrey M. Shurlock, who had succeeded

Breen as head of the PCA, wrote a memo on *Freud* in which he indicated that

> because of this highly clinical nature of this script, dealing as it does with all sorts of incestuous relations and other sexual aberrations, we would not feel justified in taking on ourselves the responsibility of issuing a Code Seal for it.
>
> Mr. Reinhardt [Wolfgang Reinhardt, the film's producer] admitted that this picture did not fall into the normal category of entertainment film and certainly would demand special handling in release.

Later, on April 21, 1961, the script was deemed "unacceptable" by the MPAA. By the next month, John Huston had authorized William Gordon, his public relations consultant, to begin an exhaustive campaign to garner support for the film, or, in the words of Gordon himself, "to circularize the script and to create the climate requisite for general acceptance of the finished picture of *Freud*."[16] Although the chronology of events might suggest that Huston's and Gordon's public relations strategy was hatched as a direct response to the rejection of the script by the PCA (and in fact Monsignor Little of the Legion of Decency counseled Huston and Gordon as to how to obtain support for the film), Gordon's words here and in other correspondence reveal a play for much broader acceptance. Instead of using technical consultancy as it had been used previously to impress Code officials and through their sanctions the general public, Huston and Gordon were prepared to bypass Code auspices and mount their appeal one step more directly through professional psychiatry to the general public.

Their public relations strategy relied on a network of opinion leaders. By the beginning of June, less than two months after the MPAA rejection, the script had been circulated to at least six eminent psychiatrists, including Dr. Martin Grotjahn, former member of the Berlin Psychoanalytic Institute and at the time training analyst for the Institute for Psychoanalytic Medicine of Southern California and author of *Psychoanalysis and the Family Neurosis*, among other books; Dr. Leo Rangell, past president of both the Los Angeles Psychoanalytic Society and the Southern California Psychiatric Society and president at the time of the American Psychoanalytic Association (one of the associations Monsignor Little had urged Huston and Gordon to cultivate), clinical professor of psychiatry at UCLA Medical School, consultant at Reiss-Davis Clinic for Child Guidance, and a training analyst at the Los Angeles Psychoanalytic Institute; and Dr. Kurt Eissler, head of the Freud Archives.

The response from the psychiatrists was generally and sometimes overwhelmingly positive. Grotjahn replied with a two-and-a-half-page single-spaced letter, written in the suitably self-reflective style of a psychoanalyst and effusively praising the script.[17] It was also at this point that Loomis wrote a lengthy response praising the script by saying, "In my own judgment, this is the most compelling presentation of the insight of the early stages of psychoanalysis that I have ever encountered. It is authentic and convincing, and it leaves one with a flavor that truth is just beginning."[18] Unlike Rangell, Loomis did have numerous substantive comments and suggestions, and he was engaged for a flat rate of four thousand dollars as technical consultant. Huston and Gordon planned to use Loomis not only as an expert reader of the script but as a "liaison with his colleagues in the field." They planned to have Loomis preside over private screenings to which would be invited psychiatric, religious, and sociological authorities. In addition, he was to act as liaison with the Protestant Film Commission. It was Loomis who was the linchpin of Huston's and Gordon's public relations push. In a letter to Huston, Gordon explained how he intended to use Loomis, saying, "All of these endeavors are to be geared to obtain approvals and perhaps even accolades for the film rather than just have it 'cleared' as unobjectionable." So, over the course of the film's production, Loomis prepared lengthy and detailed analyses of the psychoanalytic concepts and historical material dealt with in the script, and he corresponded with other professionals, conveying their responses and suggestions, and mediating their criticisms of the film.

The professionals with whom Loomis corresponded were not only psychiatric professionals. Another group to show an interest in the proposed film on Freud was the religious community. Religious leaders were viewed as appropriate advisers because they had taken the initiative to respond to the film, because of Freud's Jewishness, and more than that because it was religious leaders who presided over filmic depictions of sexuality in general, and the sexual component of the *Freud* script was its most controversial element.

Appropriately, it had been a letter from Reverend William Bier, chairman of the Department of Psychology at Fordham University, that led Gordon to Loomis in the first place. Previously, Bier had written to Gordon registering certain objections to the film. Gordon had responded by contacting two of the authorities cited in Bier's volume *Freud and Catholics*: Dr. Smiley Blanton of the American Foundation of Religion and Psychiatry and of the Norman Vincent Peale Organization of Religion and Psychiatry, and Loomis, of the Union Theological Seminary Program in Psychiatry and Religion. By consulting with theological psychiatrists, the filmmakers could satisfy two constituencies simultaneously. In September 1961 Loomis was able to report to

Gordon that "two priests, six ministers, and a rabbi approve of the play."

Two specific aspects of the *Freud* script met with frequent objection: the "prostitution theme" or the events concerning the father of Freud's hysterical patient, Cecily Koertner; and the "Magda theme," concerning Magda, a patient of Freud's depicted in the film script as having actually been an incest victim instead of having merely fantasized such events. According to the script, Cecily's father was to have frequented brothels and cheap burlesque halls and was to have met Cecily's mother when she was a dancer in such a club. Two scenes conveying this prostitution theme and singled out for attack were a brief scene of the future Frau Koertner performing a "Leda and the Swan" number (a scene that does not appear in the finished film), and the scene of Cecily passing through the corridors and rooms of a brothel on her way to identify the body of her father who had died there of a heart attack (which scene did make it into the final version of the film). This latter scene was described by Bier as being "distinctly in bad taste" and "most objectionable." Moreover, it was viewed as being irrelevant to the general subject matter of the film and as a theme that would reflect poorly on the image of Freud. According to Bier, "The prostitution theme has nothing whatever to do with Freud from the historical point of view, and this, in my opinion constitutes the most objectionable feature of the manuscript as currently conceived."[19]

But Huston wanted very much to retain the prostitution theme, which he saw, as Loomis put it, as "a symptom of a sick society and as a pathologic factor in the etiology of Cecily's neurosis."[20] And so it was Loomis's job to justify that thematic thread by giving the official stamp to Huston's psychoanalytic interpretation and by adding his own characterization of Herr Koertner's desire for prostitutes as an *illness*. In Loomis's words:

> I think it is important to work with Herr Koertner's sexual problem in such a way that it is clear to the audience that he has an illness. A major factor in his illness is his inability to love one woman in both a tender and a sexual way. He has separated love into two parts and can be only sexually active with one kind of woman whom he doesn't love. Therefore, as soon as his wife becomes pregnant he ceases to find her sexually attractive. Freud described this phenomenon in more than one of his papers. It is sometimes referred to as the virgin and prostitute syndrome: "a good woman is not sexual; a sexual woman is not good."[21]

Gordon also assured Bier that those scenes dealing with prostitution "will be handled in such a way as to be reasonably acceptable to rea-

sonable people." Interestingly, he came up with an additional way to
justify the inclusion of the objectionable material, which was to point
out that the scenes of prostitution were "phantasy segments," "played
during visualized dreams," and would "communicate a bizarre, unreal,
never-never land atmosphere which should do much to ameliorate and
mitigate the adverse effect which you [Bier] anticipate."[22] Prostitution
bracketed as dream or fantasy material was thus viewed as being less
available for imitation than prostitution subject to cinema's reality effect. The "Magda theme" also received some comment, including comment from Code personnel who specified how the memory of father-
daughter incest was to be evoked. The excision of this scene was not
required, but it did not end up in the finished film, much to Huston's
regret.[23]

Besides manifesting themselves as objections to specific themes or
scenes in the *Freud* script, the objections to the film's use of sexual
themes focused on the substance of *Freud*'s content. Because the film
centered on the discovery of the Oedipus complex and of infantile sexuality, it came under comment and sometimes censure for being so
thoroughly about sexuality and even sexual perversion. The PCA was
concerned with the explicitness of the sexual subject matter, in particular the repeated use of words such as "sexual" and "rape," and, as
Gordon put it in a letter to Universal executive Edward Muhl, with "the
harsh, blunt, sometimes clinical and unaccustomed language: prime
examples of which are whore and infantile sexuality. The objection resides," he continued, "not in the significance of the words but in their
repeated articulation."

While both centered on "excessive" sexuality, the concerns of the
PCA on one hand and of psychiatry and theological psychology on the
other hand did differ. Where PCA personnel were of course concerned
to monitor the film's morality and decency, the psychiatrists were concerned to monitor the representation not of sexuality itself but of
Freud's views of sexuality, notably of infantile sexuality and the sexual
etiology of neurosis. Freud's theories of sexuality thus became a particular area of negotiation among various psychiatrist respondents.
Consequently, the collective desire to render Freud on film influenced
the psychoanalytic interpretations of American analysts by placing
them in an arena ringed by theological contexts and community standards in general.

A significant portion of American psychiatrists believed that Freud
meant "sexuality" in a much broader sense than the colloquial meaning of the term would suggest. By "sexuality" he did not intend to indicate only issues of desire and the libido, but instead a much wider
range of emotional issues comprising virtually everything except the

death instinct. Following this interpretation, where sex was mentioned one could conceivably substitute (either in the film itself or mentally) less charged or less "sexy" terminology. According to Reverend Peter Ciklic, professor and chairman of the Department of Psychology at Loyola University:

> It is important to keep in mind that Freud construed sex in the broader sense of "life instinct" (libido, élan vital, life urge)—as opposed to "death instinct" (thanatos)—but psychologically uneducated people accept Freudian terminology on sex in a narrower sense. Therefore I would avoid wherever possible, the terms such as "infantile sexuality," "incest," etc., and substitute them with the words, "undesirable emotional attachment," or the like.[24]

In addition to taking the bite out of the term "sexuality," these particular American authorities tended to make the historical argument that Freud later rescinded his early claim as to the sexual nature of the unconscious, or, if not by Freud himself, the primacy of sexuality was later and appropriately denied by others. A Dr. Campbell stated succinctly that the film "gives the [presumably misleading] impression that 'everything is due to sex.' "[25]

Others elaborated more fully. Bier suggested that an epilogue be added to the film in which it could be pointed out that the theories portrayed were "elaborated by Freud in the *early* [my emphasis] stages of his development of psychoanalysis and that he, himself, changed some of these subsequently."[26] Both Bier and Ciklic suggested that even if Freud himself hadn't modified (and the implication is *corrected*) his theories on sexuality, this was done subsequently by his disciples: Jung, Rank, Adler, and Stakel. These eminent psychoanalysts, Ciklic argued, were "as great as Freud" himself (Jung was the first president of the International Psychoanalytic Association, Adler president of the Vienna Psychoanalytic Society), and yet they left Freud precisely because of the pansexualism of his theories.

The crux of the matter for these psychiatrists was that the *Freud* script misconstrued Freud by overemphasizing sex. "After all," wrote Bier, "the play stresses not so much Freud's emphasis on the unconscious, which was his basic contribution, as his emphasis on the *sexual nature* of the unconscious, and the latter is precisely the portion of his theory which was, subsequently, modified."[27] Ironically, this reading of the film *Freud* recapitulates the resistance with which the Freud character is met when he attempts to elaborate to the Medical Congress his theory of infantile sexuality.

It is important to remember, however, that the views of these consultants who sought to bracket off sexuality in *Freud*, while in tune with certain prevalent standards of decency, were not the views that ultimately held sway with the script. Loomis began and ended by successfully defending as true to Freud a more vibrant and less constrained depiction of psychosexual processes. In the Conclusion I will offer a reading of the complicated ideological stances with regard to psychiatric expertise and feminine sexuality that emerged out of this atmosphere of negotiation to take their place in the representational system that is the film *Freud*.

For the purposes of this chapter, however, we may conclude that whatever one's evaluation of the validity of the version of Freud's theories presented in the film, it is the very struggle for control over the discourse on sexuality in Freud, the thinker, and the discourse on feminine sexuality in *Freud,* the movie, that evidences, once again and perhaps even more directly, psychiatry's profound stake in the communication of ideas about psychoanalysis and female identity.

Conclusion
Feminine Sexuality and the Fallible Freud

The psychiatric film texts produced between the end of World War II and the mid-1960s were forged through the cinematic reinscription and reworking of themes and images that developed out of experiences of mental disturbance, professional responses to mental disturbance, and the perceived role of gender in relation to those phenomena. Although each film enjoyed a unique relationship to the swirl of ideas around psychiatry and femininity, some general discursive through lines may be discerned. We may conclude now that the relationship between American psychiatry and women in the postwar years was characterized by fluctuations in evaluations of psychiatric expertise, in the theory and practice of women's gender roles, and in views of female mental life; and these fundamental fluctuations manifested themselves cinematically in films about psychiatry and women in the importance placed on dialogue, especially the words of the expert (or, conversely, in the troubled expert's inability to articulate internal states), in the play with alternating sex and gender roles, and in the representation of female psychosexuality as a central textual problem.

John Huston's film, *Freud* (1962), because of its concentration on Freud himself, goes the furthest both to shore up and to call into question notions of psychiatric expertise and expression in relation to female mental disturbance. Its analysis will serve here to exemplify one final time the complicated relationship between filmic representation and psychiatric patterns of adjustment and resistance.

Freud develops two case histories. One history is that of a young girl (based loosely on Anna O.) suffering from a multitude of hysterical symptoms that are initially traced by Freud back to a childhood incident of paternal sexual abuse. The other case history is that of Freud's self-analysis leading to the discovery of infantile sexuality and the Oedipal complex. Played in fits and starts by Montgomery Clift, this Freud alternates between intellectual insight and the morass of neurotic subjectivity. What is particularly significant in relation to this study is the fact that the two case histories are not merely parallel, but rather thoroughly imbricated.[1] The written correspondence between psychiatrists and motion picture personnel described in chapter 6 reveals a deep concern that sexual themes, especially those developed in conjunction with the Koertner family, be downplayed so as not to affect adversely the image of Freud. Also of central importance in this correspondence is a general concern that Freud not be shown too personally or as "fallible, . . . weak, even neurotic," that he not, in short, be "taken off the pedestal."[2] Nevertheless, in the finished film Freud's self-analysis is obviously personal and it is connected to sexual themes. He must work through his own inability to mourn his father's death in order to help his young patient, Cecily Koertner (Susannah York); *and* he must reconstruct, through dreams, a serpent bracelet, and his mother's verification, "the memory of something I witnessed between my father and my sister." Psychoanalytic expertise and psychosexuality do figure, then, as the film's thematic twin engine.

Ultimately, as history seemingly has borne out, Freud realizes that it was *his own desire* for his mother and jealousy of his father that "conjured the crime against my sister," and it is this realization that leads to the discovery of the Oedipal complex and to the refutation of real childhood abuse in Cecily's case. "The false" he declaims "is often the true, standing on its head."

From a feminist point of view, one is critical of the denial of childhood seduction that has figured prominently in the writing of the history of psychoanalysis and that figures also in the resolution of the plot of *Freud*. As some have now noted, the historical Freud returned time and time again to the role of real childhood trauma in the etiology of neurosis; for him, Oedipal desire and the reality of childhood sexual abuse were not mutually exclusive.[3] The film's rendition of sexual abuse is therefore constrained by the convenient appropriation and reinscription for male subjectivity of what would otherwise have been an acknowledgment of a concrete element in the etiology of female neurosis.

But, to stand "the true" on its head, that's precisely the point and interest of *Freud* for the project at hand. Here, as becomes increasingly true of the psychiatric films of the postwar period, one finds a woman patient, a male analyst, and a certain crucial exchange of neurotic material and affect between them. The psychic life and stability of the male representative of the psychiatric profession is explored as the meat of *Freud*, and questioned, all the more pointedly, for the fact that that representative is a dreamy, nervous, mentally self-flagellating Freud himself. The visual and structural imbrication of the mental life of a neurotic girl with that of the founder of psychoanalysis portrays, then, an "interested" psychoanalysis with a stake in its own renditions of feminine psychosexuality; and portrays as well a "fallible" Freud whose truck with feminine sexuality simultaneously forms and threatens the findings and scientific status of psychoanalytic thought. *Freud*, in short, is a limit case for the simultaneous aggrandizement *and critique* of the expert status of psychiatry in the face of feminine subjectivity that it has been the project of this book to explore.

Cecily's case is fodder for Freud's successful pursuit of knowledge and as such deserves to be ranged with the other aspects of the film through which his place in history is reaffirmed. An opening narrated prologue compares Freud to Copernicus and Darwin, long dialogues with Josef Breuer[4] primarily on the subject of infantile sexuality give weight to Freud's intellectual life and discoveries, Freud's thoughts themselves are voiced in resonant tones (and voiced, moreover, by John Huston himself, thereby taking on the added legitimacy of the film's respected creator), and finally, Freud's patients, with Cecily among them, appear as the raw supporting material for his theories. The film's celebration of Freud's achievements unfolds, therefore, in the essentially logocentric passages through which his thoughts are articulated. "Thinking, after all" wrote one contemporaneous reviewer, "does not lend itself to visual representation."[5]

However, Cecily's case is also central to the film's other and primarily visual register—a register of dreams, memories, nonrealistic representations of the waking state, and pointed iconography through which Freud's mental life gets figured as brilliant but neurotic, authoritative but simultaneously implicated as subject to patriarchal law, and, finally, as feminized by association with Cecily's mental state.

The characters Freud and Cecily, though technically analyst and analysand, are in fact similarly depicted through various aspects of the film's visual scheme. Both are identified with an object filmed in close-up that symbolizes the fraught relationship of its owner to his or her father. In Freud's case the object is an heirloom pocket watch entrusted to him by his father as Freud embarks for Paris to study with Charcot. The symbolic meaning of the watch is portentously overdetermined when Freud immediately drops and cracks it in the train compartment: a breach between father and son. That the watch is symbolic of such a patrilineal break is further made clear by the fact that what a fellow passenger calls the "unhappy accident" occurs in a train compartment—the very place where Freud imagines his father's crime against his sister to have taken place during a childhood trip, a trip that had just been alluded to in barely audible offscreen dialogue by Freud's mother: "Sigi cried the whole way home. The train frightened him." At this point in the film, we are not aware of the father-son breach, nor of Freud's faulty memory of the abuse against his sister. But this early scene is marked visually, to be imbued with retrospective meaning, as Freud's self-analysis begins to unearth the memory of what took place in the train compartment. Almost immediately after it surfaces, however, this memory of abuse is discredited. It was not, after all, a father's abuse against his daughter in a train compartment that glimmered in the depths of Freud's memory, but rather a son's (Freud's) frustrated desire for his mother.

Cecily's object, a doll, is similarly marked visually and similarly connected to an abuse scenario involving the child, Cecily, and her father. This memory too, like that of Freud, is ultimately rejected as faulty, or to be more precise, as a seduction fantasy on the part of the girl herself. As Cecily skirts the memory of paternal abuse in an analytic session with Freud, the doll is shown in close-up, eyes opening and shutting, as Cecily almost imperceptibly rocks her back and forth. The fluttering eyes of the doll recall a previous moment when Cecily's own eyes fluttered as she resisted hypnosis and spurred Freud on to the invention of the talking cure. The motif of eyes opening and shutting further underlines the parallelism of Cecily's and Freud's cases since it is a sign reading "the eyes must be closed" that appears to Freud in a dream and that he must decipher to understand his inability to mourn his father.[6]

If opening and shutting eyes evoke flashing insight alternating with resistance to memory, another physical symptom extends the metaphor: that of falling. Both Freud and Cecily respond to dawning insight in dreams or reality by falling or fainting away. Freud is seen falling for the first time at the end of a dream in which his patient, a young man, embraces Freud's own mother and then pulls Freud over the edge of a cliff at the lip of a cave. Later, Freud collapses at his father's funeral at the moment he must pass through the cemetery gate. This image leads immediately to a dream about a funeral train and the sign, "the eyes must be closed." Cecily, for her part, tells of collapsing when she is taken on a shopping trip by her father to "Red Tower Street," a street of prostitution. She falls again on legs hysterically paralyzed when Freud has encouraged her to attempt to walk after he believed she had reached a crucial traumatic memory of her father's preference for prostitutes over the company of his own daughter. As Cecily falls to the ground and also out of frame, only Freud's figure is left there, there where Cecily had been.

This substitution is not anomalous, but rather indicative of a thoroughgoing structural and visual scheme through which Freud and Cecily are linked. Formally, the film unfolds through the alternation of Freud's and Cecily's visualized dreams, memories, and even scenes characterized by a dreamlike mise-en-scène but ostensibly "real" according to the plot of the film (the weirdly subjective point-of-view shots describing Freud's experience in his father's funeral procession, the oddly theatrical scene when Freud goes at night to Red Tower Street in search of Cecily, who has painted and dressed herself as a prostitute).

But beyond mere alternation, the dreams and memories of Freud and Cecily are also linked by a consistent confusion of their authorship. Two scenes are most notable in this regard. The first, the very analytic session in which Cecily reveals the memory of her sexual abuse by her father, is initially coded as *Freud's memory* of Cecily's memory. Previously, Cecily had rocked her doll and recounted her memory of the episode in which her father took her backstage at the ballet and into the dressing room of a dancer. When she got home, the nine-year-old Cecily (played not by Susannah York, but by a child actress in an obvious and almost garish blonde wig) painted her face in imitation of the dancer and was harshly scolded by her mother and then comforted by her father and promised a doll. As the scene is shot (with compositions at odd angles, a partially diffused image, and the screams of the child), two figures, mother and father, vie for control over the image of Cecily's face, which, until her discovery, had been framed solely for Cecily's own regard in a hand mirror.

Cecily's second account of this memory goes further, and it is initiated by a pensive close-up of Freud's face and a dissolve to that of Cecily framed in the mirror. This time we see Herr Koertner carrying Cecily to his own room, lying her down on his bed, and removing her shoes and socks. "Is that when he promised you the doll?" Freud asks. "Yes. No. No, it was later in the night when I woke up and cried," responds Cecily. "Why were you crying in the middle of the night?" asks Freud. As Cecily narrates we see from her point of view Cecily's father in the bathroom. He comes toward her on the bed, looming up out of a low angle shot. "Tall like a tower," she narrates. And then, after an image of her father turning out the light and as the screen fades to a brief interval of black leader, we hear Cecily's narration, "strong as a god when he embraced me." "And he promised you a doll if you wouldn't tell," finishes Freud. Not only has Freud participated in the exhumation of this memory with interspersed comments and questions, but its visualization conforms with the cinematic convention of attributing authorship of a memory to the person seen just prior to that memory. This confusion of narrational and historical authorship over the abuse scene is furthered later in the film when Cecily recants her testimony of it, telling Freud that she only told him what she thought *he* wanted to hear. Freud, in other words, through a kind of thought transference between analyst and analysand, was the memory's true source.

Undeniably, the assignation of Cecily's abuse to Freud's memory serves the film's intellectual hermeneutic. Cecily's sexual abuse can now be recruited into Freud's abandonment of the seduction "theory." Cecily still loves her doll because it was she who desired her father and not he who abused her. A second scene furthers both the interpenetration of the psychic lives of Freud and Cecily and the sense that this interpenetration functions in the service of the denial of childhood abuse. As in *The Snake Pit*, where Dr. Kik's narration calls up images of an infant at the same time Virginia and Baby Doe, here in *Freud* it is Freud's own narration that calls up a new version of Cecily's traumatic childhood memory, replayed in general and socially acceptable terms. Cecily's own memory precedes Freud's version and is now confined to one shot. We see the girl Cecily twirling to her father's piano accompaniment as her mother comes forward. "Shall I tell you a story?" offers Freud to the present-tense Cecily. In the "story" he tells, the bedroom is replaced by the parlor and a child's bed; abuse, by an accomplished and solicitous father; and a mother's anger, by her deliberate interference with a lesson in propriety. The story is Freud's. Because he was not abused, Cecily must not have been. And her case is merely a set of clues useful primarily for what it can bring to Freud's self-analysis. And yet even here in Freud's revision of Cecily's personal history a signifier of abuse may be discerned. In Freud's account, exactly as in Cecily's, the father looms forward in a low angle shot, menacing as always and dressed as he had been for the bedroom. It appears to be the identical shot, though it is now superimposed over Cecily's figure as she listens to Freud's account.

Looking at this film and this image from today's perspective, now that the reality and prevalence of sexual abuse are known, the fantasy in question would not be that of the girl, but of the analyst—the analyst's fantasy that sexual abuse is neither prevalent, nor, if prevalent, significant; the fantasy that such abuse can be rewritten as faulty memory or lying to please the analyst.[7] From the perspective of *Freud*'s own context, this alternative reading of the reality of sexual abuse would not have been so readily available. The film certainly does not provide an explicit feminist critique of the harm done women by psychiatry's failure to recognize the reality or the importance of sexual abuse. Nevertheless, by the early 1960s the popular and professional suggestions discussed herein, that psychiatry had paid too little attention to the social etiology of women's problems and conversely attributed too much to women's perceived psychological or even biological fallibility or incapacity, enable a reading of *Freud* sensitive to the full range of nuances in the film. In this light, the suggestion that the film *does broach* the problem of sexual abuse is more than feminist wish-fulfillment, either for a spectator familiar with popular and/or professional literature on the subject or for the men and women whose own experiences have been informed by a lived knowledge of sexual abuse.

A final aspect of *Freud* illustrates the film's thorough investment in exploring through one another the subjectivities of analyst and analysand. Near the end of the film Cecily bemoans the fact that she'll have to leave analysis with Freud. "But my symptoms are gone," she says sadly. "Yes. All but one," answers Freud. "Your love for me." But the transference referred to here as a symptom has a fuller life in the text as a whole. For if Cecily has stood for Freud in the film's character logic, then Cecily's transference implies at the very least Freud's countertransference, or, to extend the implication to its fullest, Freud's *transference*. For Lacan, as indicated in chapter 2, "The transference is a phenomenon in which subject and psycho-analyst are both included. To divide it in terms of transference and counter-transference—however bold, however confident what is said on this theme may be—is never more than a way of avoiding the essence of the matter."[8]

Two specific scenes suggest, then, that Cecily's desire is the desire of the analyst. In one scene Breuer is called to the bedside of Cecily, who is in the throes of a hysterical childbirth following a hysterical pregnancy. With Freud looking on, Breuer calms Cecily down and then carries on with his plans to depart on a trip "to preserve my marriage." The dominant reading of this scene would be to attribute Cecily's pregnancy to her unconscious love for and desire to manipulate Breuer. However, Lacan's analysis of the source case history of Anna O., whom he calls by her true name, Bertha Pappenheim, makes available an alternative reading. Lacan suggests that his readers and auditors suspend "the tendency to say quite simply that it was Bertha's fault":

> Why is it that we do not consider Bertha's pregnancy rather,
> according to my formula *man's desire is the desire of the Other*, as
> the manifestation of Breuer's desire? Why do you not go as far as to
> think that it was Breuer who had a desire for a child? I will give you

the beginning of a proof; namely that Breuer, setting off for Italy with
his wife, lost no time in giving her a child.[9]

Of course, the patient in question for our purposes is Cecily and not
Bertha, but still Lacan's formulation is suggestive. In this light one
might attribute the filmic Breuer's hurried flight and his wife's suspi-
cions to a reciprocal transference rather than to the unfounded paranoia of a jealous wife.

In a follow-up scene, Freud's wife, Martha, is troubled in her turn by
the white carnations Cecily now sends to Freud instead of Breuer, for
they seem to signify here again a love relationship.[10] But Freud explains their psychological weight to Martha, saying that for Cecily, "her
attachments are also symptoms." If that is the case, Martha queries,
what about Freud's love for her? Must it too be deromanticized and
deindividualized by being placed within an Oedipal context? Yes, replies Freud. "It may be you bear a likeness to some image in my heart.
Some forgotten image." Thus, in this passage Freud's desire is suggested not only because transference desire is always the desire of the
analyst as well as of the analysand, but because, in responding to Martha,
Freud has put himself in Cecily's place and given credence to her
transference. He has explained Cecily's desire for him in reference to
his own desire for his wife. By virtue of this substitution as well as the
thoroughgoing imbrication of Cecily and Freud in the film, Freud's role
as authoritative analyst is qualified—he embodies very precisely Lacan's
"subject *presumed* to know" (emphasis added).

In addition to epitomizing the postwar psychiatric film concerned with
femininity, the case of *Freud* illustrates certain changes in the cinematic depiction of psychiatry and women from the 1940s to the 1960s,
which may be summarized as follows. Where in the 1940s female subjectivity surfaced intermittently through breaches of convention (the
missed exchange of point-of-view shots in *Whirlpool*, the "Beautiful
Psychiatrist" in *Spellbound*), subjective interludes (Virginia's hallucination of the lapping waves in *The Snake Pit*), or semicovert references (the denial of a dress used to characterize Ann Sutton's childhood privation in *Whirlpool*), the 1950s and 1960s saw explicit
references to aspects of female subjectivity and sexuality: childhood
sexual abuse (*Tender Is the Night*, *Freud*), divorce (*The Three Faces of
Eve*), incestuous relationships (*Lilith*), and lesbian alternatives (*Lilith*
again). Where in the 1940s feminine resistance in psychiatric cinema
is primarily legible as a textual adjunct to incipient but mainly unpop-
ularized debates on the limitations of psychiatric efficacy and rigid
gender roles, by the 1960s the blooming social critique of authoritarian

psychiatry in relation to problems of women's psychic and social life had gained cinematic expression in the figure of the "fallible" (as distinguished from the criminal) psychiatrist and in reference to an etiology of female mental illness and independent subjectivity grounded in material experience.

In his 1947 article, "Psychiatry and the Films," Lawrence Kubie wrote that cinema can influence "the sense of reality by which we humans must try to live."[11] This effect is redoubled, he argued, in the case of psychological films:

> Guilt and anger and fear are deeply buried in all of us; and in everyone there is some intimation of jeopardy, however remote, from conflicting inner stresses. Yet these very internal conflicts at the same time give rise to a fearful fascination with mental disorders, and to the need to dispose of that fear in some comforting fashion.
> *Consequently, whenever mental frailty is portrayed in the films, whether as minor neurotic quirks or as frank insanity, a considerable part of any audience is both fascinated and terrified on levels deeper than the plot alone would stir.*[12] (emphasis added)

This quote is of consequence both for its indication that psychiatrists had by the late forties identified the phenomenon of the psychiatric film, and for its indication that psychiatrists, however naively in light of Althusserian Marxism, had given weight to the dynamic ability of the films of this particular corpus to inspire different and specific *unconscious* audience effects.

Though we must not overlook the political context of this psychiatrist's words (he was arguing, after all, for a motion picture industry–endowed and psychiatrist-run research foundation to study "the special uses of films in emotional and intellectual education"), neither must we ignore the clear sense of the material and political stakes of certain cinematic representations that this psychiatrist's words bring out. For, as seen in the analysis of *Freud*, the psychiatric film concerned also with femininity does couch the promise to represent contemporaneous social cultural conflicts in such a way as to engage the conscious and unconscious "fascination" and "terrors" of audience members, or alternatively, to ameliorate public fears concerning mental illness and its treatment. There is a semipermeable boundary between representations of psychiatry and women and the lives of real viewers. And it is at this boundary that the analyses presented here have tried to abide.

Today I would not turn to psychiatry or cinema as examples of institutions crucially formative of feminine subjectivity. Today the fragmented and commodity-based texts of broadcast, cable, and home video media received at home and in the car (consider especially MTV, reality programming, and very notably talk radio) would seem to offer greater purchase than contemporary institutional psychiatry or contemporary cinema on continually produced social, political, and sexual identities. But what I have tried to offer feminism and film studies today, along with a discrete historical analysis of the interactions between women and two institutions in their heyday, is an example of reading the intertextual construction of femininities. The elaboration of resistant discourses has been pursued here as a feminist analytical terrain and strategy that is not negatory, but rather equal to and alive to dissident thought and action even when it is not already couched in purely feminist terms. Perhaps the various ways and means of resistance identified here, especially the formal textual resistance to classical patterns of visual dominance and professional psychiatric resistance to notions of feminine essence and the authoritarian tendency of expertise, can be put toward the more expansive feminism where gender is viewed as one among many salient variables of subjectivity in relation to oppression and resistance. There is no "woman spectator" pure and simple. One aims, then, toward a sense of subject positioning conceived not only in terms of gender differences and racial, ethnic, national, class, and other such differences, but in terms of gender differences and the quite *specifically historical differences* of the female psychiatric professionals, of the antiauthoritative psychiatrists in an era of the hegemony of the authoritative, of the writers who were feminists before the second wave of feminism gave them a context for struggle and, too, of the resolutely independent viewers of the always somewhat innovative Hollywood classical film.

Notes

Introduction

1. Patrice Petro, *Joyless Streets: Women and Melodramatic Representation in Weimar Germany* (Princeton, N.J.: Princeton University Press, 1989), p. 224.

2. Sacvan Bercovitch, *Reconstructing American Literary History* (Cambridge: Harvard University Press, 1986), p. viii.

3. A discourse for Foucault is "a totality, in which the dispersion of the subject and his discontinuity with himself may be determined . . . a space of exteriority in which a network of distinct sites is deployed" (Michel Foucault, *The Archaeology of Knowledge and the Discourse on Language* [1972], trans. A. M. Sheridan Smith [New York: Pantheon, 1982], p. 55). In other words, Foucault does not conceive of discourse as the ideological product of the economic mode of production as in Marxist thought, nor does he conceive of it as the expression of man's ideas as in traditional intellectual history. Discourses are not expressions of power. They are not the by-product of "real," or non-discursive domains parenthetically identified by Foucault as "institutions, political events, economic practices and processes" (p. 162), and they do not reside in cultural products only, such as films, books, paintings, etc. Instead, discursive operations generate meaning, and this meaning becomes a tangible organizing principle of the aggregate of social relations that Foucault calls the social formation. In short, discourses *are* power.

4. Foucault, *Archaeology of Knowledge*, pp. 193-94.

5. In addition to *The Archaeology of Knowledge*, see Michel Foucault, *Madness and Civilization*, trans. Richard Howard (New York: Random House, 1965), and Foucault, *The Birth of the Clinic*, trans. A. M. Sheridan Smith (New York: Random House, 1973).

6. Foucault, *Archaeology of Knowledge*, p. 164.

7. Ibid., pp. 148-49.

8. Russell Jacoby, *Social Amnesia: A Critique of Contemporary Psychology from Adler to Laing* (Boston: Beacon Press, 1975); and Diane Waldman, "Horror and Domesticity: The Modern Gothic Romance Film of the 1940s" (Ph.D. dissertation, University of Wisconsin, Madison, 1981). See also Russell Jacoby, *The Repression of Psychoanalysis: Otto Fenichel and the Political Freudians* (New York: Basic Books, 1983).

9. *A Psychiatric Glossary*, 5th ed., American Psychiatric Association (Boston: Little, Brown, 1980), p. 2.

10. Ellen Herman, "The Impact of Postwar Psychology on the Emergence and Growth of Feminism" (paper presented at the Sixteenth National Conference of the Association of Women in Psychology, March 9, 1991, Hartford, Conn.).

11. In a sense, I am proposing to read the *history* of postwar American psychiatry with the same attention to the gaps and fissures in the institution's discursive practices that European and Continentally influenced feminist theorists have paid to the gaps and fissures of psychoanalytic *theory*. For examples of books that examine closely the relationship between psychoanalysis and feminism, see Jacqueline Rose's *Sexuality in the Field of Vision* (London: Verso, 1986); *Feminism and Psychoanalysis*, ed. Richard Feldstein and Judith Roof (Ithaca, N.Y.: Cornell University Press, 1989); or *Between Feminism and Psychoanalysis*, ed. Teresa Brennan (New York: Routledge, 1989).

12. I am relying here on the excellent summary of the term "resistance" provided by J. LaPlanche and J.-B. Pontalis in *The Language of Psychoanalysis*, trans. Donald Nicholson-Smith (New York and London: Norton, 1973), pp. 394-96.

13. Sigmund Freud, "The Interpretation of Dreams" (1900), in *The Standard Edition of the Complete Psychological Works of Sigmund Freud*, ed. and trans. James Strachey (London: Hogarth Press, 1953-74), vol. 5, p. 517.

14. LaPlanche and Pontalis, *Language of Psychoanalysis*, p. 395.

15. John Clarke, Stuart Hall, Tony Jefferson, and Brian Roberts, "Subcultures, Cultures and Class," *Resistance through Ritual: Youth Subcultures in Post-War Britain*, ed. Stuart Hall and Tony Jefferson (London: Hutchinson, 1976), p. 47. First published in 1975 as *Working Papers in Cultural Studies*.

16. John Clarke, "Style," in *Resistance through Ritual*, ed. Hall and Jefferson, p. 178.

17. Laura Mulvey, "Visual Pleasure and Narrative Cinema," *Screen* 16, no. 3 (Autumn 1975): 57-68; also reprinted in *Feminism and Film Theory*, ed. Constance Penley (New York: Routledge, 1988).

18. See, for example, Waldman, "Horror and Domesticity"; *Home Is Where the Heart Is: Studies in Melodrama and the Woman's Film*, ed. Christine Gledhill (London: British Film Institute, 1987); Mary Ann Doane, *The Desire to Desire: The Woman's Film of the 40's* (Bloomington: Indiana University Press, 1987); and Doane, *Femmes Fatales: Feminism, Film Theory, Psychoanalysis* (New York and London: Routledge, 1991).

19. *Camera Obscura* 20-21 (1989), "The Spectatrix," ed. Janet Bergstrom and Mary Ann Doane.

20. Linda Williams's article, " 'Something Else Besides a Mother': *Stella Dallas* and the Maternal Melodrama," *Cinema Journal* 24, no. 1 (Fall 1984): 2-27, served as a touchstone for this debate, argued in issues of *Cinema Journal* subsequent to the publication of the Williams piece. For more recent reflections on the question, see *Camera Obscura* 20-21 (1989).

21. See also Diane Waldman, "Theory and the Gendered Spectator: The Female or the Feminist Reader?" *Camera Obscura* 18 (1989): 80-94; and Tania Modleski, "Some Functions of Feminist Criticism, or the Scandal of the Mute Body," *October* 49 (Summer 1989): 3-24.

22. Stephen Heath, "Film and System: Terms of Analysis, Part I," *Screen* 16, no. 1 (Spring 1975): 7-77, and "Part II," *Screen* 16, no. 2 (Summer 1975): 91-113.

23. Dana Polan, *Power and Paranoia: History, Narrative and the American Cinema, 1940-1950* (New York: Columbia University Press, 1986).

24. Foucault, *Archaeology of Knowledge*, p. 33.

25. Krin Gabbard and Glen O. Gabbard, *Psychiatry and the Cinema* (Chicago and London: University of Chicago Press, 1987).

26. Films that have psychological themes but that do not fit into the specific problematic of psychiatry and women being studied here include numerous films in which psychiatrists, psychoanalysts, psychotherapists, or psychologists appear in bit parts (*Bringing Up Baby* [1938], *That Uncertain Feeling* [1941]). One also finds (1) films in which a general practitioner performs a similar function to that of the specialist (*Johnny Belinda* [1948], *All That Heaven Allows* [1955], *Beyond the Forest* [1949]); (2) films in which a hypnotist performs the psychiatrist's function (*The Pirate* [1948], *Black Magic* [1949]); (3) films centering on female neurosis but not on the curative process per se (*Guest in the House* [1944], *Don't Bother to Knock* [1952], *The Long Hot Summer* [1958]); (4) amnesia films that do not involve psychiatric treatment (*Her Panelled Door* [1951], *Love Letters* [1945]); and (5) films set not in mental institutions or hospitals but in institutions where the deviant behavior depicted is close to that which mental illness might engender (*So Young, So Bad* [1950]) (see Filmography B).

But perhaps the most significant category of psychiatric films eliminated from this study are those pertaining to male neurosis, psychosis, or psychopathology (see Filmography C). Under this rubric are found (1) films centering on male neurosis (*Fear Strikes Out* [1957]); (2) films portraying male mental illness in a wartime or military setting (*Captain Newman, M.D.* [1963], *The High Wall* [1947], *Home of the Brave* [1949]); (3) that prolific subcategory of films dealing with the actions of a psychopathic killer clearly identified as deranged (*Phantom of the Rue Morgue* [1954], *The Dark Past* [1948], *Specter of the Rose* [1946], *The Couch* [1962]); and (4) films depicting psychosurgery on male subjects, usually for international political ends (*Crisis* [1950], *Man in the Dark* [1953]). A survey of the corpus shows that films depicting male instead of female madness are more apt to ascribe the origins of madness to precipitating events and factors outside individual psychical and familial structure—war trauma, alcoholism, and drug abuse, for example. The etiology of female madness is described differently, as we shall see.

27. See, for example, Lawrence Kubie, "Psychiatry and the Films," *Hollywood Quarterly* (Jan. 1947): 113-17; and Franklin Fearing, "The Screen Discovers Psychiatry," *Hollywood Quarterly* (Jan. 1947): 154-58.

28. Mark Poster, "The Future According to Foucault: *The Archaeology of Knowledge* and Intellectual History," chap. 5 in *Modern European Intellectual History: Reappraisals and New Perspectives*, ed. Dominick LaCapra and Steven L. Kaplan (Ithaca, N.Y., and London: Cornell University Press, 1982), p. 148.

29. Fearing (psychologist), "Screen Discovers Psychiatry"; and Keith Sward (clinical psychologist), "Boy and Girl Meet Neurosis," *Screen Writer* (Sept. 1948): 8-26.

30. Manny Farber, "Film," *Nation* 169 (July 9, 1949): 45-46.

31. Fearing, "Screen Discovers Psychiatry," p. 157.

32. Marc Vernet, "Freud: effets speciaux—Mise en scène: U.S.A.," *Communications* 23 (1975): 223–34.

33. Polan, *Power and Paranoia*, pp. 162-64.

34. Mary Ann Doane, "Clinical Eyes: The Medical Discourse," chap. 2 in *The Desire to Desire* (Bloomington: Indiana University Press, 1987), p. 46; Waldman, "Horror and Domesticity"; and Diane Waldman, " 'At Last I Can Tell It to Someone!': Feminine Point of View and Subjectivity in the Gothic Romance Film of the 40s," *Cinema Journal* 23, no. 2 (Winter 1984): 29-40.

35. Polan, *Power and Paranoia*, p. 164.
36. Waldman, "Horror and Domesticity," p. 5.
37. Doane, "Clinical Eyes," p. 68.
38. Polan, *Power and Paranoia*, p. 178.
39. That the ideological import of psychiatric films on women is undecidable outside of its wider cultural context is illustrated by the reversals of emphasis in various readings of the same films. For example, in Mary Ann Doane's doctoral dissertation ("The Dialogical Text: Filmic Irony and the Spectator" [University of Iowa, 1979]) she employs *Spellbound* precisely to illustrate the operations of textual irony. Although she indicates that psychoanalysis in *Spellbound* (and *Marnie*) "provides the grammar which generates the narratives of the two films," psychoanalysis is also "subjected to an ironical reading." In these films, "The activity at the level of the enunciation (which we have specified as a 'reading')," writes Doane, "manifests itself as a resistance to the material and the logic of the story presented." Later, in "Clinical Eyes: The Medical Discourse" (1987), Doane grouped *Spellbound* with other films of the medical gaze, which she sees as the "most fully recuperated form of the woman's film." In both instances of reading *Spellbound*, Doane is sensitive to textual contradictions or "resistances," but she weights their significance differently; initially emphasizing textual irony and later emphasizing recuperation.

The solution is not to decide finally on one "preferred reading." Rather, it would seem to me productive to take further the filmic contradictions themselves, to take them into the light of cultural context, where they may be discussed in relation to the wider cultural contradictions of which they are the cinematic transposition.
40. Ad published in *American Journal of Psychiatry* 109, no. 2 (Aug. 1952).

1. Psychiatry after World War II: The Stake in Women

1. See the following histories for detailed accounts of the economic and social problems of the era: Mary P. Ryan, *Womanhood in America: From Colonial Times to the Present* (1975), 2nd edition (New York: New Viewpoints, 1979); Lois Banner, *Women in Modern America: A Brief History* (New York: Harcourt Brace Jovanovich, 1974); William Chafe, *The American Woman: Her Changing Social, Economic, and Political Roles, 1920-1970* (New York: Oxford University Press, 1972); Susan M. Hartmann, *The Home Front and Beyond: American Women in the 1940s* (Boston: Twayne, 1982); Marty Jezer, *The Dark Ages: Life in the U.S., 1945-1960* (Boston: South End Press, 1982); Douglas T. Miller and Marion Nowak, *The Fifties: The Way We Really Were* (New York: Doubleday, 1977); Nancy Woloch, *Women and the American Experience* (New York: Knopf, 1984); Howard Zinn, *Postwar America: 1945-1971* (Indianapolis: Bobbs-Merrill, 1973).

As social historian Marty Jezer argues (p. 4), the much-vaunted economic prosperity was in fact predicated on the perceived necessity for military readiness, and military spending and economic imperialism were in turn supported by Cold War propaganda that whipped up fears of Soviet Communist infiltration. From the perspective of this global context, the United States was, according to Howard Zinn, a "corporate-controlled juggernaut," with disastrous ramifications for the noncorporate, nonsuburban, nonmale, nonwhite, most populous sectors of the population.

Misogyny and antifeminism were defined as central social problems of the era by historians Ryan, Chafe, and Banner, among others who revealed the repressive sex discrimination disguised by the rhetoric of optimism. The labor force was a prime arena of hidden and not-so-hidden sex discrimination. In *The American Woman*, William Chafe provides a new historical analysis of women in the labor force during the years when received history and its early feminist critique had it that women were locked in at home up to their elbows in soap suds. Chafe argues that there may have been widespread firing of women *immediately* after the war, but that by 1946 there were one million *more* women in factories than there had been in 1940 (Chafe, *American Woman*, p. 181; see also Woloch, *Women and the American Experience*, app. 6). But Chafe points to what he calls a "paradox" or what has also been called the "work myth." While unprecedented numbers of women were joining the work force, only minimal progress was made in the areas of greatest concern to women's rights advocates—employment in the professions, child-care centers, and a uniform wage scale. According to Chafe, "A job for a wife over thirty-five became normal—at least by a statistical standard—but most Americans continued to subscribe to the belief that women were (and should remain) primarily homemakers" (p. 189). That women at work for pay outside their homes were overlooked by the rhetoric of optimism allowed the perpetuation of economic and social disadvantages. An ideology defining the optimal female roles as exclusively wife and mother justified an economic need, in this case the need for a casual work force.

Michael Zuckerman's "Dr. Spock: The Confidence Man," in *The Family in History*, ed. Charles E. Rosenberg (Denver: University of Denver Press, 1975), pp. 171-207, illuminates yet another chink in the logic of prescribed female roles in noting the inconsistencies of Dr. Benjamin Spock's *Baby and Child Care*. On one hand, Spock urges mothers to trust their instincts, implying that women possess natural internal directives for child-rearing. On the other hand, Spock details with mind-boggling rigor the day-to-day necessities of child management. According to Zuckerman, this internally contradictory view—that women are "naturally" bred for child-rearing above all else and yet in need of professional regulation—is basic to the fifties. As Zuckerman points out, Spock's obsession with both confidence and management is less paradoxical in light of the requirement of a labor force capable of easy confidence and camaraderie along with subordination to company values.

2. Betty Friedan, in *The Feminine Mystique* (1963; New York: Dell, 1974), points out that sociopolitical problems, while acknowledged in some quarters, were simultaneously being omitted from mainstream outlets directed toward women. Mass-circulation magazines such as *Ladies' Home Journal* and *McCall's* had carried hundreds of articles on political topics in the 1930s and 1940s ("The First Inside Story of American Diplomatic Relations Preceding Declared War" and "Can the U.S. Have Peace after This War?" by Walter Lippmann, for example). But by the 1950s they "printed virtually no articles except those that serviced women as housewives, or described women as housewives, or permitted a purely female identification" (p. 45). Here, women and social problems were designated separate spheres and they received separate treatment. What is missing is the *joint consideration* of social problems and "women's issues." In this connection, see Chuck Kleinhans's discussion of the filmic adoption of the separation of public and private spheres that Marx described as necessary under capitalist social arrangement, in "Notes on Melodrama and the Family under Capitalism," *Film Reader* 3 (Feb. 1978): 40-47.

3. Banner, *Women in Modern America*, p. 212.

4. The terrain of psychiatric history has been carved up in numerous ways, each with its own methodology and concomitant object of study. For example, some historians have traced the history of psychiatry or branches of psychiatry *as a profession* (Oberndorf, Fine, Rogow; see below for full citations), and in an oft-related approach, the history of psychiatry has been written through the biographies of its most notable practitioners (Alexander et al., *Psychoanalytic Pioneers*). Of obvious importance is the history of psychiatric ideas, research, and treatment. Indicative of such approaches, which often include "psychotherapy" in their titles, are Alexander (*History of Psychiatry*), Ehrenwald, Bergmann and Hartman, Walker, and Hendrick. The history of psychiatry as

an institution centers on the history of the mental institution as a wider metaphor for the authoritative control of patients in general (Foucault, Castel et al.). There are also those sociological or epidemiological studies concerned with actual patients or clients or with American society as a patient (Veroff et al., Albert Deutsch, Pugh and MacMahon). Finally, certain works pursue the history of psychiatry as social history in the historiographical sense of the term (Starr, Grob, Hale, Quen). Mora and Brand take a self-reflexive approach, which they see as essential to the understanding of the institutionalization of psychiatry.

In spite of the vastness and breadth of this literature, sorely underrepresented within it is any substantive consideration of psychiatry in relation to the role of women and the study of femininity.

Franz Alexander, Samuel Eisenstein, and Martin Grotjahn, *Psychoanalytic Pioneers* (New York and London: Basic Books, 1966); Franz Alexander, M.D., and Sheldon T. Selesnick, M.D., *The History of Psychiatry: An Evaluation of Psychiatric Thought and Practice from Prehistoric Times to the Present* (New York: Harper and Row, 1966); Martin S. Bergmann and Frank R. Hartmann, *The Evolution of Psychoanalytic Technique* (New York: Basic Books, 1976); Robert Castel, Franceoise Castel, and Anne Lovell, *The Psychiatric Society*, trans. Arthur Goldhammer (1979; New York: Columbia University Press, 1982); Albert Deutsch, *The Mentally Ill in America: A History of Their Care and Treatment from Colonial Times*, 2nd ed., revised and enlarged (1937; New York: Columbia University Press, 1949); Jan Ehrenwald, M.D., ed., *The History of Psychotherapy: From Healing Magic to Encounter* (New York: Aronson, 1976); Reuben Fine, *A History of Psychoanalysis* (New York: Columbia University Press, 1979); Michel Foucault, *The Birth of a Clinic: An Archaeology of Medical Perception*, trans. A. M. Sheridan Smith (1963; New York: Vintage Books, 1973); Gerald N. Grob, *Mental Illness and American Society, 1875-1940* (Princeton, N.J.: Princeton University Press, 1983); Nathan Hale, *Freud and the Americans: The Beginnings of Psychoanalysis in the U.S., 1876-1917* (New York: Oxford University Press, 1971); Ives Hendrick, M.D., *Facts and Theories of Psychoanalysis*, 2nd ed., revised and enlarged (1934; 1939; reprint, New York: Knopf, 1947); George Mora, M.D., and Jeanne L. Brand, eds., *Psychiatry and Its History: Methodological Problems in Research* (Springfield, Ill.: Thomas, 1970); Clarence Oberndorf, *A History of Psychoanalysis in America* (New York: Harper and Row, 1953); Thomas F. Pugh, M.D., and Brian MacMahon, M.D., *Epidemiologic Findings in United States Mental Hospital Data* (Boston: Little, Brown, 1962); Jacques M. Quen, M.D., and Eric T. Carlson, M.D., eds., *American Psychoanalysis: Origins and Development: The Adolf Meyer Seminars* (New York: Brunner/Mazel, 1978); Arnold Rogow, *The Psychiatrists* (New York: Putnam, 1970); Paul Starr, *The Social Transformation of American Medicine* (New York: Basic Books, 1982); Joseph Veroff, Richard A. Kulka, and Elizabeth Douvan, *Mental Health in America: Patterns of Help-seeking from 1957-1976* (New York: Basic Books, 1981); and Nigel Walker, *A Short History of Psychotherapy in Theory and Practice* (London: Routledge and Kegan Paul, 1957).

5. According to Paul Starr, *Social Transformation*, p. 335, the number of people working in medicine grew from 1.2 million to 3.9 million between 1950 and 1970, and expenditures on health care across the nation grew from $12.7 billion to $71.6 billion. At the same time, penicillin and the broad-spectrum antibiotics, such as tetracycline and sulfa drugs, and the polio vaccine were developed and hailed as "wonder drugs."

6. Starr, *Social Transformation*, p. 337.

7. See, for example, Oberndorf, *History of Psychoanalysis in America*, p. 208; and Starr, *Social Transformation*, pp. 337-47. Also see the following sources: Ernest Havemann, *The Age of Psychology* (New York: Simon and Schuster, 1957), p. 16; Edward A. Strecker, M.D., Sc.D., Litt.D., LL.D., *Their Mothers' Sons: The Psychiatrist Examines*

an American Problem (New York: Lippincott, 1947), chap. 1; and *International Encyclopedia of Psychiatry, Psychology, Psychoanalysis and Neurology*, ed. Benjamin B. Wolman (New York: Produced for Aesculapius Publishers by Van Nostrand Reinhold, 1977), s.v. "shellshock."

8. Starr, *Social Transformation*, p. 344.

9. William Menninger, *Psychiatry in a Troubled World: Yesterday's War and Today's Challenge* (New York: Macmillan, 1948), p. vii and "Part I: In War," pp. 3-42.

10. Starr, *Social Transformation*, p. 345.

11. Fine, *History of Psychoanalysis*, p. 148.

12. Starr, *Social Transformation*, p. 345.

13. Psychiatry is a branch of medicine dealing with mental and emotional illness; it is classified, like pediatrics or internal medicine, as a specialty with specific residency requirements. Psychoanalysis is a theory and therapeutic methodology derived from the work of Sigmund Freud.

14. Robert P. Knight, M.D., "The Present Status of Organized Psychoanalysis in the United States," *Journal of the American Psychoanalytic Association* 1, no. 2 (April 1953): 197-221; Oberndorf, *History of Psychoanalysis in America*; and Fine, *History of Psychoanalysis*. This claim is generally acknowledged, but for a specific example, see Veroff, Kulka, and Douvan, *Mental Health in America*, p. 10.

15. Knight, "Present Status," p. 206.

16. Sanford Gifford, "History of Psychoanalysis in the United States," in *International Encyclopedia*, p. 380; and Knight, "Present Status," p. 208.

17. The case of Los Angeles is particularly significant for this study, since it was there that most of the films under discussion were planned and executed. The fact that Los Angeles had the eighth highest ratio in the United States of psychoanalysts and analytic students to members of the total population (Knight, "Present Status," p. 208) may have contributed to the availability for film scripts of psychological subject matter. And the fact that the inception of organized psychoanalysis occurred significantly later in Los Angeles than on the East Coast, where psychoanalytic societies had existed since the early 1930s, meant that the rise of psychoanalysis in Los Angeles coincided with rather than prefigured Hollywood's production of a profusion of films about the subject.

18. Gifford, *History of Psychoanalysis in the United States*, p. 379.

19. Russell Jacoby, *The Repression of Psychoanalysis: Otto Fenichel and the Political Freudians* (New York: Basic Books, 1983); and Sigmund Freud, "The Question of Lay Analysis" (1926), in *The Standard Edition of the Complete Psychological Works of Sigmund Freud*, ed. and trans. James Strachey (London: Hogarth Press, 1953-74), vol. 20, pp. 177-250.

20. Knight, "Present Status," p. 216.

21. Eugene Pumpian-Mindlon, "Psychoanalysis," in *Encyclopedia of Mental Health*, ed. Albert Deutsch (New York: Watts, 1963), p. 1599.

22. Oberndorf, *History of Psychoanalysis in America*, p. 4.

23. S. Goodman, ed., *Psychoanalytic Education and Research* (New York: International Universities Press, 1977), p. 347; and Oberndorf, *History of Psychoanalysis in America*, p. 164.

24. H. Strassman et al., "The Impact of Psychiatric Residency on Choice of Analytic Training," originally published in *Journal of the American Psychoanalytic Association* 24 (1976): 347-55; quoted in Fine, *History of Psychoanalysis*, p. 11. The entry by Pumpian-Mindlon under "psychoanalysis" in the *Encyclopedia of Mental Health* asserts, "Psychiatry is a branch of medicine that deals with mental and emotional illness. Psychoanalytic concepts have profoundly affected all areas of psychiatry—indeed they have affected medicine as a whole" (p. 159).

25. Gifford, "History of Psychoanalysis in the United States," p. 380.

26. Pumpian-Mindlon, "Psychoanalysis," *Encyclopedia of Mental Health*, p. 1585.

27. This argument of Hale's is also recapped by Diane Waldman in "Horror and Domesticity: The Modern Gothic Romance Film of the 1940s" (Ph.D. dissertation, University of Wisconsin, Madison, 1981).

28. Diane Waldman, "Horror and Domesticity," sketches the early history of popular treatment of psychoanalysis in literature and magazines in preparation for her discussion of a film that reworks psychoanalytic material (*Secret beyond the Door*). Drawing on the work of Nathan Hale, Waldman argues that the years between 1908 and 1918 saw the first real evidence of the popularization of psychoanalysis. By 1915, the mass-circulation magazines were publishing fictional stories featuring psychoanalysis. *Mrs. Marden's Ordeal*, the first American psychoanalytic novel, was published in 1917. Interest increased after World War I to the point where historian William Leuchtenberg argued that "psychology became a national mania" (Waldman, p. 230).

David Sievers, author of *Freud on Broadway: A History of Psychoanalysis and the American Drama* (New York: Hermitage House, 1955), drew the pattern of diffusion of psychoanalytic concepts in American theater in a similar fashion. *The Fatted Calf* (1912), by Arthur Hopkins, about a mother's love and fear for her child, was the first American theatrical psychoanalytic effort. The 1920s in American drama deserved to be called "The Psychological Era," argues Sievers (p. 65). The trend continued in the 1930s as more and more plays with psychological themes were produced.

29. Havemann, *Age of Psychology*.

30. Lucy Freeman, *Fight against Fears* (New York: Pocket Books, 1952); Robert Lindner, *The Fifty-Minute Hour* (1954; New York: Dell, 1986); Havemann, *Age of Psychology*, pp. 8-9.

31. Hendrik M. Ruitenbeek, *Freud and America* (New York: Macmillan, 1966), and *Psychoanalysis and the Social Sciences* (New York: Dutton, 1962); and Richard LaPiere, *The Freudian Ethic: An Analysis of the Subversion of American Character* (New York: Duell, Sloan, and Pearce, 1959).

32. Friedan, "The Sexual Sell," chap. 9 in *Feminine Mystique*, p. 204. Here Friedan quotes advertisers discussing how to get housewives to consume more products. Also see Marty Jezer's discussion of Dichter (Jezer, *Dark Ages*, pp. 124-29).

33. Two examples are Ferdinand Lundberg and Marynia F. Farnham, M.D., *Modern Woman: The Lost Sex* (New York: Harper Brothers, 1947); and Strecker, *Their Mothers' Sons*.

34. Havemann, *Age of Psychology*, front cover.

35. Ibid., pp. 6-8.

36. In identifying certain psychiatric discursive practices with essentialist ideas about women, I am speaking at the level of institutionalized practices based on shared social values. Not every individual psychiatrist steered the women in his or her practice away from outside jobs. I assume that some did, whether consciously or unconsciously, and some did not. Such important differences in therapeutic technique will be discussed in the following chapter.

37. Fine, for example, mentions the "flood of publications" on the mother-child relationship that followed the discovery of neuropsychiatric disabilities of draftees (*History of Psychoanalysis*, p. 152), yet, typically, he doesn't pose this relationship as a historical factor in the growth of psychoanalysis.

38. Menninger, *Psychiatry in a Troubled World*, pp. 393-94.

39. The word "essentialism" has now gained currency in theoretical work in the humanities. It is used to describe the notion that "sexual difference has its roots in the

biological and thus that anything produced by women will exhibit the mark of this 'essence.' " Editorial, *Camera Obscura* 11 (1983), p. 4.

40. Lundberg and Farnham, *Modern Woman*. Friedan mentions that this work was paraphrased "ad nauseam in magazines and marriage courses" (*Feminine Mystique*, p. 111). The book is also mentioned by recent historians Banner (*Women in Modern America*, p. 213), Chafe (*American Woman*, pp. 202-6), and Woloch (*Women and the American Experience*, p. 474). Marynia Farnham even appears in the film *Rosie the Riveter* (Connie Field, 1980) in a newsreel presented as an example of World War II propaganda against the working woman.

41. Strecker, *Their Mothers' Sons*.

42. Ibid., pp. 219-20. In fact, Farnham and Lundberg and Strecker complain about overprotective mothers as well as working mothers. Their ideas contain, therefore, a certain element of contradiction: women are inadequate mothers because they are overly involved outside the home *and* also inadequate as mothers because they are overly involved with their children.

43. Lundberg and Farnham, *Modern Woman*, p. 71.

44. Ibid., chap. 7, "The Feminist Complex."

45. Philip Wylie, *Generation of Vipers* (New York: Rinehart, 1942).

46. See Lundberg and Farnham, *Modern Woman*, chap. 14, "Ways to a Happier End."

47. There were a few women psychiatrists, of which more later.

48. The idea that women greatly outnumbered men in therapy and mental institutions might also be derived from *Women and Madness* by Phyllis Chesler (Garden City, N.Y.: Doubleday, 1972). Chesler uses the disproportion of institutionalized women to men to argue that incarceration of women stemmed from a misogynist and punitive social impetus in mental health where independent or assertive women were treated as mentally ill. Chesler's masterly use of statistical research (she combines healthy skepticism with great interpretive facility) and her original analyses make for a thoroughly convincing argument that has taken on the status of a feminist milestone. But in order to generalize her argument, Chesler underemphasizes the fact that her statistics are actually drawn mostly from the period extending from the early 1960s to the time of her book's publication in 1972. Thus, she is for the most part writing about a later period than the one delineated in my own study, a period when, if Chesler's statistics are to be believed, women really were more often subject to psychiatric intervention than men.

Chesler argued that women's decreased presence in the home and increased visibility in society at large were responsible for the increase in the number of women seeking psychiatric help in the early 1960s: "Traditionally, most women performed both rites of madness and childbirth more invisibly—at home—where, despite their tears and hostility, they were still needed. While women live longer than men, there is less and less use and literally no place for them in the only place they 'belong'—within the family" (p. 33). Assuming Chesler is correct that women were being displaced from the home, one might say that the period of which she is writing, the late 1960s, or the *end* of the period I am considering, represents the final phase of the "progress" from the "madwoman in the attic" (to borrow from Sandra Gilbert and Susan Gubar's *The Madwoman in the Attic: The Woman Writer and the Nineteenth-Century Literary Imagination* [New Haven, Conn.: Yale University Press, 1978]) to the madwoman in the asylum, a phase accompanied by a shift in the gender of the largest group of psychiatric patients from male to female.

49. Lawrence S. Kubie, "A Pilot Study of Psychoanalytic Practice in the United States: With Suggestions for Future Studies," *Psychiatry* 113 (1950): 227-45.

50. Ibid., pp. 231-32.

51. Nathaniel H. Siegel, "Characteristics of Patients in Psychoanalysis (A Study of Patients of Members of the American Psychoanalytic Association)," *Journal of Nervous and Mental Disease* 135 (1962): 155-58.

52. If the patients who were themselves psychiatrist candidates in training analysis (the majority of whom were men) were discounted, women probably would outnumber men as patients. Male physicians might indeed be discounted because they did not purport to be seeking psychoanalysis because of illness, but rather in preparation for practice. Yet, why should they be discounted? They were, after all, a significant patient group. I suspect that, as Freud has noted, many are drawn to the field of helping others because of their own neuroses. It is interesting that this group of patients was rarely portrayed in popular accounts. Doing so would perhaps have undermined the crucial authority of the occupation.

53. H. Aronson and Walter Weintraub, M.D., "A Survey of Patients in Classical Psychoanalysis: Some Vital Statistics," *Journal of Nervous and Mental Disease* 146, no. 2 (1968): 91-97.

54. A report by D. A. Hamburg, *Report of the Ad Hoc Committee on Data* (New York: American Psychoanalytic Association, 1967), summarized data including data collected by the Central Fact-Gathering Committee of the APA established in 1952 and disbanded in 1957 due to "methodological difficulties." Hamburg explained the discrepancy between studies by noting that candidates in training, mostly male, tend to be analyzed by more experienced analysts, of which a higher proportion were represented in Aronson and Weintraub's study.

55. These studies are more prevalent, undoubtedly because of the funding structure of mental institutions (government agencies have to know where their money is going, and other government bodies get grants to study agencies of the first sort) and because of the more public, pragmatic, and scientific nature of psychiatry as a branch of medicine.

56. Pugh and MacMahon, *Epidemiologic Findings*.

57. Veroff, Kulka, and Douvan, *Mental Health in America*. This book is particularly rich in interpreted information on demographic differences in help-seeking. I am aware of how little of the information contained therein I am able to touch upon here.

58. Ibid. This point is argued throughout the book, but see, in particular, p. 159.

59. Ibid., p. 120.

60. Pugh and MacMahon, *Epidemiologic Findings*, p. 52.

61. Hannah Lerman, *A Mote in Freud's Eye: From Psychoanalysis to the Psychology of Women* (New York: Springer, 1986), p. 256. Juliet Mitchell ("Introduction I," in *Feminine Sexuality: Jacques Lacan and the* école freudienne, ed. Juliet Mitchell and Jacqueline Rose, trans. Jacqueline Rose [London: Macmillan, 1982]) also posits sort of a latency period for work on feminine psychosexuality. However, Mitchell doesn't argue that work on feminine sexuality was *absent* in this period, but that the work which was being done merely rehashed earlier debates and is therefore unimportant: "By 1935 the positions have clarified and the terms of the discussion on sexual differences do not change importantly, though the content that goes to fill out the argument does so" (p. 15).

62. Deutsch had completed vols. 1 and 2 of *The Psychology of Women* by 1945 (New York: Grune and Stratton, 1944, 1945), after which she turned to other areas, and Lerman speculates that Deutsch considered the volumes definitive. Karen Horney, M.D., *Feminine Psychology*, ed. Harold Kelman, M.D. (New York: Norton, 1967), contains articles written between 1922 and 1936.

63. See Nancy Chodorow's symposium paper, "History and Life Histories of Early Women Psychoanalysts," delivered at "In Symposium: Women and Psychoanalysis: Historical and Clinical Perspectives," Berkeley, Calif., March 16-17, 1984. Chodorow's ar-

ticle is also anthologized in *Women Physicians in Leadership Roles*, ed. Leah J. Dickstein and Carol C. Nadelson (Issues in Psychiatry Series of the American Psychiatric Association, 1986).

64. See, for example, Judith Kestenberg, "Vicissitudes of Female Sexuality," *Journal of the American Psychoanalytic Association* 4, no. 3 (July 1956): 453-76, and "On the Development of Maternal Feelings in Early Childhood: Observations and Reflections," *Psychoanalytic Study of the Child* 11 (1956): 257-91; and Therese Benedek, *Studies in Psychosomatic Medicine: Psychosexual Functions in Women* (New York: Ronald Press, 1952).

Lerman mentions only the later work of Benedek and Kestenberg in the context of their debate with Mary Jane Sherfey over the vaginal orgasm. Furthermore, Lerman explains away Marie Bonaparte's work as a 1950s contribution, saying that it belongs "in spirit" to the debate of the twenties and thirties. My own view is that these books testify to the ongoing nature of this debate. Finally, Nancy Chodorow herself, in a conversation of March 1986, disagreed with Lerman's thesis as I explained it, saying that, indeed, much work was done on feminine sexuality during this era.

Although I disagree with Lerman on this issue, I would like to point out that her book is a notable scholarly contribution. I would also like to express my gratitude for her encouragement, suggestions, and time.

65. Marie Bonaparte, *Female Sexuality* (New York: International Universities Press, 1953).

66. See, for example, G. Bibring, "Some Considerations of the Psychological Processes in Pregnancy," *Psychoanalytic Study of the Child* 14 (1959), and "A Study of the Psychological Processes in Pregnancy and the Earliest Mother-Child Relationship," *Psychoanalytic Study of the Child* 16 (1961); Marcel Heiman, "Sexual Response in Women," *Journal of the American Psychoanalytic Association* 2, no. 2 (April 1963); and S. Keiser, "Psychopathology of Orgasm," *Psychoanalytic Quarterly* 16 (1947).

67. Clara Thompson, "The Role of Women in This Culture," *Psychiatry* 4 (1941): 1-8; "Cultural Pressures in the Psychology of Women," *Psychiatry* 5 (1942): 331-39; "Penis Envy in Women," *Psychiatry* 6 (1943): 123-25; "Some Effects of the Derogatory Attitude toward Female Sexuality," *Psychiatry* 13 (1950): 349-54; and "Cultural Complications in the Sexual Life of Women," in *Symposium on Feminine Psychology* (New York: New York Medical College, 1950), p. 54.

68. Lerman, *Mote in Freud's Eye*, p. 258.

69. Susan Quinn, *A Mind of Her Own: The Life of Karen Horney*, chaps. 16 and 17 (New York: Basic Books, 1987).

70. Fine, *History of Psychoanalysis*, p. 152.

71. Helene Deutsch, *The Psychology of Women*.

72. Sigmund Freud, "Femininity" (1933), in *The Standard Edition of the Complete Psychological Works of Sigmund Freud*, ed. James Strachey (London: Hogarth Press, 1953-74), vol. 22, pp. 112-33. There is a very revealing methodological problem encountered by psychoanalytic theory. It too results from the fact that the child's first object is female (the mother) whether the child is a boy or a girl. The boy takes his mother as a sexualized love object, becomes the rival of his father, and through the castration complex learns to identify with his father to avoid competing with him. He identifies with his father with regard to his father's sexual attachment to another person — the mother — and assumes that someday he will find a woman like her for his own. In the case of the girl, however, she must reject her love for the mother and wish for the father's child. In other words, she fantasizes herself not only as the sexual partner of the father, but as *the mother* of his child. The girl's sexuality is spoken of in relation to the maternal figure and also *as* a neophyte mother. I am not attempting to make Chodorow's argument that the

girl's psychical structure is ordered by a merging-separation function where she desires the mother and identifies with the mother (*The Reproduction of Mothering: Psychoanalysis and the Sociology of Gender* [Berkeley: University of California Press, 1978]). What I am trying to point to is a resulting theoretical determinism in which to talk about female sexuality is to talk about her ultimate motherhood, and motherhood not as a *choice*, as fatherhood seems to be for the boy, but as the *realization of sexual development*.

Compare this conflation vis-à-vis women with an interesting paper by Heinz Lichtenstein, M.D. ("Identity and Sexuality: A Study of Their Interrelationship in Man," *Journal of the American Psychoanalytic Association* 9, no. 2 [April 1961]), in which, dealing with the male, he carefully separates the sexual function from the procreative function.

73. Michel Foucault, *The Archaeology of Knowledge and the Discourse on Language*, trans. A. M. Sheridan Smith (New York: Pantheon Books, 1972), pp. 149, 151-52.

74. David Reisman, Nathan Glazer, and Reuel Denny, *The Lonely Crowd* (New Haven, Conn.: Yale University Press, 1950); William H. Whyte, *The Organization Man* (New York: Simon and Schuster, 1956); C. Wright Mills, *The Power Elite* (New York: Oxford University Press, 1956); and Robert Dahl, *A Preface to Democratic Theory* (Chicago: University of Chicago Press, 1956).

75. Ruth Herschberger, *Adam's Rib* (New York: Pellegrini & Cudahy, 1948).

76. Monique Plaza, " 'Phallomorphic Power' and the Psychology of 'Woman': A Patriarchal Chain," in *Human Sexual Relations*, ed. Mike Brake (New York: Pantheon Books, 1982), pp. 323-60.

77. Walter Lippmann, "Stereotypes as Defense," chap. 7 in *Public Opinion* (1922; New York: Harcourt Press, 1957).

78. Simone de Beauvoir, *The Second Sex* (1949), trans. and ed. H. M. Parshley (New York: Vintage Books, 1974); first published in English by Knopf, 1952.

79. Chafe, *American Woman*, also notes this *Life* feature spread.

80. Friedan, *Feminine Mystique*, p. 35.

81. Elizabeth Bragdon, ed., *Women Today: Their Conflicts, Their Frustrations and Their Fulfillments* (Indianapolis: Bobbs-Merrill, 1953).

82. Ibid., p. 310.

83. See Chafe's (*American Woman*) summary of the work of these social scientists.

84. Mirra Komarovsky, "Cultural Contradictions and Sex Roles," *American Journal of Sociology* 52, no. 3 (Nov. 1946): 184-89.

85. Juliet Mitchell in *Psychoanalysis and Feminism: Freud, Reich, Laing and Women* (New York: Vintage Books, 1974); and Russell Jacoby in *Social Amnesia: A Critique of Contemporary Psychology from Adler to Laing* (Boston: Beacon Press, 1975) and *The Repression of Psychoanalysis: Otto Fenichel and the Political Freudians* are notable among those who have argued that the culturalism of those social scientists and psychoanalysts who emphasize the effects on an individual of structural social conficts over biologism is a misguided or "flat" culturalism that misses the point of what is radical about Freud's ideas: namely their generalizability and their instinctual and sexual depths. In the following chapter I will address this claim by giving close attention to aspects of theoretical American psychoanalysis. Here, it will have to suffice to say that however short the culturalists fell from radical Freudian theories of personality, their concrete look at the social roots of women's oppression evinced a political courage at a time when the watchword of the day was "anatomy is destiny."

86. Recall that in 1954, the Supreme Court reversed a constitutional amendment to rule that segregation of the public schools was unconstitutional, and, in an atmosphere of backlash in which the Ku Klux Klan reemerged, President Eisenhower sent the army to Arkansas to enforce a desegregation order. In 1961, President Kennedy was inaugu-

rated after having campaigned on a platform including a strong civil rights plank. There was a massive grass-roots movement behind civil rights legislation and governmental support. Rosa Parks, who in 1955 refused to give up her bus seat to a white man, inspired a black bus boycott that was almost 100 percent effective and that resulted, one year later, in the integration of the Montgomery, Alabama, bus system. The civil rights march on Washington (August 28, 1963) was attended by 200,000 people. Another march on Washington, this time the March on Washington to End the War in Vietnam (April 17, 1965), is evidence of another major protest that was articulated through mass activism. See Jezer, *Dark Ages*, pp. 296-303; Zinn, *Postwar America*; Allen J. Matsusow, *The Unravelling of America: A History of Liberalism in the 1960s* (New York: Harper and Row, 1984); Todd Gitlin, *The Whole World Is Watching: Mass Media in the Making and Unmaking of the New Left* (Berkeley: University of California Press, 1980); Sohnya Sahyers, Anders Stephanson, Stanley Aronowitz, and Fredric Jameson, eds., *The Sixties without Apology* (Minneapolis: University of Minnesota Press, 1985); and *The Twentieth Century: An Almanac* (New York: World Almanac Publications, 1985), p. 85.

87. Walter R. Gove and Jeannette F. Tudor, "Adult Sex Roles and Mental Illness," in *Changing Women in a Changing Society*, ed. Joan Huber (Chicago and London: University of Chicago Press, 1973), p. 53. Gove and Tudor cite a study by Dean Knudsen: "The Declining Status of Women: Popular Myths and the Failure of Functionalist Thought," *Social Forces* 48 (Dec. 1969).

88. Gifford, *History of Psychoanalysis in the United States*, p. 382. Gifford writes that a "sense of deceleration" in the forward motion of American psychoanalysis was evident from the early 1960s. Arnold Rogow (*Psychiatrists*) locates the period of rapid growth in American psychoanalysis between 1940 and 1960, and states that by 1964 a notable decline in applications for membership in the American Psychoanalytic Association was evident.

89. Gifford, *History of Psychoanalysis in the United States*.

90. This panel is reported on in the *Journal of the American Psychoanalytic Association* 9, no. 3 (1961): 571-84.

91. Alfred C. Kinsey, Wardell B. Pomeroy, Clyde E. Martin, Paul H. Gebhard, *Sexual Behavior in the Human Female* (1953; New York: Pocket Books, 1965), p. 582.

92. William H. Masters and V. E. Johnson, *Human Sexual Response* (Boston: Little, Brown, 1966).

93. Mary Jane Sherfey, "The Evolution and Nature of Female Sexuality in Relation to Psychoanalytic Theory," *Journal of the American Psychoanalytic Association* 14 (1966): 28-128.

94. Mary Jane Sherfey; quoted in Lerman, p. 264.

95. Given the propensity of American feminists to rely on Friedan's work when rejecting Freudian psychoanalysis, the actual critique of Freud presented by Friedan is surprisingly moderate. She argues that Freudian psychology itself was far less oppressive for women than the American practice of psychoanalytic therapy and the concomitant appropriation of the field by American social science functionalists, sex-directed educators, and popularizers.

96. Beauvoir, *Second Sex*; and Chesler, *Women and Madness*.

97. P. Susan Penfold and Gillian Walker, *Women and the Psychiatric Paradox* (Montreal and London: Eden Press, 1983).

98. Such feminist attacks on Freudian psychoanalysis are very common in the United States, but for a specific source of them see back issues of the journal *Signs*.

99. Seymour L. Halleck, M.D., *The Politics of Therapy* (New York: Science House, 1971). Also see Jay Haley, *Strategies of Psychotherapy* (New York: Grune and Stratton, 1963); and David Ingleby, ed., *Critical Psychiatry* (New York: Pantheon, 1980), as two

other sources of various ideas around the central notion that psychiatry could act as an oppressive social force.

100. Halleck, *Politics of Therapy*, p. 13.

101. Ibid., p. 238.

102. Jezer, *Dark Ages*, p. 232.

103. See, for example, Abraham Maslow (1962), *Toward a Psychology of Being* (Princeton, N.J.: Van Nostrand, 1968). Other proponents of the "sick society" thesis, such as Rousseau, Marx, and Veblen, and more recent writers such as Lawrence K. Frank, *Society as the Patient: Essays on Culture and Personality* (New Brunswick, N.J.: Rutgers University Press, 1948), had been speaking their ideas before Maslow's work attained currency, but I cite Maslow precisely because it was his work that represented the contemporary version of the thesis.

104. For a useful account of the relationship between humanistic psychology and "the social movements of the 1960s, especially the second wave of feminism," see Ellen Herman, "Being and Doing: Humanistic Psychology and the Spirit of the 1960s," in *Sights on the Sixties*, ed. Barbara Tischler (New Brunswick, N.J.: Rutgers University Press, forthcoming). However, a view of the move from First Force to Third Force psychology as offering an unqualified social critique must be at least partially questioned. The historical move was perhaps progressive to the extent that First Force Freudian psychoanalysis engaged in authoritarian tactics while denying that fact and to the extent that Third Force humanistic psychology provided a materialist social critique of a troubled society. But, to the extent that Third Force psychology lacks a complex model of psychic structure and thereby weakens the crucial notions of the unconscious and the sexual etiology of mental illness, its vision is quite limited. Mitchell also makes this argument in *Psychoanalysis and Feminism*, where she shows why feminism cannot afford to reject Freudian thought. Also see Jacoby, *Social Amnesia* and *Repression of Psychoanalysis*.

105. Maslow, *Psychology of Being*, p. 8; quoted in Herman, "Being and Doing."

2. Women and Psychiatric Technique

1. Stanley Joel Reiser, *Medicine and the Reign of Technology* (Cambridge: Cambridge University Press, 1978).

2. Interestingly, Reiser notes that a physician writing in 1899 concluded that medicine was "gradually relegating hearing to a lower intellectual plane than sight" (p. 68). I find this point compelling both in view of cinema's date of inception and its early prioritization of the visual, and in view of the current theoretical critique of the supposed primacy of the visual in sound cinema. See, for example, Stephen Heath, "Difference," *Screen* 19, no. 3 (Autumn 1978): 51-112.

3. I am drawing on the historical research of Elliot S. Valenstein, *Great and Desperate Cures: The Rise and Decline of Psychosurgery and Other Radical Treatments for Mental Illness* (New York: Basic Books, 1986), and that of Elaine Showalter, *The Female Malady: Women, Madness and English Culture, 1830-1980* (New York: Pantheon, 1985) for this discussion of psychosurgery.

4. Showalter, *Female Malady*, p. 209; Valenstein, *Great and Desperate Cures*, p. 322n.

5. Valenstein, *Great and Desperate Cures*, p. 252.

6. According to Charles C. Limburg ("A Survey of the Use of Psychosurgery [lobotomy] with Mental Patients," *Proceedings of the First Research Conference on Psychosurgery* [New York, Nov. 17 and 18, 1949], Public Health Service Publication 16 [1951]: 165-73), a 1949 survey of mental patients operated on in veterans' hospitals, state men-

tal hospitals, county and city hospitals, psychopathic hospitals, private mental hospitals, the psychiatric wards of general hospitals, and medical schools found that 3,310 patients were males and 3,775 were females.

If these numbers seem equal, a closer look at the data reveals that wherever physicians had a choice between a male and a female lobotomy candidate, the woman was selected. In institutions where the vast majority of the patients were men, as in veterans' hospitals, where 95 percent of patients were male, men were given lobotomies. Of 1,125 lobotomies performed at these institutions 1,085 were done on men. However, in institutions where there were male and female patients, female patients were operated on with much greater frequency than were male patients. The preponderance of women grew even more imbalanced after the development of the transorbital procedure because of the rapidity with which it could be performed.

7. Showalter, *Female Malady*, p. 204.

8. Ibid., p. 213. Showalter acknowledges recent studies that show that schizophrenia was *not* statistically a predominantly female disease in the postwar period. The studies to which Showalter refers find schizophrenia equally divided between men and women (p. 281, n. 21). However, she argues that the treatments for schizophrenia have strong *symbolic* association with feminization and the female role (p. 205). Other, mostly earlier, studies claimed that schizophrenia was primarily diagnosed in women. See, for example, studies cited in Saul K. Levine, M.D., FRCP(C), Louisa E. Kamin, M.D., and Eleanor Lee Levnice, M.S.W., "Sexism and Psychiatry," *American Journal of Orthopsychiatry* 44, no. 3 (April 1974): 327-36; and Phyllis Chesler, *Women and Madness* (Garden City, N.Y.: Doubleday, 1972). Chesler sees schizophrenia as more prevalent in women and classes it as a "female disease."

9. See, for example, Lothar B. Kalinowsky, M.D., and John E. Scarff, M.D., "The Selection of Psychiatric Cases for Prefrontal Lobotomy," *American Journal of Psychiatry* 105, no. 1 (July 1948): 81-85.

10. Walter Freeman and James Watts, quoted in Valenstein, *Great and Desperate Cures*, p. 228. The economic problem of overcrowding in mental institutions was alleviated by lobotomy because, after a lobotomy, the patient could go home. Roy Grinker, a Chicago psychoanalyst, noted, however, that costs were not really being curbed. They were merely being "borne by another agency, namely the home rather than the state." Quoted in Valenstein, p. 185.

11. Walter Freeman and James W. Watts, *Psychosurgery: In the Treatment of Mental Disorders and Intractable Pain*, 2nd ed. (Springfield, Ill.: Thomas, 1950), p. x; quoted in Valenstein, *Great and Desperate Cures*, p. 229.

12. Percival Bailey, an American neurosurgeon, quoted in Valenstein, *Great and Desperate Cures*, p. 91.

13. Valenstein, *Great and Desperate Cures*, p. 190.

14. For the former, see Marilyn French, *The Woman's Room* (New York: Jove/HBJ Books, 1977).

15. Virginia Woolf, *Three Guineas* (1938; Middlesex, England: Penguin, 1979), p. 5; and Freeman and Watts quoted in Valenstein, *Great and Desperate Cures*, p. 228.

16. Morris Fraser, *ECT: A Clinical Guide* (Chichester, England: Wiley, 1982). Fraser asserts that in spite of the adverse reaction to shock therapy it has never been " 'in fashion,' or 'out.' "

17. Showalter, *Female Malady*, p. 207. It's an apt rather than an accidental historical coincidence that Edward Strecker, retired military man and accusor of inadequate moms, operated one of the "best equipped shock clinics in the United States." Valenstein, *Great and Desperate Cures*, p. 58, quoting "Death for Sanity," *Time*, Nov. 1939, pp. 39-40.

18. Peter R. Breggin, *Electroshock: Its Brain-Disabling Effects* (New York: Springer, 1979); quoted in Showalter, *Female Malady*, p. 207.

19. Lothar B. Kalinowsky, M.D., and Paul H. Hoch, M.D., *Shock Treatment* (New York: Grune and Stratton, 1949), p. 13.

20. Fraser, *ECT*, p. xiv. Note that the quote speaks of the patient's illness as depression rather than schizophrenia. This is because the quote is taken from a recent text. In contemporary times, as psychotropic drugs have become available for the treatment of schizophrenia, ECT has been used more and more in cases of depressive illness. In addition, recent years have seen the alteration of diagnostic categories themselves. Symptoms previously associated with schizophrenia may now be classed as depressive illness of the psychotic type.

21. Kalinowsky and Hoch, *Shock Treatment*, p. 13.

22. *American Journal of Psychiatry* 109, no. 7 (Jan. 1953), p. 541.

23. Franz Alexander, M.D., and Sheldon T. Selesnick, M.D., *The History of Psychiatry: An Evaluation of Psychiatric Thought and Practice from Prehistoric Times to the Present* (New York: Harper and Row, 1966), p. 29.

24. I examined drug ads in the *American Journal of Psychiatry* (hereafter *AJP*) between 1944, when the first ad in the publication appeared, and 1964. Before November 1946, each issue contains one ad on the back of the front cover. No ads at all are published between November 1946 and 1952. Suddenly, in July 1952, the number and variety of ads mushroom. Ads for sleeping pills, tranquilizers, mood elevators, narcosynthetic drugs, weight control drugs, drugs for the control of alcohol and drug abuse, for epilepsy, asthma control, and cardioneurosis abound. Also found are ads for electroshock machines, for security sanitarium windows that are without bars, and for private sanitariums. Each ad was frequently run in several issues.

25. *AJP* 117, no. 1 (July 1960).

26. *AJP* 114, no. 11 (May 1958).

27. *AJP* 112, no. 11 (May 1956).

28. *AJP* 109, no. 1 (July 1952).

29. Ibid.

30. See, for example, the ad for Sparine in *AJP* 115, no. 4 (Oct. 1958), or the ad for Ritalin in *AJP* 114, no. 11 (May 1958).

31. *AJP* 112, no. 7 (Jan. 1956).

32. Marie N. Robinson, M.D., *The Power of Sexual Surrender* (New York: Signet, 1959); Frank S. Caprio, M.D., *The Sexually Adequate Female* (New York: Citadel Press, 1953); Maxine Davis, *The Sexual Responsibility of Woman* (New York: Permabooks, 1956); and Fritz Wittels, M.D., *The Sex Habits of American Women* (New York: Eton Books, 1951).

33. Th. H. van de Velde, M.D., *Ideal Marriage: Its Physiology and Technique* (1926; New York: Random House, 1930, 1957).

34. Robinson, *Sexual Surrender*, p. 28.

35. Caprio, *Sexually Adequate Female*, pp. 43-44.

36. Robinson, *Sexual Surrender*, p. 157.

37. Wittels, *Sex Habits*, p. xiii. One basic theme is often taken as the focus in marriage manuals: female sexual frigidity, or "sexual anesthesia," in the terms of Havelock Ellis. The psychiatrist author of *The Sexually Adequate Female*, Caprio, shocks his readers with a wealth of statistics to prove that 20 percent to 30 percent of all women are frigid and that this frigidity is responsible for the majority of divorces. Here frigidity means failure to achieve *vaginal* as opposed to clitoral orgasm, and so this book, among others, exhorts women to an ideal of mature sexuality that would later, as indicated above, be deemed physically impossible.

38. Chris Costner Sizemore and Elen Sain Pittillo, *I'm Eve* (1977; New York: Jove, 1983), p. 411. Also see Gene Tierney's autobiography with Mickey Herskowitz, *Self-Portrait* (New York: Wyden Books, 1979), as an unintentional revelation of sexism in psychiatry.

39. Norman Reider, M.D., "Problems in the Prediction of Marital Adjustment," in *Neurotic Interaction in Marriage,* ed. Victor W. Eisenstein, M.D. (New York: Basic Books, 1956), pp. 311-25.

40. Ibid., pp. 311-12.

41. Ibid., p. 311.

42. Ibid., p. 312.

43. Robert Lindner, "Solitaire," in *The Fifty-Minute Hour: A Collection of True Psychoanalytic Tales,* new edition ed. and intro. Samuel Shem, M.D. (1954; New York: Rinehart, 1986), pp. 84-124.

44. In the 1970s and 1980s bulimia was reinterpreted by feminist scholars and media critics as an understandable if self-destructive response to the rigid social standards of female attractiveness furthered by the media. See Luli Barzman McCarroll, "Media/ Bulimia, or the Politics of Cleanliness," *On Film* 13 (Fall 1984): 14-24.

45. Another illustration of the issues brought up by this analysis of Lindner's work is the book by Ludwig Eidelberg, M.D., *Take Off Your Mask* (1948; New York: Pyramid Books, 1960).

46. Robert Lindner, *Must You Conform?* (1956; New York: Grove Press, 1971), and *Prescription for Rebellion* (1952; Westport, Conn.: Greenwood Press, 1975). For a lengthier discussion of Lindner's work as an argument against adjustment psychiatry, see Russell Jacoby, "The Americanization of Psychoanalysis," chap. 7 in *The Repression of Psychoanalysis: Otto Fenichel and the Political Freudians* (New York: Basic Books, 1983).

47. For summaries of this debate, see the panel reports on annual meetings of the American Psychoanalytic Association in 1952 and 1953 in the "Scientific Proceedings" section of the *Journal of the American Psychoanalytic Association* (as well as the published papers themselves noted below, as discussed): "I. Psychoanalysis and Dynamic Psychotherapy — Similarities and Differences," reported by Leo Rangell, M.D., *Journal of the American Psychoanalytic Association* 2, no. 1 (Jan. 1954): 152-62; and "I. The Traditional Psychoanalytic Technique and Its Variations," reported by Elizabeth R. Zetzel, M.D., *Journal of the American Psychoanalytic Association* 1, no. 1 (July 1953): 526-37.

48. Interestingly, this professional ambivalence is reflected in Stanley Reiser's history of medical evidence gathering in that he sometimes seems to characterize psychoanalysis as a welcome return to older models of medical practice where the doctor relied on the patient's subjective account of his or her symptoms, while at other times he characterizes psychoanalysis as a form of alienating technology where the doctor uses his or her unconscious as an instrument and treats the patient as an object.

49. Lawrence Kubie, M.D., "A Pilot Study of Psychoanalytic Practice in the United States: With Suggestions for Future Studies," *Psychiatry* 113 (1950), p. 235.

50. In fact, there are no ready sources of material that answer questions about the analyst's words in analytic sessions. For reasons of confidentiality, among other reasons, case literature typically consisted of detailed psychodynamic interpretations and metapsychological conclusions and omitted altogether the exact part played by the analyst. This confidentiality is notorious. To give one example of it, Robert Knight ("Evaluation of the Results of Psychoanalytic Work," *American Journal of Psychiatry* 98 [1941]: 434-41, and "The Present Status of Organized Psychoanalysis in the United States," *Journal of the American Psychoanalytic Association* 1, no. 2 [April 1953]: 197-221) mentions the resistance of analysts to filling out questionnaires on the age, marital status, and gen-

der of their patients, let alone regarding the content of the ongoing exchanges. My account of the dynamics of psychotherapy relies, therefore, on my interpretation of the professional literature that does exist and on case literature written for the general public, where the format required the creation of "dialog" placed in the mouth of the physician.

51. Franz Alexander, "Psychoanalysis and Psychotherapy," *Journal of the American Psychoanalytic Association* 2, no. 4 (Oct. 1954), p. 728. Also see summaries of his work in the conference reviews noted above.

52. Ibid., p. 726.

53. There is a contradiction in Alexander's argument that does not disturb my own, but that is interesting to note. Early on, he implies that psychoanalysis is the least supportive and most "uncovering" therapy using insight. Later, in discussing transference, it seems that psychoanalysis is most supportive because of the fundamental nature of the transference relationship. He goes on to propose a move from the daily appointments of classical analysis to a schedule of less frequent appointments as a way to lessen "support." Normally, such a move would be interpreted as a move toward less analytic, more supportive therapy.

54. Phyllis Greenacre, M.D., "The Role of Transference: Practical Considerations in Relation to Psychoanalytic Therapy," *Journal of the American Psychoanalytic Association* 2, no. 4 (Oct. 1954): 671-84.

55. Ibid., p. 676.

56. Leo Stone, "The Widening Scope of Indications for Psychoanalysis," *Journal of the American Psychoanalytic Association* 2, no. 4 (Oct. 1954): 567-620 (hereafter *JAPA*).

57. "Borderline" designates "those patients who present largely neurotic syndromes, sometimes quite conventional, who nevertheless induce in the clinician the conviction or strong suspicion of more grave illness," according to Stone, "Widening Scope," p. 581.

58. Ibid., p. 585.

59. J. LaPlanche and J.-B. Pontalis, *The Language of Psycho-Analysis* (1967), trans. Donald Michelson-Smith (New York: Norton, 1973), p. 259.

60. Stone, "Widening Scope," p. 583.

61. Sigmund Freud, "Psycho-Analysis" (1922), *Collected Papers* (London: Hogarth Press, 1950), vol. 5, pp. 107-30; quoted in Merton Gill, M.D., "Psychoanalysis and Exploratory Psychotherapy," *JAPA* 2, no. 4 (Oct. 1954): 771-97.

62. Sigmund Freud, *An Outline of Psychoanalysis* (1939; New York: Norton, 1949), p. 67; quoted in Gill, "Exploratory Psychotherapy," p. 777.

63. Gill, "Exploratory Psychotherapy," p. 775.

64. Edward Bibring, M.D., "Psychoanalysis and the Dynamic Psychotherapies," *JAPA* 2, no. 4 (Oct. 1954): 745-69.

65. Gill uses the terms "exploratory" and "interpretive," and Bibring the term "interpretive."

66. Gill, "Exploratory Psychotherapy," p. 776.

67. LaPlanche and Pontalis, *Language of Psychoanalysis*, p. 92.

68. Douglas Orr, M.D., "Transference and Countertransference: A Historical Survey," *JAPA* 2, no. 4 (Oct. 1954): 621-70; and Benjamin Wolstein, *Countertransference* (New York: Grune and Stratton, 1959).

69. LaPlanche and Pontalis, *Language of Psychoanalysis*, p. 455. Freud's concept of transference also comprises the notion of transference-*resistance*. This notion is crucial for me, and I will take it up later. For now, my interest is in moving on from Freudian concepts to American popular and professional concepts.

70. Ibid., p. 92.

71. See the summary provided by Douglas Orr, "Transference and Countertransference." Also see the work of the following authors on transference/countertransference: Greenacre, "Role of Transference"; Lucia E. Tower, M.D., "Countertransference," *JAPA* 4, no. 2 (April 1956): 224-55; René A. Spitz, M.D., "Countertransference," *JAPA* 4, no. 2 (April 1956): 256-65; Therese Benedek, "Dynamics of the Countertransference," *Bulletin of the Menninger Clinic* 17 (1953): 201-8; and Maxwell Gitelson, M.D., "The Emotional Position of the Analyst in the Psycho-Analytic Situation," *International Journal of Psychoanalysis* 33 (1952): 1-10.

72. Orr, "Transference and Countertransference," p. 646. Tower agrees with Orr on this point ("Countertransference," p. 224).

73. Tower, "Countertransference," p. 226. Similar statements on countertransference quoted in Tower are as follows: " 'The [countertransference mistake] should be admitted, to allow the patient to express his anger, and he is entitled to some expression of regret from the analyst.' . . . 'It is not safe to let even subtle manifestations of the counter-transference creep inadvertently into the interpersonal climate. The analyst must recognize and control these reactions' " (p. 226).

74. Spitz, "Countertransference."

75. Jacques Lacan, *The Four Fundamental Concepts of Psycho-Analysis* (1973), trans. Alan Sheridan (New York: Penguin Books, 1977), chaps. 10-20.

76. Ibid., pp. 231-32.

77. Such work is particularly notable in that its existence challenges Juliet Mitchell's claim that American psychoanalysis amounted to mere adjustment therapy because it stripped psychoanalysis of its fundamental theories of infantile sexuality. Juliet Mitchell, *Psychoanalysis and Feminism: Freud, Reich, Laing and Women* (New York: Vintage Books, 1975).

78. Tower, "Countertransference," p. 225.

79. Ibid., p. 230.

80. The training analysis itself is a relatively radical aspect of psychoanalysis, because it gives the analyst a solid knowledge of what it is like to be in the patient's position. This is usually missing in the conventional doctor-patient relationship. In *Bedside Manners: The Troubled History of Doctors and Patients* (New York: Simon and Schuster, 1985), Edward Shorter gives an example of a doctor who experienced for the first time the powerlessness of his patients when he collapsed to the ground suffering from Lou Gehrig's disease and a fellow physician refused to acknowledge him lying there, for to do so would have been to encounter the weakness of one like himself.

81. Roland H. Berg, "The Couch vs. the Pill," *Look* (Feb. 2, 1960), p. 46.

82. Ibid., p. 46.

83. Alexander Reid Martin, M.D., "Why Psychoanalysis?" in *Are You Considering Psychoanalysis?* ed. Karen Horney (New York: Norton, 1946), p. 25.

84. Nancy Lynch, "A Walk in a Dark Room," *Mademoiselle*, Oct. 1957; pp. 98, 146-49.

85. Josef Breuer and Sigmund Freud, *Studies on Hysteria* (1893-95), trans. and ed. James Strachey (New York: Basic Books, 1955), p. 305.

86. Jeffrey D. Blum, "On Changes in Psychiatric Diagnosis over Time," *American Psychologist* 11 (Nov. 1978): 1017-31.

87. H. J. Eysenck, *Reader's Digest*, Jan. 1960, p. 39.

88. Karen Horney, M.D., ed., *Are You Considering Psychoanalysis?* (New York: Norton, 1946), p. 13.

89. Dorothy Ferman, "The Psychoanalytical Joy Ride," *Nation*, Aug. 26, 1950, pp. 183-85.

90. Gregory Zilboorg, M.D., *Nation*, Sept. 2, 1950, pp. 205-9.

91. Lucy Freeman, *Fight against Fears* (1951; New York: Pocket Books, 1953), p. 161.

92. The American culturalist school had its roots in the 1920s, when Otto Rank and Sandor Ferenczi shifted attention from infantile experiences to the way those past experiences were affecting the patient's current existence. Karen Horney, Harry Stack Sullivan, Erich Fromm, and Abraham Kardiner are usually regarded as major contributors to this school.

93. See articles collected in Jean Strouse, ed., *Women and Analysis* (New York: Grossman, 1974).

94. Entry in *International Encyclopedia of Psychiatry, Psychology, Psychoanalysis and Neurology*, ed. Benjamin B. Wolman (New York: Produced for Aesculapius Publishers by Van Nostrand Reinhold, 1977).

95. Although Horney wrote many of her articles on feminine sexuality in the 1920s in Berlin, where she was a colleague of Franz Alexander at the Berlin Institute for Psycho-Analysis before emigrating to the United States in 1932, the influence of her ideas was very strong in the United States in the postwar period of interest here. See Nellie Louise Buckley, "Women Psychoanalysts and the Theory of Feminine Development: A Study of Karen Horney, Helene Deutsch, and Marie Bonaparte" (Ph.D. dissertation, University of California, Los Angeles, 1982), p. 43; Susan Quinn, *A Mind of Her Own: The Life of Karen Horney* (New York: Summit Books, 1987); and Marcia Westkott, *The Feminist Legacy of Karen Horney* (New Haven, Conn.: Yale University Press, 1986).

96. See, for example, Clara Thompson, M.D., "Cultural Pressures in the Psychology of Women," in *Psychoanalysis and Women: Contributions to New Theory and Therapy*, ed. Jean Baker Miller, M.D. (New York: Brunner/Mazel, 1972). Also see Karen Horney, *Feminine Sexuality* (New York: Norton, 1967), a collection of essays from the 1920s and 1930s.

97. Thompson, "Cultural Pressures in the Psychology of Women" (1942), in *Psychoanalysis and Women*, ed. Miller.

98. See Harry Stack Sullivan, "The Inefficient Wife" (1956), and Karen Horney, "The Ever-Tired Editor" (1942), in *Great Cases in Psychoanalysis*, ed. Harold Greenwald (New York: Armson, 1973).

99. Sullivan, "Inefficient Wife," p. 204.

100. Ibid.

101. Horney, "Ever-Tired Editor," p. 192.

102. This argument is put forth by Nellie Buckley, who also notes that Horney's biographer, Jack L. Rubins (*Karen Horney: Gentle Rebel of Psychoanalysis* [New York: Dial Press, 1978]), calls Horney's portrait of Clare "semifictitious."

3. Marriage and Psychiatry; or, Transference-Countertransference as a Love Affair

1. Lea Jacobs, "*Now Voyager*: Some Problems of Enunciation and Sexual Difference," *Camera Obscura* 7 (1981): 89-109; and Maria LaPlace, "Bette Davis and the Ideal of Consumption: A Look at *Now Voyager*," *Wide Angle* 6, no. 4 (1985): 34-43.

2. One might say that the most excessive example of mental vulnerability shared by the male psychiatrist occurs in the "mad doctor" films. However, I have chosen not to work with these films here precisely because they do feature male madness rather than female madness. In a film of the exact title, *The Mad Doctor* (1941), a psychiatrist marries and murders women for their money. In *Hollow Triumph* a man murders and takes the place of a psychiatrist, filling in by spouting psychoanalytic jargon. Regardless of the male psychoses depicted, these films do not indict the psychiatric institution so much as

they bracket off isolated, individual men—actual criminals—without whom the authority of the institution would be better preserved. Indeed, the psychopathic killer of *Hollow Triumph* is not really the psychiatrist at all, but an imposter.

My point, again, is analogous to that Diane Waldman makes in "Horror and Domesticity: The Modern Gothic Romance Film of the 40s" (Ph.D. dissertation, University of Wisconsin, Madison, 1981). Individual psychopathic male characters are used in certain films to disguise misogyny as the exception and not the norm. While the plots of the "mad psychiatrist" films turn the tables on mental illness, they actually function as apologia for the mental health of the psychiatric institution as a whole. This pattern of justifying the system by indicting the individual may be compared more generally to Hollywood's treatment of political subject matter. For example, the film *Missing* broaches the issue of "the disappeared" victims of South American military juntas. But instead of showing how economic and military motives encourage the United States to look the other way in the face of violations of human rights by totalitarian regimes, the film blames "bad" men in powerful positions for U.S. involvement. The implication is that if only we could get good men in the CIA, the Pentagon, the government, everything would be fine.

3. Sigmund Freud, "Katharina," in Josef Breuer and Sigmund Freud, *Studies on Hysteria*, trans. and ed. James Strachey (New York: Basic Books, 1955), pp. 125-34.

4. Ibid., p. 127.

5. *Whirlpool* opens when Ann Sutton (Gene Tierney) is caught shoplifting at the Wilshire Store in Los Angeles. In the store offices a stranger comes to her aid, revealing that Sutton is the nonworking and independently wealthy wife of a distinguished psychoanalyst, Dr. William Sutton (Richard Conte). Ann feels compelled to hide her kleptomania from her husband for fear he will no longer love her. The stranger turns out to be "Doctor" David Korvo (José Ferrer), a self-described human scientist who specializes in hypnosis. He convinces Ann that he can cure her problems, which to his mind run far deeper than kleptomania and insomnia. Ann begins to receive treatment by hypnosis from Dr. Korvo, although she is warned away from him by a former patient and former lover of his, Theresa Randolph, who is now in analysis with Dr. William Sutton. One night when Dr. Sutton is away at a conference, Ann, following a posthypnotic suggestion, takes a recording of Randolph's analytic session from her husband's office and goes to Terry Randolph's home. There she finds Randolph dead. She is discovered at the home and arrested. She remembers nothing of these events. Dr. Sutton begins to come to her aid but then becomes convinced that Ann was the lover of Korvo and is covering for him. But Korvo has a good alibi. He was postoperative at the time of the murder. Ann finally "confesses" to the police. But the story she tells is not of the crime, but of her kleptomania, which she sees as having originated in rebellion against a parsimonious father who didn't love her. Dr. Sutton finally realizes that Ann's basically good character couldn't have altered in a flash. He figures out that Korvo could have killed Randolph if he used self-hypnosis to gather the strength to leave his hospital bed. So Sutton persuades a kindly detective to let him take Ann back to the scene of the crime, saying, "The solution's hidden in her brain and I can bring it out." Dr. Sutton shows Ann that his insistence that she start marriage with him as a poor doctor's wife, instead of spending money left her by her father, brought back her illness. Her renewed trust in her husband removes the power of Korvo from her mind, and she remembers the night of the murder and where she hid Dr. Sutton's recordings of the analytic session in which Randolph accused Korvo of swindling her. Korvo has been hiding in the house. He accosts the Suttons and Detective Colton. But he is bleeding from his surgery and collapses. Ann and her husband embrace.

6. See Mary Ann Doane's theoretical explanation of this problematic in "Clinical Eyes: The Medical Discourse," chap. 2 in *The Desire to Desire: The Women's Film of the 1940s* (Bloomington and Indianapolis: Indiana University Press, 1987).

7. See Pam Cook, "Duplicity in *Mildred Pierce*," in *Women in Film Noir*, ed. E. Ann Kaplan (London: British Film Institute, 1978), pp. 68-82; Joyce Nelson, "*Mildred Pierce* Reconsidered," *Film Reader* 2 (Jan. 1977): 65-70; Janet Walker, "Feminist Critical Practice: Female Discourse in *Mildred Pierce*," *Film Reader* 5 (1982): 164-72; Pamela Robertson, "Structural Irony in *Mildred Pierce*, or How Mildred Lost Her Tongue," *Cinema Journal* 30, no. 1 (Fall 1990): 42-54; and Linda Williams, "Feminist Film Theory: *Mildred Pierce* and the Second World War," in *Female Spectators*, ed. E. Dierdre Pribram (London and New York: Verso, 1988), 12-30.

8. Freud initially thought that hypnosis might be useful in relieving hysterical patients of their unpleasant symptoms and in gaining access to unconscious material, so he tried to "suggest" symptoms out of existence (Josef Breuer and Sigmund Freud, *Studies on Hysteria* [1893-95], trans. and ed. James Strachey with the collaboration of Anna Freud [New York: Basic Books, 1955]). Clearly such suggestions amount to behavioral interventions, and Freud soon discarded the use of hypnosis in favor of the "talking cure" or free association (Milton Kline, *Freud and Hypnosis: The Interaction of Psychodynamics and Hypnosis* [New York: Julian Press, 1958]). But Freud's initial interest in hypnosis was rejuvenated in postwar America (*Encyclopedia of Medical History*, s.v. "hypnosis").

9. Lawrence Kubie, M.D., and Sydney Margolin, M.D., "The Process of Hypnotism and the Nature of the Hypnotic State," *American Journal of Psychiatry* 100, no. 5 (March 1944): 611.

10. Ibid.

11. J. LaPlanche and J.-B. Pontalis, *The Language of Psycho-Analysis* (1967), trans. Donald Nicholson-Smith (New York: Norton, 1973), pp. 455-64.

12. Andrew Sarris points out that all of Preminger's films resist point-of-view shots in favor of presenting their issues and problems "as [the] single-take two-shot, the stylistic expression of the eternal conflict" (*The American Cinema* [New York: Dutton, 1968], p. 106). Since this book is not about authorship, I'll have to leave aside the discussion of *Whirlpool*'s style in that context. But the question of authorship does not exhaust the issues brought up by style. In fact, auteur approaches, when at their worst, have served to close down the kinds of questions I would like to bring up here.

13. Mary Ann Doane, "*Caught* and *Rebecca*: The Inscription of Femininity as Absence," *Enclitic* 5/6 (1981/1982): 75-89, presents a discussion of *Whirlpool*'s style in this context.

14. See Laura Mulvey, "Visual Pleasure and Narrative Cinema" (1975), in *Feminism and Film Theory*, ed. Constance Penley (New York and London: Routledge, 1988), pp. 57-68; and Raymond Bellour, "Hitchcock the Enunciator," *Camera Obscura* 2 (Fall 1977): 69-94, discuss composition and editing and the (real or fictional) man's possession of the image of the woman. Bellour points out that the first shot of Marnie is motivated by a shot of Mark (Sean Connery) staring into space, daydreaming of her. Also see Mary Ann Doane, "*Gilda*: Epistemology as Striptease," *Camera Obscura* 11 (1983): 7-28.

15. C. F. Keppler, *The Literature of the Second Self* (Tucson: University of Arizona Press, 1972).

16. Dana Polan, *Power and Paranoia: History, Narrative, and the American Cinema, 1940-1950* (New York: Columbia University Press, 1986), p. 182.

17. François Roustang, *Psychoanalysis Never Lets Go*, trans. Ned Lukacher (Baltimore and London: Johns Hopkins University Press, 1980).

18. Ibid., p. 88.

19. Ibid., p. 89.

20. Sigmund Freud, *The Standard Edition of the Complete Psychological Works of Sigmund Freud*, ed. and trans. James Strachey (London: Hogarth Press and the Institute of Psychoanalysis, 1953-74), vol. 16, p. 446 (hereafter *SE*); quoted in Roustang, *Psychoanalysis Never Lets Go*, p. 90.

21. Roustang, *Psychoanalysis Never Lets Go*, p. 89.

22. Ibid.

23. Corbett H. Thigpen and Hervey M. Cleckley, *The Three Faces of Eve* (New York: Popular Library, 1957); and Chris Costner Sizemore and Elen Sain Pittillo, *I'm Eve* (1977; New York: Jove Publications, 1983). Of course, it would be unsound reasoning to accept Sizemore's account of her life as the pure truth that "sets the record straight" and that discredits Thigpen's and Cleckley's case history. Clearly, Sizemore's own version is produced through processes of mediation different from but every bit as complex as those which figure into the production of the film and book *The Three Faces of Eve*. For example, I see *I'm Eve* as having emerged out of the sociocultural currents of the late 1970s, crucially the feminist movement (which must have spurred Sizemore's desire to speak for herself) and out of the growing deemphasis on psychoanalytic therapy in the mental health professions. My intention in this study is to utilize three documents, reading them against one another, to tease out some of the mediations or pressures that shaped the 1950s versions of the events of Sizemore's life.

24. The book says nothing, however, about any childhood sexual abuse, although current research suggests overwhelmingly that childhood sexual abuse is a central etiological factor in multiple personality disorder. See Richard P. Kluft, "Making the Diagnosis of Multiple Personality Disorder (MPD)," *Directions in Psychiatry* 5, lesson 23, p. 3; and C. W. Wilbur, "The Effect of Child Abuse on the Psyche," in *Childhood Antecedents of Multiple Personality*, ed. Richard P. Kluft (Washington, D.C.: American Psychiatric Press, 1985).

25. Thigpen and Cleckley, *Three Faces of Eve*.

26. Morton Prince, *The Dissociation of a Personality: The Hunt for the Real Miss Beauchamp* (1905; Great Britain: Fletcher and Son, 1978).

27. Richard P. Kluft, "The Treatment of Multiple Personality Disorder," *Psychiatry Clinics of North America* 7 (1984): 9-30; and F. W. Putnam et al. "100 Cases of MPD" (paper presented at the Annual Meeting of the American Psychiatric Association as New Research Abstract no. 77, New York, 1983).

28. See Marc Vernet's and Diane Waldman's discussions of this similarity between narrative structure and the Freudian cathartic model in Marc Vernet, "Freud: effets speciaux—Mise en scène: U.S.A.," *Communications* 23 (1975): 223-34; and Waldman, "Horror and Domesticity."

For further discussion of the flashback and psychology, see Raymond Borde and Etienne Chaumeton, "The Sources of Film Noir," *Film Reader* 3 (Feb. 1978): 58-66; and Maureen Turim, "Flashbacks and the Psyche in Melodrama and Film Noir," chap. 5 in *Flashbacks in Film: Memory and History* (New York and London: Routledge, 1989), pp. 143-88.

29. Sigmund Freud, "Some Psychical Consequences of the Anatomical Distinction between the Sexes" (1925), *SE* 19, pp. 241-60; "Female Sexuality" (1931), *SE* 21, pp. 221-46; and "Femininity" (1933), *SE* 22, pp. 112-33.

30. Sizemore and Pittillo, *I'm Eve*, p. 493.

31. Ibid., p. 505. Hollywood conventions are not the only ones to realize narrative closure through personality synthesis. The history of "Eve's" case proceeds via a one-upmanship of synthetic personalities. Like Hollywood endings, the authority of psychological accounts depends on closure. Sizemore's first ghostwritten autobiography was titled *The Final Face of Eve*. It introduced an additional personality only to reconfirm a new synthesis. In *I'm Eve*, however, Sizemore confirms a *Life* magazine report that she was not really integrated, and provides an account of how Drs. Thigpen and Cleckley pressured the ghostwriter and Sizemore herself to conform, for the most part, to their conclusions and support reports of her cure.

32. Polan, *Power and Paranoia*, p. 168.

33. Sizemore herself recognizes that power is often expressed as the power to tell a story. In *I'm Eve*, she exposes Thigpen's and Cleckley's conspiracy to reserve for themselves the rights to her life story. In 1953, Thigpen got her to sign a document including the following clause: "[I give to Thigpen and Cleckley] all world-wide rights forever in my life story (including without limitation publication and other rights in all versions of the story written by or for them and those published aforesaid), and I have reserved unto myself no rights of any kind whatsoever in my life story." In view of this history, Sizemore's urge to write her autobiography was all the more charged.

34. Woodward herself praised Nunnally Johnson's direction because he gave her "total freedom to try anything"; quoted in Nora Johnson, *Nora Johnson on Nunnally Johnson* (Garden City, N.Y.: Doubleday, 1979), p. 262. Woodward received an Academy Award for Best Actress for her performance in *The Three Faces of Eve*.

35. A question arises as to the validity of taking *Tender Is the Night* as an example of a 1960s film when in fact it is based on an F. Scott Fitzgerald novel written in 1932. I would defend this 1960s historicization of the film on the grounds that the very fact that the novel was already in existence prior to the postwar profusion of films about women and psychoanalysis, and yet was not developed into a film project until the 1960s, lends credence to the notion that the narrative was more appropriate to, or more consistent with, ideas about women and psychoanalysis current in the 1960s than those of the period immediately following World War II.

36. Another example, from later in the film (although the fact that this scene occurs within a flashback makes it chronologically earlier in terms of story events), spatially indicates that Nicole is on the mend. Dr. Diver has suggested that they go out for a walk in Zurich, and, having accepted, Nicole is shown in a wide shot running full force down the street with Dick trailing.

37. The term "incest" is not directly spoken in the film, but I don't see how Baby's words could be interpreted any other way. It would be interesting to look at the implications of the omission of the word itself, but I think such a project would be of more central importance to a study of film censorship.

38. J. LaPlanche and J.-B. Pontalis confirm Freud's neglect of this term (*The Language of Psycho-Analysis*, p. 92). Recent scholars, however, have shown that the *concept* of countertransference is absolutely integral to Freud's work. See, for example, *In Dora's Case: Freud-Hysteria-Feminism*, ed. Charles Bernheimer and Claire Kahane (New York: Columbia University Press, 1985).

39. Appropriately, the term "countertransference," used in the film *Tender Is the Night*, is not present in the 1932 novel.

40. *Spellbound* (1945), an early film in which we see the gruesome sight of the younger brother of the hero impaled on a wrought iron fence, is perhaps an exception.

41. Turim, "Flashbacks and the Psyche," p. 151.

42. Freud, *Studies on Hysteria*, p. 134.

4. The Institutional Edifice

1. Michel Foucault, "The Great Confinement" and "The Insane," chaps. 2 and 3 in *Madness and Civilization* (1961), trans. Richard Howard (New York: Vintage Books, 1973), pp. 38-64 and 65-84. According to Foucault, the mad, the poor, and the criminal were all confined together from the first mass confinement of the seventeenth century to as late as the nineteenth century. L'Hôpital Général of Paris and its counterparts were not medical establishments so much as prisons (p. 40).

The film *Bedlam* presents a character who seems to be based on William Tuke, who founded the York Retreat in the late eighteenth century and was among the first to argue that the violence of patients came from their ill treatment. (Also see Elaine Showalter, *The Female Malady: Women, Madness, and English Culture, 1830-1980* [New York: Pantheon, 1985]). Through this Quaker character, the incarcerated woman learns to lavish care, kindness, and cleanliness on madhouse inhabitants.

2. See, for example, the plays *Chamber Music* by Arthur Kopit, *Johnny Johnson* by Paul Johnson with music by Kurt Weil, *One Flew over the Cuckoo's Nest* by Ken Kesey, *Marat/Sade* by Peter Weiss, *The Physicists* by Friedrich Dürrenmat, and *The Dayroom* by Don DeLillo.

3. Shoshana Felman, *Writing and Madness* (*Literature/Philosophy/Psychoanalysis*) (1978), trans. Martha Noel Evans and Shoshana Felman with the assistance of Brian Massumi (Ithaca, N.Y.: Cornell University Press, 1985), pp. 13-14.

4. Maria LaPlace, "Producing and Consuming the Woman's Film: Discursive Struggle in *Now, Voyager*," in *Home Is Where the Heart Is: Studies in Melodrama and the Woman's Film*, ed. Christine Gledhill (London: British Film Institute, 1987), pp. 138-66; and Lea Jacobs, "*Now Voyager*: Some Problems of Enunciation and Sexual Difference," *Camera Obscura* 7 (1981): 89-110.

5. Mary Ann Doane, "Clinical Eyes: The Medical Discourse," in *The Desire to Desire: The Woman's Film of the 1940s* (Bloomington and Indianapolis: Indiana University Press, 1987), pp. 40-41.

6. Felman, *Writing and Madness*, p. 14.

7. Paul Starr (*The Social Transformation of American Medicine* [New York: Basic Books, 1982]) cited *The Snake Pit* as evidence of public concern over mental hospital conditions. Also see reviews by Jack Spears, "The Doctor on the Screen," *Films in Review* 6, no. 9 (Nov. 1955): 436-44; and Martin Dworkin, "Movie Psychiatrics," *Antioch Review* (Winter 1954-55): 484-91, written closer to the time of the film's release.

8. Doane, "Clinical Eyes," p. 46.

9. Foucault, *Madness and Civilization*, p. 247.

10. Ibid., p. 250.

11. Honoré de Balzac, *L'Illustre Gaudissart*, in *La Comédie humaine* (Paris: Editions du Seuil, Collection "L'Intégrale," 1966).

12. Felman, *Writing and Madness*, pp. 105-6.

13. Ibid., p. 106.

14. Ibid., p. 113.

15. Ibid., p. 112.

16. Ibid., p. 109.

17. Ibid., p. 110.

18. Shoshana Felman, "Women and Madness: The Critical Phallacy," *Diacritics* 5 (Winter 1975): 2-10.

19. My discussion of *The Cobweb* has been greatly influenced by prior work on the film done in the context of studies of melodrama and its specific Hollywood incarnation. See Thomas Elsaesser's seminal "Tales of Sound and Fury: Observations on the Family

Melodrama," in *Home Is Where the Heart Is*, pp. 43-69; Geoffrey Nowell-Smith, "Minnelli and Melodrama," *Screen* 18, no. 2 (Summer 1977): 113-18; and D. N. Rodowick, "Madness, Authority, and Ideology in the Domestic Melodrama of the 1950's," *The Velvet Light Trap* 19 (1982): 40-45. Elsaesser was the first of the three authors to make the essential point that melodrama is concerned with the representation of bourgeois social relations and the problem of individual identity. Furthermore, as all three of the authors suggest, the form was particularly sensitive to the internal contradictions of bourgeois ideology. Elsaesser and Rodowick have both encouraged my own area of interest by discussing the centrality to its focus on identity and familial relations of the Freudian themes running throughout 1940s and 1950s melodrama.

20. David Rodowick's discussion of "institutional and familial authority" in *The Cobweb* is relevant here.

21. Rodowick cites Geoffrey Nowell-Smith's claim that the problem of melodrama is always that of the acquisition of individual identity within the symbolic order of patriarchal society, and he quotes a line from the film as support: "In all institutions, something of the individual gets lost." Rodowick then goes even further to indicate that the "problem is especially crucial in the representation of women," and that "feminine sexuality is always in excess of the social system which seeks to contain it" ("Madness, Authority, and Ideology," p. 42).

22. Elsaesser's article ("Tales of Sound and Fury") in its original place of publication (*Monogram* 4 [1973]: 2-15) is illustrated with a still from this scene carrying the caption, "Dappling the Dawn with Desire."

23. Elsaesser argues that the melodramas of Sirk, Ray, and Minnelli in particular are characterized by a "heightening of the ordinary gesture and a use of setting and decor so as to reflect the characters' fetishist feelings" ("Tales of Sound and Fury," p. 56), or that psychological symbolization emerged from decor and from "vertiginous drops in the emotional tension" (p. 60). (Page numbers here are taken from the Gledhill volume.)

24. In a UCLA graduate seminar, Robert Vianello named this film "The Drapes of Wrath," succinctly expressing the transference of emotion to scenic decor or, speaking psychoanalytically, to the scene of the decor.

25. In this respect, the film reveals a bias toward legalized heterosexual monogamy; however, it can at least broach a sexual model for *that* union.

26. Nowell-Smith describes this scene as a "hysterical" one in which the "realist convention breaks down" ("Minelli and Melodrama," p. 119).

27. Felman, "Women and Madness."

28. See Pam Cook's discussion of the work of J. J. Bachofen in "Duplicity in *Mildred Pierce*," *Women in Film Noir*, ed. E. Ann Kaplan (London: British Film Institute, 1978), pp. 68-82. The work of Bachofen cited is *Myth, Religion and Mother Right* (1861), selected writings (Princeton, N.J.: Princeton University Press/Bollingen Foundation, 1973). Also see Susan Griffin, *Women and Nature: The Roaring inside Her* (New York: Harper and Row, 1979).

29. Elaine Showalter, *Female Malady*, p. 3.

30. *Webster's New Collegiate Dictionary* (Springfield, Mass.: Merriam, 1977), s.v. "Lilith."

31. Other aspects of the film's representational system coordinate our identification with Lilith. To take the sound track as an example, the opening title sequence is accompanied by a haunting melody played by a single flute, which is later identified as music played by Lilith on a flute she has crafted.

32. Beatty's performance in *Lilith* is similar to the one he gives in Arthur Penn's *Mickey One* (1965), another film in which there is the suggestion that the Beatty character is highly unstable.

33. Mary Ann Doane makes a similar point in a fascinating discussion where she argues that the light doctors train on the women in *Dark Victory*, *Lady in the Dark*, *Cat People*, and *The Snake Pit*, among other films, "is the mechanism by means of which the films of the medical discourse insure the compatibility of rationality and desire" ("Clinical Eyes," p. 61).

5. Psychiatry and the Working Woman

1. Mary Ann Doane, "Clinical Eyes: The Medical Discourse," in *The Desire to Desire* (Bloomington and Indianapolis: University of Indiana Press, 1987), p. 41.

2. See Laurel Samuels, "Female Psychotherapists as Portrayed in Film Fiction and Nonfiction," *Journal of the American Academy of Psychoanalysis* 13, no. 3 (July 1985): 367-78; Krin Gabbard and Glen O. Gabbard, *Psychiatry and the Cinema* (Chicago and London: University of Chicago Press, 1987), especially pp. 21-30 and 61-67; Irving Schneider, M.D., "Images of the Mind: Psychiatry in the Commercial Film," *American Journal of Psychiatry* 134, no. 6 (June 1977): 613-20; and Martin S. Dworkin, "Movie Psychiatrics," *Antioch Review* (Winter 1954-55): 484-91. Samuels has located forty-one films in which a female psychiatrist plays a lead role, including sixteen such films falling within the time frame under study here.

3. The Samuels ("Female Psychotherapists") and Gabbard and Gabbard (*Psychiatry and the Cinema*) texts both make this point in their sex role analyses of *Spellbound*.

4. William H. Chafe, *The American Woman: Her Changing Social, Economic, and Political Roles, 1920-1970* (London and New York: Oxford University Press, 1971).

5. Leila J. Rupp, "Woman's Place Is in the War: Propaganda and Public Opinion in the United States and Germany, 1939-1945," in *Women of America: A History*, ed. Carol Ruth Berkin and Mary Beth Norton (Boston: Houghton Mifflin, 1979), pp. 343-59.

6. Gabbard and Gabbard, *Psychiatry and the Cinema*, p. 21.

7. Ibid., p. 25.

8. In a parenthetical comment Mary Ann Doane points out that although Constance Peterson (Ingrid Bergman) in *Spellbound* is the psychoanalyst and J. B. (Gregory Peck) her patient, Peterson is in fact "ultimately constituted as analysand" (*Desire to Desire*, p. 46).

9. See Gabbard's and Gabbard's discussion of how Jerry Morgan (Danny Kaye) in *Knock on Wood* masters psychoanalytic principles overnight (*Psychiatry and the Cinema*, pp. 21-29).

10. Sigmund Freud, "I: The Sexual Aberrations" (1905), in *Three Essays on the Theory of Sexuality*, trans. James Strachey (New York: Avon Books, 1962), p. 42, or "Fetishism" (1927), in *Sexuality and the Psychology of Love*, ed. Philip Rieff (New York: Collier Books, 1963), pp. 214-19.

11. Of course, according to the plot of *Spellbound*, the white lines on the bathrobe are disturbing because they threaten to invoke the repressed memory of ski tracks in the snow, which in turn threaten to invoke J. B.'s further repressed memory of the grisly death of his little brother, who slid down a stone stair railing to be impaled on a wrought iron stake. But, if the ski tracks function as a kind of (especially horrific) screen memory for the childhood incident, that incident in its turn may be viewed as a kind of (especially horrific) *Hollywood* screen memory for the primal scene. As Marc Vernet has noted ("Freud: effets speciaux—Mise en scène: U.S.A.," *Communications* 23 [1975], p. 225), following a consideration of the evacuation of the Oedipus complex in *The Snake Pit*, "Sexuality in effect hardly appears in this type of film as compared with no matter what other genre."

12. Sigmund Freud, "From the History of an Infantile Neurosis" (1919), in *Three Case Histories*, ed. Philip Rieff (New York: Collier Books, 1963), pp. 187-317.

13. Sigmund Freud, "Family Romances" (1908), in *The Standard Edition of the Complete Works of Sigmund Freud*, ed. and trans. James Strachey (London: Hogarth Press, 1953-74), vol. 9, pp. 235-41.

14. The "male madness" films listed in Filmography C and mentioned in the Introduction would provide a productive corpus for the further investigation of masculine specularization.

15. Mary Ann Doane, "Clinical Eyes."

16. See Mary Ann Doane, "*Gilda*: Epistemology as Striptease," *Camera Obscura* 11 (1983): 8-28.

17. Richard Dyer, "Resistance through Charisma: Rita Hayworth and *Gilda*," in *Women in Film Noir*, ed. E. Ann Kaplan (London: British Film Institute, 1978), pp. 91-99.

18. According to Scott Bukatman, "What Mary Ann Doane has called 'the desire to desire,' whereby female desire is thwarted and repressed through the absence of a legitimate figuration system for the expression and legitimation of that desire, might be perversely adapted to describe the disruptive polylingualism of the Lewis text. Jerry, taking on the persona of the female hysteric, acts out his own ambivalence towards an inscribed and proscribed social position (masculinity)" ("Paralysis in Motion: Jerry Lewis's Life as a Man," *Camera Obscura* 17 [1988], p. 196). In this connection also see Thyrza Goodeve's paper entitled, "The Female Man: Hysterical Jerry Professes Desire," presented on her Jerry Lewis panel at the Society for Cinema Studies Conference in New Orleans, April 3-6, 1986.

19. See Bukatman's discussion ("Paralysis in Motion") of Lewis's *The Nutty Professor*.

20. See Joan Riviere, "Womanliness as a Masquerade," *International Journal of Psycho-Analysis* 10 (1929): 303-13.

6. Psychiatrists and Cinema: A Correspondence

1. Letter to Eric Johnston from Karl M. Bowman, M.D., president of the American Psychiatric Association, March 19, 1946, Production Code Administration files, Margaret Herrick Library of the Academy of Motion Picture Arts and Sciences, Los Angeles.

2. Letter to Joseph Breen from Samuel Feigin, M.D., president of the New York Society for Clinical Psychiatry, March 14, 1946, Production Code Administration files.

3. Letter to Francis Harmon, vice-president of the MPAA, from Iago Galdston, M.D., March 5, 1946, Production Code Administration files.

4. See, for example, the letter to Iago Galdston from S. Bernard Wortis, M.D., director, Bellevue Psychiatric Hospital, February 8, 1946, Production Code Administration files; and the letter to Johnston from Bowman, March 19, 1946.

5. This review was quoted in the letter from Bowman to Johnston, March 19, 1946.

6. Letter from Joseph Breen to Karl Bowman, April 5, 1946, Production Code Administration files.

7. Letter from Joseph Breen to Iago Galdston, March 14, 1946, Production Code Administration files.

8. Ibid.

9. Letter to Karl Bowman from Joseph Breen, April 5, 1946, Production Code Administration files. Brophy was in fact unknown to Bowman and his immediate colleagues until inquiries revealed him to be not a psychiatrist at all but a surgeon on the hospital staff who did not "profess to know psychiatry" (letter from Karl Bowman to C. C. Bur-

lingame, M.D., Langley Porter Clinic, University of California Medical School, June 20, 1946, Production Code Administration files). (Bowman seems to have found it significant to report the information provided by a colleague of a colleague that Brophy was not only not a psychiatrist, but had no practice of his own and was independently wealthy to boot, with a home in a "fashionable Bel-Air [*sic*] district"—a dilettante by implication.)

10. Letter from Joseph Breen to Jason S. Joy, head of the MPAA department of public relations, July 30, 1947, Production Code Administration files.

11. Letter to Joseph Breen from C. C. Burlingame, chairman, Committee on Public Education, American Psychiatric Association, Aug. 6, 1947, Production Code Administration files.

12. Letter from "A Motion Picture Patron" to the Association of Motion Picture Producers, June 12, 1947, Production Code Administration files.

13. Quoted in Michael Shortland, "Screen Memories: Towards a History of Psychiatry and Psychoanalysis in the Movies," *British Journal of the History of Science* 20 (1987), p. 426.

14. Script conference notes on *The Snake Pit*, Dec. 2, 1946, Special Collections, University of Southern California. Zanuck's words are paraphrased in these notes by his secretary, Molly Mandaville.

15. Letter to E. E. Muhl from William Gordon, Aug. 15, 1961, "*Freud*; Letters from William Gordon—General," John Huston Collection, Margaret Herrick Library of the Academy of Motion Picture Arts and Sciences, Los Angeles. In view of Huston's concern for historical detail, it was ironic that certain historical liberties were necessitated by the Freud family's opposition to the film. For example, Freud had to be portrayed as childless due to the legal prohibition against portraying any living member of the Freud family contrary to his or her wishes. Diane Waldman and I explore the ideological ramifications of this omission in "Huston's *Freud*: A Psychoanalytic Feminist Reading," in *Close Viewings: An Anthology of New Film Criticism*, ed. Peter Lehman (Tallahassee: Florida State University Press, 1990), pp. 282-99.

16. Letter to John Huston from William Gordon, May 25, 1961, "*Freud*; William Gordon re: script analysis," Huston Collection.

17. Letter from Martin Grotjahn, M.D., to William Gordon, June 20, 1961, Huston Collection.

18. Letter from Earl A. Loomis, Jr., M.D., to William Gordon, June 8, 1961, Production Code Administration files.

19. Letter from William Bier to William Gordon, June 28, 1961, Huston Collection.

20. Letter from Earl Loomis to William Gordon, Aug. 16, 1961, "*Freud*; Dr. Stephen Black, comments on script," Huston Collection.

21. Ibid.

22. Letter from William Gordon to William Bier, July 3, 1961, Huston Collection.

23. John Huston, *An Open Book* (New York: Viking, 1980), pp. 341-42.

24. Letter to William Gordon from Peter Ciklic, professor and chairman, Department of Psychology, Loyola University, May 5, 1961, Huston Collection.

25. Campbell's views are paraphrased by Loomis in a letter to Gordon, Aug. 16, 1961, Huston Collection.

26. Letter from Bier to Gordon, June 28, 1961.

27. Ibid.

Conclusion

1. A number of the points made in this conclusion about the film *Freud* were also made in "John Huston's *Freud* and Textual Repression: A Psychoanalytic Feminist Reading," an article I coauthored with Diane Waldman (in *Close Readings: An Anthology of*

New Film Criticism, ed. Peter Lehman [Tallahassee: Florida State University Press, 1991], pp. 282-99). In that article we discussed the contradictions inherent in the depiction of Freud as a troubled man of science, the importance of the interrelationship of Freud's own and Cecily's case history, and, centrally, the film's ambivalence about sexual abuse, which we examined in the context of changes in the figuration of abuse seen in a comparison of the various script stages, in two cuts of the film, and in the context of Freud's own writings on the etiology of neurosis. Here, I would like to develop further certain of those ideas in relation to the larger corpus discussed in this book and with special consideration of the role of dream and memory in the exploration of male and female subjectivities. A great debt is due Diane Waldman for the ideas about *Freud* she generated and shared with me, and for her role in helping me to develop my own ideas about the film.

2. This objection, presumably that of a colleague, was expressed in a letter from Earl A. Loomis, Jr., M.D. (credited for "Technical Advice" on *Freud*) to William Gordon (Huston's public relations director), June 8, 1961, Production Code Administration files.

3. Walker and Waldman ("Huston's *Freud*") cite the following examples, among others, of points in Freud's work where he returned to the significance of actual seduction: Sigmund Freud, "Introductory Lectures on Psychoanalysis" (1916), in *The Standard Edition of the Complete Psychological Works of Sigmund Freud*, ed. and trans. James Strachey (London: Hogarth Press and Institute of Psychoanalysis, 1953-74), vol. 16, p. 370 (hereafter *SE*); "Female Sexuality" (1931), *SE*, vol. 21, p. 238; and "Femininity" (1933), *SE*, vol. 22, p. 120. These examples are also cited in Jeffrey Masson, *The Assault on Truth: Freud's Suppression of the Seduction Theory* (New York: Penguin, 1984). Also see Jane Gallop, *The Daughter's Seduction: Feminism and Psychoanalysis* (Ithaca, N.Y.: Cornell University Press, 1982).

4. Though these dialogues between Freud and Breuer remain prominent in the final edited version of *Freud*, they were even longer in the original, and presumably less commercial, cut of the film.

5. "Twinkle-Think," *Newsweek*, Sept. 24, 1962, p. 63.

6. Throughout the film the metaphor of letting in the light works in tandem with the metaphor of seeing or not seeing to connote intellectual discovery. The opening narration states, "This is the story of Freud's descent into a region almost as black as hell itself, man's unconscious, and *how he let in the light*." Later, Freud's wife, Martha, enters his study saying, "I saw the light," just as Freud has remembered his childhood desire for his mother.

7. Florence Rush's *The Best Kept Secret: Sexual Abuse of Children* (Englewood Cliffs, N.J.: Prentice-Hall, 1980) is the touchstone work revealing and studying the sexual abuse of children and its psychosexual implications. In that work she cites examples of psychoanalytic literature that attempted to downplay the assaults and emphasize "victim participation." See, for example, Cindy Burton, *Vulnerable Children* (London: Routledge and Kegan Paul, 1968).

8. Jacques Lacan, *Four Fundamental Concepts of Psycho-Analysis* (1973), trans. Alan Sheridan, ed. Jacques-Alain Miller (New York: Penguin Books, 1977), p. 231.

9. Ibid., pp. 157-58.

10. And the Oedipal import of the carnation has been clarified for the spectator as well as for Freud by the sight of a portrait, hung prominently in the hall of the Koertner home, of Herr Koertner with a white carnation in his lapel.

11. Lawrence S. Kubie, M.D., "Psychiatry and the Films," *Hollywood Quarterly*, Jan. 1947, p. 114.

12. Ibid., pp. 114-15.

Filmography A

Psychoanalytic Psychiatry and Female Mental Illness
(in chronological order according to release date)

Private Worlds (Gregory La Cava, Paramount, 1935; Claudette Colbert, Charles Boyer, Joan Bennett, Joel McCrea)

Carefree (Mark Sandrich, RKO, 1938; Fred Astaire, Ginger Rogers)

King's Row (Sam Wood, Warner Brothers, 1941; Ann Sheridan, Robert Cummings, Ronald Reagan)

Now, Voyager (Irving Rapper, Warner Brothers, 1942; Bette Davis, Claude Rains, Paul Henreid)

Cat People (Jacques Tourneur, RKO, 1942; Simone Simon, Tom Conway)

Lady in a Jam (Gregory La Cava, Universal, 1942; Irene Dunne, Patrick Knowles)

So Proudly We Hail! (Mark Sandrich, Paramount, 1943; Claudette Colbert, Paulette Goddard, Veronica Lake)

Lady in the Dark (Mitchell Leisen, Paramount, 1943; Ginger Rogers, Barry Sullivan, Ray Milland)

The Seventh Veil (Compton Bennett, GB, British Lion, 1945; James Mason, Ann Todd, Herbert Lom)

She Wouldn't Say Yes (Alexander Hall, Warner Brothers, 1945; Rosalind Russell, Lee Bowman)

Spellbound (Alfred Hitchcock, Selznick, 1945; Ingrid Bergman, Gregory Peck, Michael Chekhov, Leo G. Carroll)

Bedlam (Mark Robson, RKO, 1946; Boris Karloff, Anna Lee)

The Dark Mirror (Robert Siodmak, Universal, 1946; Olivia de Havilland, Lew Ayres)

The Locket (John Brahm, RKO, 1946; Laraine Day, Brian Aherne, Robert Mitchum)

Shock (Alfred L. Werker, Fox, 1946; Vincent Price, Lynn Bari)

Nightmare Alley (Edmund Goulding, Fox, 1947; Tyrone Power, Helen Walker)

Possessed (Curtis Bernhardt, Warner Brothers, 1947; Joan Crawford, Stanley Ridges, Van Heflin)

Hollow Triumph, retitled *The Scar* (Steve Sekely, Eagle Lion, 1948; Paul Henreid, Joan Bennett)

The Snake Pit (Anatole Litvak, Fox, 1948; Olivia de Havilland, Leo Genn, Mark Stevens)

Whirlpool (Otto Preminger, Fox, 1949; Gene Tierney, José Ferrer, Richard Conte)

Shadow on the Wall (Patrick Jackson, MGM, 1950; Nancy Davis, Ann Sothern, Zachary Scott)

I, the Jury (Harry Essex, UA, 1953; Biff Elliot, Preston Foster, Peggie Castle)

Marry Me Again (Frank Tashlin, RKO, 1953; Robert Cummings, Marie Wilson)

Knock on Wood (Norman Panama, Melvin Frank, Paramount, 1954; Danny Kaye, Mai Zetterling)

The Cobweb (Vincent Minnelli, MGM, 1955; Richard Widmark, Gloria Grahame, Lauren Bacall)

The Shrike (José Ferrer, Universal, 1955; June Allyson, José Ferrer)

The Opposite Sex (David Miller, MGM, 1956; June Allyson, Joan Collins, Ann Sheridan, Ann Miller, Joan Blondell, Dolores Gray, Agnes Moorehead)

The Search for Bridey Murphy (Noel Langley, Paramount, 1956; Teresa Wright)

Lizzie (Hugo Haas, MGM, 1957; Eleanor Parker, Richard Boone)

Oh, Men! Oh, Women! (Nunnally Johnson, Fox, 1957; Ginger Rogers, David Niven, Dan Dailey, Barbara Rush, Tony Randall)

The Three Faces of Eve (Nunnally Johnson, Fox, 1957; Joanne Woodward, Lee J. Cobb)

Home before Dark (Mervyn LeRoy, Warner Brothers, 1958; Jean Simmons)

Suddenly Last Summer (Joseph L. Mankiewicz, Columbia, 1959; Elizabeth Taylor, Montgomery Clift, Katharine Hepburn)

Splendor in the Grass (Elia Kazan, Warner Brothers, 1961; Natalie Wood, Warren Beatty)

The Chapman Report (George Cukor, Warner Brothers, 1962; Jane Fonda, Efrem Zimbalist, Jr.)

David and Lisa (Frank Perry, Continental, 1962; Keir Dullea, Janet Margolin)

Freud (John Huston, Universal, 1962; Montgomery Clift, Susannah York)

Tender Is the Night (Henry King, Fox, 1962; Jason Robards, Jennifer Jones, Joan Fontaine)

Lilith (Robert Rossen, Columbia, 1964; Jean Seberg, Warren Beatty)

Marnie (Alfred Hitchcock, UA, 1964; Tippi Hedren, Sean Connery)

Shock Treatment (Denis Sanders, Fox, 1964; Lauren Bacall, Roddy McDowall)

The Slender Thread (Sydney Pollack, Paramount, 1965; Anne Bancroft, Sidney Poitier)

Three on a Couch (Jerry Lewis, Columbia, 1966; Jerry Lewis, Janet Leigh)

Note: For reasons explained in the text, I have included here films depicting female psychiatrists. I have also included a small number of relevant Hollywood films that slightly predate the period in question.

Selected Filmography B

Mental Disturbance
(in chronological order according to release date)

That Uncertain Feeling (Ernst Lubitsch, UA, 1941)

Experiment Perilous (Jacques Tourneur, RKO, 1944)

Gaslight (George Cukor, MGM, 1944)

Guest in the House (John Brahm, UA, 1944)

Love Letters (William Dieterle, Paramount, 1945)

The Pirate (Vincent Minnelli, MGM, 1945)

Johnny Belinda (Jean Negulesco, Warner Brothers, 1948)

Sleep, My Love (Douglas Sirk, UA, 1948)

Beyond the Forest (King Vidor, Warner Brothers, 1949)

Black Magic (Gregory Ratoff, 1949)

The Secret Fury (Mel Ferrer, RKO, 1950)

So Young, So Bad (Bernard Vorhaus, UA, 1950)

Her Panelled Door (Ladislas Vajda, GB, Associated British, 1951)

Don't Bother to Knock (Roy Ward Baker, Fox, 1952)

Problem Girls (E. A. Dupont, Columbia, 1953)

All That Heaven Allows (Douglas Sirk, Universal, 1955)

Strange Lady in Town (Mervyn LeRoy, Warner Brothers, 1955)

Women's Prison (Lewis Seiler, Columbia, 1955)

The Long Hot Summer (Martin Ritt, Fox, 1958)

Bells Are Ringing (George Cukor, MGM, 1958)

A Child Is Waiting (John Cassavetes, prod. Stanley Kramer, 1962)

Strait-Jacket (William Castle, Columbia, 1964)

Mirage (Edward Dmytryk, Universal, 1965)

Selected Filmography C

Male Madness
(in chronological order according to release date)

The Amazing Dr. Clitterhouse (Anatole Litvak, Warner Brothers, 1938)

Blind Alley (Charles Vidor, Columbia, 1939)

The Mad Doctor (Tim Whelan, Paramount, 1941)

Hangover Square (John Brahm, Fox, 1945)

My Name Is Julia Ross (Joseph H. Lewis, Columbia, 1945)

Specter of the Rose (The Scarf) (Ben Hecht, Republic, 1946)

Crossfire (Edward Dymtryk, RKO, 1947)

Fear in the Night (Maxwell Shane, 1947)

The High Wall (Curtis Bernhardt, MGM, 1947)

The Dark Past, remake of *Blind Alley* (Rudolph Maté, Columbia, 1948)

Mine Own Executioner (Anthony Kimmins, GB, Fox release, 1948)

The Quiet One (Sidney Meyers, 1948)

Secret beyond the Door (Fritz Lang, Universal, 1948)

Home of the Brave (Mark Robson, UA, 1949)

The Astonished Heart (Terence Fisher, GB, Universal-International, 1950)

Crisis (Richard Brooks, MGM, 1950)

Harvey (Henry Koster, Universal, 1950)

The Hidden Room (Edward Dmytryk, GB, Eagle Lion, 1950)

Fourteen Hours (Henry Hathaway, Fox, 1951)

The Scarf (E. A. Dupont, UA, 1951)

The Second Woman (James V. Kern, UA, 1951)

Shadow in the Sky (Fred M. Wilcox, MGM, 1951)

Teresa (Fred Zimmerman, MGM, 1951)

Night without Sleep (Roy Baker, Fox, 1952)

Man in the Dark (Lew Landers, Columbia, 1953)

The Lonely Night (Irving Jacoby, Arthur May–Edward Kingsley, 1954)

The Long Wait (Victor Saville, UA, 1954)

Phantom of the Rue Morgue (Roy Del Ruth, Warner Brothers, 1954)

The Purple Plain (Robert Parrish, General Film Distributors, 1954)

The Sleeping Tiger (Joseph Losey, GB, Angle Amalgamated, 1954)

The Seven Year Itch (Billy Wilder, Fox, 1955)

Autumn Leaves (Robert Aldrich, Columbia, 1956)

Nightmare, remake of *Fear in the Night* (Maxwell Shane, UA, 1956)

Strange Intruder (Irving Rapper, Allied Artists, 1956)

The Unguarded Moment (Harry Keller, Universal, 1956)

Chain of Evidence (Paul Landers, Allied Artists, 1957)

Fear Strikes Out (Robert Mulligan, Paramount, 1957)

The Night Runner (Abner Biberman, Universal, 1957)

The Sad Sack (George Marshall, Paramount, 1957)

Pressure Point (Hubert Cornfield, prod. Stanley Kramer, 1962)

The Couch (Owen Krump, Warner Brothers, 1962)

Captain Newman, M.D. (David Miller, Universal, 1963)

Paranoiac (Freddie Frances, GB, J. Arthur Rank, 1963)

Shock Corridor (Sam Fuller, Allied Artists, 1963)

A Fine Madness (Irvin Kershner, Warner Brothers, 1966)

Blindfold (Philip Dunne, Universal, 1966)

Selected Bibliography

Banner, Lois. *Women in Modern America: A Brief History*. New York: Harcourt Brace Jovanovich, 1974.

Beauvoir, Simone de. *The Second Sex*. 1949. Translated and edited by H. M. Parshley. New York: Vintage, 1974.

Bellour, Raymond. "Hitchcock the Enunciator." *Camera Obscura* 2 (Fall 1977): 69-94.

Bercovitch, Sacvan, ed. *Reconstructing American Literary History*. Cambridge, Mass.: Harvard University Press, 1986.

Bergstrom, Janet. "Alternation, Segmentation, Hypnosis: Interview with Raymond Bellour." *Camera Obscura* 3-4 (Summer 1979): 71-104.

———. "The Logic of Fascination: Fritz Lang and Cinematic Conventions." Ph.D. dissertation, University of California, Los Angeles, 1980.

Berkhofer, Robert, Jr. "The Challenge of Poetics to (Normal) Historical Practice." *Poetics Today* 9 (1988): 435-52.

———. "A New Context for a New American Studies." *American Quarterly* 41, no. 4 (December 1989): 588-612.

Blum, Jeffery D. "On Changes in Psychiatric Diagnosis over Time." *American Psychologist* 33, no. 11 (November 1978): 1017-31.

Borde, Raymond, and Etienne Chaumeton. "The Sources of Film Noir." *Film Reader* 3 (February 1978): 58-66.

Bragdon, Elizabeth, ed. *Women Today: Their Conflicts, Their Frustrations and Their Fulfillments*. Indianapolis: Bobbs-Merrill, 1953.

Brennan, Teresa, ed. *Between Feminism and Psychoanalysis*. New York and London: Routledge, 1989.

Castel, Robert, Franceoise Castel, and Anne Lovell. *The Psychiatric Society*, 1979. Translated by Arthur Goldhammer. New York: Columbia University Press, 1982.

Chafe, William. *The American Woman: Her Changing Social, Economic, and Political Roles, 1920-1970*. New York and London: Oxford University Press, 1972.

———. *The Paradox of Change: American Women in the 20th Century*. New York and London: Oxford University Press, 1991.

Chesler, Phyllis. *Women and Madness*. Garden Grove, N.Y.: Doubleday, 1972.

Doane, Mary Ann. "*Caught* and *Rebecca*: The Inscription of Femininity as Absence." *Enclitic* 5/6 (1981-82): 75-89.

———. *The Desire to Desire: The Woman's Film of the 1940s*. Bloomington and Indianapolis: Indiana University Press, 1987.

———. *Femmes Fatales: Feminism, Film Theory, Psychoanalysis*. New York and London: Routledge, 1991.

Ehrenreich, Barbara. *The Hearts of Men*. Garden City, N.Y.: Anchor Press, 1983.

Eisenstein, Victor, ed. *Neurotic Interaction in Marriage*. New York: Basic Books, 1956.

Elsaesser, Thomas. "Tales of Sound and Fury: Observations on the Family Melodrama." *Monogram* 4 (1973): 2-15. Reprinted in *Home Is Where the Heart Is: Studies in Melodrama and the Woman's Film*, edited by Christine Gledhill, pp. 43-69. London: British Film Institute, 1987.

Fearing, Franklin. "The Screen Discovers Psychiatry." *Hollywood Quarterly*, January 1947, pp. 154-58.

Feldstein, Richard, and Judith Roof, eds. *Feminism and Psychoanalysis*. Ithaca, N.Y.: Cornell University Press, 1989.

Felman, Shoshana. "Women and Madness: The Critical Phallacy." *Diacritics* 5 (1975): 2-10.

———. *Writing and Madness: Literature/Philosophy/Psychoanalysis*. Translated by Martha Noel Evans and Shoshana Felman. Ithaca, N.Y.: Cornell University Press, 1985.

Fine, Reuben. *A History of Psychoanalysis*. New York: Columbia University Press, 1979.

Foucault, Michel. *The Archaeology of Knowledge and the Discourse on Language*. 1972. Translated by A. M. Sheridan Smith. New York: Pantheon, 1982.

———. *The History of Sexuality, Volume I: An Introduction*. 1976. Translated by Robert Hurley. New York: Vintage Books, 1980.

———. *Madness and Civilization: A History of Insanity in the Age of Reason*. 1961. Translated by Richard Howard. New York: Vintage Books, 1973.

Freeman, Lucy. *Fight against Fears*. New York: Pocket Books, 1953.

Freud, Sigmund. *The Standard Edition of the Complete Psychological Works of Sigmund Freud*. 23 vols. Edited and translated by James Strachey. London: Hogarth Press and Institute of Psychoanalysis, 1953-1974.

———. "Family Romances" (1908). In *Standard Edition*, vol. 9, pp. 235-44.

———. "Femininity" (1933). In *Standard Edition*, vol. 22, pp. 112-33.

———. "The Question of Lay Analysis" (1926). In *Standard Edition*, vol. 20, pp. 177-250.

———. *Sexuality and the Psychology of Love*. 1905-38. Edited by Philip Rieff. New York: Collier Books, 1963.

———. *Therapy and Technique*. 1888-1937. Edited by Philip Rieff. New York: Collier Books, 1963.

Freud, Sigmund, and Josef Breuer. *Studies on Hysteria*. 1893-95. Translated and edited by James Strachey, with the collaboration of Anna Freud. New York: Basic Books, 1955.

Friedan, Betty. *The Feminine Mystique*. 1963; New York: Dell, 1974.

Gabbard, Krin, and Glen O. Gabbard. *Psychiatry and the Cinema*. Chicago and London: University of Chicago Press, 1987.

Gitlin, Todd. *The Whole World Is Watching: Mass Media in the Making and Unmaking of the New Left*. Berkeley: University of California Press, 1980.

Greenacre, Phyllis. "The Role of Transference: Practical Considerations in Relation to Psychoanalytic Therapy." *Journal of the American Psychoanalytic Association* 2, no. 4 (October 1954): 671-84.

Grob, Gerald N. *Mental Illness and American Society, 1875-1940*. Princeton, N.J.: Princeton University Press, 1983.

Hale, Nathan. *Freud and the Americans: The Beginnings of Psychoanalysis in the U.S., 1876-1917*. New York and London: Oxford University Press, 1971.

Haley, Jay. *Strategies of Psychotherapy*. New York: Grune and Stratton, 1963.

Hall, Stuart, and Tony Jefferson, eds. *Resistance through Ritual: Youth Subcultures in Post-War Britain*. London: Hutchinson, 1976.

Halleck, Seymour L. *The Politics of Therapy*. New York: Science House, 1971.

Hartman, Susan. *The Home Front and Beyond: American Women in the 1940s*. Boston: Twayne, 1982.

Havemann, Ernest. *The Age of Psychology*. New York: Simon and Schuster, 1957.

Heath, Stephen. "Difference." *Screen* 19, no. 3 (Autumn 1978): 51-112.

———. "Film and System: Terms of Analysis: Part I." *Screen* 16, no. 1 (Spring 1975): 7-77.

———. "Film and System: Terms of Analysis: Part II." *Screen* 16, no. 2 (Summer 1975): 91-113.

Herschberger, Ruth. *Adam's Rib*. New York: Pellegrini and Cudahy, 1948.

Horney, Karen. *Are You Considering Psychoanalysis?* New York: Norton, 1946.

———. *Feminine Psychology*. Edited by Harold Kelman. New York: Norton, 1967.

Jacobs, Lea. "*Now Voyager*: Some Problems of Enunciation and Sexual Difference." *Camera Obscura* 7 (1981): 89-110.

Jacoby, Russell. *The Repression of Psychoanalysis: Otto Fenichel and the Political Freudians*. New York: Basic Books, 1983.

———. *Social Amnesia: A Critique of Conformist Psychology from Adler to Laing*. Boston: Beacon Press, 1975.

Jezer, Marty. *The Dark Ages: Life in the U.S., 1945-1960*. Boston: South End Press, 1982.

Kaplan, E. Ann, ed. *Psychoanalysis and Cinema*. New York and London: Routledge, 1990.

Keppler, C. F. *The Literature of the Second Self*. Tucson: University of Arizona Press, 1972.

Kinsey, Alfred C., Wardell B. Pomeroy, Clyde E. Martin, and Paul H. Gebhard. *Sexual Behavior in the Human Female*. New York: Pocket Books, 1965.

Kleinhans, Chuck. "Notes on Melodrama and the Family under Capitalism." *Film Reader* 3 (February 1978): 40-47.

Knight, Robert. "The Present Status of Organized Psychoanalysis in the United States." *Journal of the American Psychoanalytic Association* 1, no. 2 (April 1953): 197-221.

Komarovsky, Mirra. "Cultural Contradictions and Sex Roles." *American Journal of Sociology* 52, no. 3 (November 1946): 184-89.

Kovel, Joel. "The American Mental Health Industry." In *Critical Psychiatry*, edited by David Ingleby. New York: Pantheon, 1980.

Kubie, Lawrence. "A Pilot Study of Psychoanalytic Practice in the United States: With Suggestions for Future Studies." *Psychiatry* 113 (1950): 227-45.

———. "Psychiatry and the Films." *Hollywood Quarterly*, January 1947, pp. 113-17.

Kubie, Lawrence, and Sydney Margolin. "The Process of Hypnotism and the Nature of the Hypnotic State." *American Journal of Psychiatry* 100, no. 5 (March 1944): 611-22.

Kuhn, Annette. *Cinema, Censorship and Sexuality: 1909-1925*. New York and London: Routledge, 1988.

———. "Transcending Text and Context in a Film History Project." Paper delivered at the Society for Cinema Studies Conference in New York, June 12-15, 1985.

Lacan, Jacques. *The Four Fundamental Concepts of Psycho-Analysis*. 1973. Edited by Jacques-Alain Miller and translated by Alan Sheridan. New York and Harmondsworth, Middlesex: Penguin Books, 1977.

LaCapra, Dominick, and Steven L. Kaplan, eds. *Modern European Intellectual History: Reappraisals and New Perspectives*. Ithaca, N.Y., and London: Cornell University Press, 1982.

LaPiere, Richard. *The Freudian Ethic: An Analysis of the Subversion of the American Character*. New York: Duell, Sloan, and Pearce, 1959.

LaPlace, Maria. "Bette Davis and the Ideal of Consumption: A Look at *Now Voyager*." *Wide Angle* 6, no. 4 (1985): 34-43.

LaPlanche, J., and J.-B. Pontalis. *The Language of Psycho-Analysis*. 1967. Translated by Donald Nicholson-Smith. New York: Norton, 1973.

Lerman, Hannah. *A Mote in Freud's Eye: From Psychoanalysis to the Psychology of Women*. New York: Springer, 1986.

Liebman, Nina. "Sexual Misdemeanor/Psychoanalytic Felony." *Cinema Journal* 26, no. 2 (Winter 1987): 27-38.

Lindner, Robert. *The Fifty-Minute Hour: A Collection of True Psychoanalytic Tales*. 1954; New York: Dell, 1986.

———. *Must You Conform?* 1956; New York: Grove Press, 1971.

———. *Prescription for Rebellion*. 1952; Westport, Conn.: Greenwood Press, 1975.

Lundberg, Ferdinand, and Marynia Farnham. *Modern Woman: The Lost Sex*. New York: Harper Brothers, 1947.

Malcolm, Janet. *Psychoanalysis: The Impossible Profession*. New York: Vintage, 1980.

Menninger, William. *Psychiatry in a Troubled World: Yesterday's War and Today's Challenge*. New York: Macmillan, 1948.

Miller, Douglas T., and Marion Nowak. *The Fifties: The Way We Really Were*. New York: Doubleday, 1977.

Miller, Jean Baker, ed. *Psychoanalysis and Women: Contributions to New Theory and Therapy*. New York: Brunner/Mazel, 1972.

Mills, C. Wright. *The Power Elite*. New York and London: Oxford University Press, 1956.

Mitchell, Juliet. *Psychoanalysis and Feminism: Freud, Reich, Laing and Women*. New York: Vintage Books, 1975.

Mitchell, Juliet, and Jacqueline Rose, eds. *Feminine Sexuality: Jacques Lacan and the école freudienne*. Translated by Jacqueline Rose. London: Macmillan, 1982.

Modleski, Tania. "Some Functions of the Feminist Critic, or the Scandal of the Mute Body." *October* 49 (Summer 1989): 3-24.

Mulvey, Laura. "Afterthoughts on 'Visual Pleasure and Narrative Cinema' Inspired by *Duel in the Sun* (King Vidor, 1946)." *Framework*, nos. 15-17 (Summer 1981): 12-15. Reprinted in *Feminism and Film Theory*, edited by Constance Penley, pp. 69-79. New York and London: Routledge, 1988.

———. "Visual Pleasure and Narrative Cinema." *Screen* 16, no. 3 (Autumn 1975): 6-18. Reprinted in *Feminism and Film Theory*, edited by Constance Penley, pp. 57-68. New York and London: Routledge, 1988.

Newfield, Bradford. "Prescribing Autonomy: Physicians and the Professional Autonomy Ideal in American Culture." Ph.D. dissertation. University of California, Los Angeles, 1991.

Nowell-Smith, Geoffrey. "Minnelli and Melodrama." *Screen* 18, no. 2 (Summer 1977): 113-18.

Oberndorf, Clarence. *A History of Psychoanalysis in America*. New York: Harper and Row, 1953.

Penfold, Susan P., and Gillian Walker. *Women and the Psychiatric Paradox*. Montreal and London: Eden Press, 1983.

Penley, Constance, ed. *Feminism and Film Theory*. New York and London: Routledge, 1988.

Petro, Patrice. *Joyless Streets: Women and Melodramatic Representation in Weimar Germany*. Princeton, N.J.: Princeton University Press, 1989.

Plaza, Monique. " 'Phallomorphic Power' and the Psychology of 'Woman': A Patriarchal Chain." In *Human Sexual Relations*, edited by Mike Brake, pp. 323-60. New York: Pantheon, 1982.

Prince, Morton. *The Dissociation of a Personality: The Hunt for the Real Miss Beauchamp*. 1905; Great Britain: Fletcher, 1978.

Reiser, Stanley Joel. *Medicine and the Reign of Technology*. Cambridge: Cambridge University Press, 1978.

Reisman, David, Nathan Glazer, and Reuel Denny. *The Lonely Crowd*. New Haven, Conn.: Yale University Press, 1950.

Renov, Michael. *Hollywood's Wartime Woman: A Study of Historical/Ideological Determination*. Ann Arbor: University of Michigan Press, 1987.

Riviere, Joan. "Womanliness as a Masquerade." *International Journal of Psycho-Analysis* 10 (1929): 303-13. Reprinted in *Formations of Fantasy*, edited by James Donald and Cora Kaplan, pp. 35-44. London: Methuen, 1986.

Robinson, Marie N. *The Power of Sexual Surrender*. New York: Signet, 1959.

Rodowick, D. N. "Madness, Authority, and Ideology in the Domestic Melodrama of the 1950's." *Velvet Light Trap* 19 (1982): 40-45. Reprinted in *Home Is Where the Heart Is: Studies in Melodrama and the Woman's Film*, edited by Christine Gledhill, pp. 268-82. London: British Film Institute, 1987.

Roustang, François. *Psychoanalysis Never Lets Go*. Translated by Ned Lukacher. Baltimore and London: Johns Hopkins University Press, 1980.

Runyan, William McKinley, ed. *Psychology and Historical Interpretation*. New York and London: Oxford University Press, 1988.

Rupp, Leila J. *Mobilizing Women for War: German and American Propaganda, 1939-1945*. Princeton, N.J.: Princeton University Press, 1978.

Ryan, Mary P. *Womanhood in America: From Colonial Times to the Present*. 1975; New York: New Viewpoints, 1979.

Sahyers, Sohnya, Anders Stephenson, Stanley Aronowitz, and Frederic Jameson, eds. *The Sixties without Apology*. Minneapolis: University of Minnesota Press, 1985.

Schneider, Irving. "Images of the Mind: Psychiatry in the Commercial Film." *American Journal of Psychiatry* 134, no. 6 (June 1977): 613-17.

Shorter, Edward. *Bedside Manners: The Troubled History of Doctors and Patients*. New York: Simon and Schuster, 1985.

Showalter, Elaine. *The Female Malady: Women, Madness and English Culture, 1830-1980*. New York: Pantheon, 1985.

Sizemore, Chris Costner, and Elen Sain Pittillo. *I'm Eve*. 1977; New York: Jove, 1983.

Smith, Mickey C. *Pharmacy and Medicine on the Air*. Metuchen, N.J.: Scarecrow Press, 1989.

Starr, Paul. *The Social Transformation of American Medicine*. New York: Basic Books, 1982.

Strecker, Edward A. *Their Mothers' Sons: The Psychiatrist Examines an American Problem*. New York: Lippincott, 1947.

Strouse, Jean, ed. *Women and Analysis*. New York: Grossman, 1974.

Thigpen, Corbett H., and Hervey M. Cleckley. *The Three Faces of Eve*. New York: Popular Library, 1957.

Tierney, Gene, with Mickey Herskowitz. *Self-Portrait*. New York: Wyden Books, 1979.

Turim, Maureen. *Flashbacks in Film: Memory and History*. New York and London: Routledge, 1989.

Valenstein, Elliot S. *Great and Desperate Cures: The Rise and Decline of Psychosurgery and Other Radical Treatments for Mental Illness*. New York: Basic Books, 1986.

Vernet, Marc. "Freud: effets speciaux—Mise en scène: U.S.A." *Communications* 23 (1975): 223-34.

Waldman, Diane. " 'At Last I Can Tell It to Someone!': Feminine Point of View and Subjectivity in the Gothic Romance Film of the 40s." *Cinema Journal* 23, no. 2 (Winter 1984): 29-40.

_____ . "Horror and Domesticity: The Modern Gothic Romance Film of the 1940s." Ph.D. dissertation, University of Wisconsin, Madison, 1981.

Walker, Janet. "Couching Resistance: Women, Film, and Postwar Psychoanalytic Psychiatry." In *Psychoanalysis and Cinema*, edited by E. Ann Kaplan, pp. 143-62. New York: Routledge, 1990.

_____ . "Hollywood, Freud and the Representation of Women: Regulation and Contradiction, 1945–early 60s." In *Home Is Where the Heart Is: Studies in Melodrama and the Woman's Film*, edited by Christine Gledhill, pp. 197-216. London: British Film Institute, 1987.

Walker, Janet, and Diane Waldman. "John Huston's *Freud* and Textual Repression: A Psychoanalytic Feminist Reading." In *Close Viewings: An Anthology of New Film Criticism*, edited by Peter Lehman, pp. 282-99. Tallahassee: Florida State University Press, 1990.

Welter, Barbara. "The Cult of True Womanhood: 1820-1860." *American Quarterly* 18 (Summer 1966): 151-74.

Whyte, William H. *The Organization Man*. New York: Simon and Schuster, 1956.

Wolfenstein, Martha, and Nathan Leites. *Movies: A Psychological Study*. Glencoe, Ill.: Free Press, 1950.

Woloch, Nancy. *Women and the American Experience*. New York: Knopf, 1984.

Wylie, Philip. *Generation of Vipers*. New York: Farrar and Rinehart, 1942.

Zinn, Howard. *Postwar America: 1945-1971*. Indianapolis: Bobbs-Merrill, 1973.

Zuckerman, Michael. "Dr. Spock: The Confidence Man." In *The Family in History*, edited by Charles E. Rosenberg, pp. 171-207. Denver: University of Denver Press, 1975.

Index

Abraham, Karl, 41, 51
adjustment therapy. *See* American psychiatry
Adler, Alfred, 149
Alexander, Franz, 40, 178nn51, 53
Allport, Gordon, 21
American cultural school of psychoanalysis, 48-50, 180n92
American Foundation of Religion and Psychiatry, 146
American Journal of Psychiatry, xxivfig., 18, 27, 30fig., 32-36figs., 60fig.
American Medical Association, 4
American medicine, 2
American Psychiatric Association, 4, 76, 139, 142-45
American psychiatry: adjustment orientation in, xvi, 7-10, 14-15, 23-37; aspects not oriented toward adjustment, xvi, xvii, xxv, 15-22, 37-50; feminist critique of, xv, xvi, 19-20; history of, xiii, xxiii, 2-5, 18-22; identity crisis of, xxiii; ideological critique of, 20-22; influence on film production, 139-40, 142-43; and mental health professions, 2; popularization of, 6-7; psychoanalytic basis of, 3-5; as

thematic material in films, xiv, xxiii, xxiv, xxv, 86-87; in wartime, 2; and women patients, xiii, xiv, 2, 7-15. *See also* psychiatric themes; psychiatrists; therapeutic technique; women; individual film entries
American psychoanalysis. *See* American psychiatry
American Psychoanalytic Association, 3-4, 10-11, 14, 19
Aronson, H., 11
Atlantic, 6

Bacall, Lauren, 108, 109fig.
Balzac, Honoré de, 103-6
Banner, Lois, 1
Bartemeier, Leo, 3
Beatty, Warren, 115-16
Beauvoir, Simone de, 16, 20
Bedlam (1946), 88-91
Bel Geddes, Barbara, 63
Bellevue Psychiatric Hospital, 140
Benedek, Therese, 13, 171n64
Bercovitch, Sacvan, xiv
Bergman, Ingrid, xxi, 123, 130
Bergstrom, Janet, xix
Berlin Psychoanalytic Institute, 145
Bethlem Hospital, 89

205

Janet Walker resides in Los Angeles and teaches at the University of Southern California and the University of California.